FRANZ BARDON · INITIATION INTO HERMETICS

INITIATION INTO HERMETICS

A COURSE OF INSTRUCTION OF MAGIC THEORY AND PRACTICE

by

FRANZ BARDON

1993

Publishers:
RÜGGEBERG-VERLAG
Postfach 130844, D-42035 Wuppertal · Germany

Title of the German original Edition:
"Der Weg zum wahren Adepten"

First Edition 1956 by Verlag Hermann Bauer, Freiburg / Breisgau
Germany

English Translation by A. Radspieler, Graz / Austria

1. Edition 1962 Graz / Austria
2. Edition 1971 Wuppertal / Germany
3. Edition 1976 Wuppertal / Germany
4. Edition 1981 Wuppertal / Germany
5. Edition 1987 Wuppertal / Germany
6. Edition 1993 Wuppertal / Germany

8/95

ISBN 3-921338-01-8

Printed by Otto Zluhan, Bietigheim / Germany
Printed in Germany

DEDICATION

This work I dedicate in sincere friendship to my faithful co-worker and.
dear disciple

Mrs. Otti Votavova.

FOREWORD

There is no doubt that every one who has been searching for the true and authentic cognition, in vain looked round for years, if not even for lifetime, to find a reliable method of training. The ardent desire for this noble aim made people again and again collect a mass of books, from near and far, supposed to be the best ones, but which were lacking a great deal for real practice. Not one, however, of all the seekers could make any sense from all the stuff collected in the course of time, and the goal aimed at so fervently vanished more and more in nebulous distances. Provided the one or the other did start to work on the progress after instuctions so highly praised, his good will and diligence never saw any satisfactory results. Apart from that, nobody could reliably answer to his pressing questions, wether or not just this way he had selected, was the correct one for his individual case.

Just at this time Divine Providence decided to help all those seekers who have been searching with tough endurance to find means and ways for their spiritual development. Through this book universal methods are given into the hands of mankind by a highest initiate who was chosen by Divine Providence for this special task.

Without exaggeration can be said that never before these complete magical methods have been accessible for the public.

Otti Votavova

INTRODUCTION

Anyone who should believe to find in this work nothing else but a collection of recipes, with the aid of which he can easily and without any effort attain to honour and glory, riches and power and aim at the annihilation of his enemies, might be told from the very inception, that he will put aside this book, being very dissappointed.

Numerous sects and religions do not understand the expression of "magic" otherwise than black art, witchcraft or conspiracy with evil powers. It is therefore not astonishing that many people are frightened by a certain horror, whenever the word "magic" is pronounced. Jugglers, conjurers and charlatans have discredited this term and, considering this circumstance, there is no surprise that magic knowledge has always been looked upon with a slight disregard.

Even in the remotest times the MAGUS has been regarded as one of the highest adepts and it might be of interest to learn that, as a matter of fact, the word "magic" is derived from this word. The so called "sorcerers" are by no means initiates but only imitators of the mysteries, who are counting partly on the ignorance and partly on the credulity of the individual or a whole nation in order to reach their selfish aims by lies and fraud. The true magician will always despise such practices.

In reality, magic is a sacred science, it is, in the very true sense the sum of all knowledge because it teaches how to know and utilize the sovereign rules. There is no difference between magic and mystic or any other conception of the name. Where ever authentic initiation is at stake, one has to proceed on the same basis, according to the same rules, irrespective of the name given by this or that creed. Considering the universal polarity rules of good and evil, active and passive, light and shadow, each science can serve good as well as bad purposes. Let us take the example of a knife, an object which virtually ought to be used for cutting bread only, which, however can become a dangerous weapon in the hands of a murderer. All depends on the character of the individual. This principle goes just as well for all the spheres of the occult sciences. In my book I have chosen the term of "magician" for all of my disciples, it being a symbol of the deepest initiation and the highest wisdom.

Many of the readers will know of course, that the word *"Tarot"* does not mean a game of cards, serving mantical purposes, but a symbolic book of initiation which contains the greatest secrets in a symbolic form. The first tablet of this book introduces the magician representing him as the master of the elements and offering the key to the first *arcanum,* the secret of the ineffable name of *Tetragrammaton**) the quabbalistic *Yod-He-Vau-He.* Here we will, therefore, find the gate to the magician's initiation. The reader will easily realise, how significant and how manifold the application of this tablet is. Not one of the books published up to date does describe the true sense of the first Tarot-card so distinctly as I have done in my book. It is—let it be noted—born from the own practice and destined for the practical use of a lot of other people and all my disciples have found it to be the best and most serviceable system.

But I would never dare to say that my book describes or deals with all the magic or mystic problems. If anyone should like to write all about this sublime wisdom, he ought to fill folio volumes. It can, however, be affirmed positively that this work is indeed the gate to the true initiation, the first key to using the universal rules. I am not going to deny the fact of fragments being able to be found in many an author's publications, but not in a single book will the reader find so exact a description of the first Tarot-card.

I have taken pains to be as plain as possible in the course of the lectures to make the sublime Truth accessible to everybody, although it has been a hard task sometimes to find such simple words as are necessary for the understanding of all the readers. I must leave it to the judgement of all of you, whether or not my efforts have been successful. At certain points I have been forced to repeat myself deliberately to emphasize some important sentences and to spare the reader any going back to a particular page.

There have been many complaints of people interested in the occult sciences that they had never got any chance at all to be

---

*) Tetragrammaton literally means "the four-letter word". It was a subterfuge to avoid the sin of uttering the sacred name YHVH (Yahveh) or Jehova as it later became when the vowels of an other word were combined with the consonants of Y H V H.

initiated by a personal master or leader *(guru)*. Therefore only people endowed with exceptional faculties, a poor preferred minority seemed to be able to gain this sublime knowledge. Thus a great many of serious seekers of the truth had to go through piles of books just to catch one pearl of it now and again. The one, however, who is earnestly interested in his progress and does not pursue this sacred wisdom from sheer curiosity or else is yearning to satisfy his own lust, will find the right leader to initiate him in this book. No incarnate adept, however high his rank may be, can give the disciple more for his start than the present book does. If both the honest trainee and the attentive reader will find in this work all they have been searching for in vain all the years, then the book has fulfilled its purpose completely.

The author.

PART I
THEORY

PICTURE OF THE MAGICIAN

The first Tarot-card

Interpretation of the Symbolism

Below you will find the mineral, vegetable and animal kingdoms expressed in a symbolic manner.

The female on the left side and the male on the right hand are the plus (positive) and the minus (negative) in every human being.

In their middle is to be seen a hermaphrodite, a creature personifying the male and female combined in one as the sign of concinnity between the male and the female principle.

The electrical and magnetical fluids are shown in red and blue colours, electrical fluid being red, magnetical fluid blue.

The head region of the female is electrical, therefore red, the region of the genitals is magnetical, consequently blue. As for the male, it happens to be in inverted order.

Above the hermaphrodite there is the globe as a sign of the earth-sphere, above which the magician is illustrated with the four elements.

Above the male, there are the active elements, that of the fire in red and the airy-element in blue colour. Above the female there are the passive elements, the water-element in green and the element of the earth in yellow colour.

The middle along the magician up to the globe is dark purple, representing the sign of the *akasha*-principle.

Above the magicians's head, with an invisible ribbon for a crown, there is a gold-edged silvery white lotus-flower as a sign of the divinity. In the inside there is the ruby-red philosophers' stone symbolising the quintessence of the whole hermetic science. On the right side in the background there is the sun, yellow like gold and on the left side we see the moon, silvery-white, expressing plus and minus in the macro- and microcosm, the electrical and the magnetical fluids.

Above the lotus-flower, Creation has been symbolized by a ball, in the interior of which are represented the procreative positive and negative forces which stand for the creating act of the universe.

The eternal, the infinite, the boundless, and the uncreated have been expressed symbolically by the word AUM and the dark-purple to black colour.

INITIATION I

THEORY

The great Secret of the Tetragrammaton
or
The quabbalistical YOD-HE-VAU-HE

*Device: That which is above
is also that which
is below.*

Hermes Trismegistos

About the Elements

Every thing which has been created, the macro-cosm as well as the micro-cosm, consequently the big and the small world have been achieved by the effect of the elements. For this reason, right from the beginning of the initiation, I shall attend to these powers and underline their deep and manifold significance in particular. In the occult literature very little has been said about the powers of the elements up to now so that I made it my business to treat this field of knowledge still unknown and to lift the veil covering these rules. It is absolutely not very easy to enlighten the uninitiated so that they are not only fully informed about the existence and the activity of the elements, but will be able to work with these powers in the future practically.

The whole universe is similar to a clockwork with all its wheels in mesh and inter-dependent from each other. Even the idea of the Godhead as the highest comprehensible entity may be divided in aspects analogous to the elements. Details about it are found in the chapter concerning the God-idea.

In the oldest oriental scriptures, the elements are designated as *tattwas*. In our European literature, they are only considered in that their good effects receive our attention and we are warned against their unfavourable influences which means that certain actions can be undertaken under the influence of the tattwas or else must be omitted. The accuracy of this fact is not to be doubted, but all that has been published up to date points to a slight aspect of the effects of elements only. How to find out about the effects of elements resp. the tattwas for any personal use, may be sufficiently learned from astrological books.

I am penetrating far deeper into the secret of the elements and therefore I have chosen a different key which, although being analogous to the astrological key, has, as a matter of fact, nothing to do with it. The reader, to whom this key is completely unknown, shall be taught to use it in various ways. As for the single tasks, analogies and effects of the elements, I shall deal with them by turns and in detail in the following chapters, which will not only unveil the theoretical part of it, but point directly to the practical use, because it is here that the greatest *arcanum* is to be found.

In the oldest book of wisdom, the Tarot has already been written something about this great mystery of the elements. The first card of this work represents the magician pointing to the knowledge and mastery of the elements. On this first card the symbols are: the sword as the fiery element, the rod as the element of the air, the goblet as that of the water and the coins as the element of the earth. This proves without any doubt that already in the mysteries of yore, the magician was destined for the first Tarot-card, mastery of the elements having been chosen as the first act of initiation. In honour of this tradition I shall give my principal attention to the elements for, as you will see, the key to the elements is the panacea, with the help of which all the occurring problems may be solved.

According to the Indian succession of the *tattwas* it runs as follows:

akasha — principle of the ether
tejas — principle of the fire
waju — principle of the air
apas — principle of the water
prithivi — principle of the earth

In accordance with the Indian doctrine, it has been said that the four somehow grosser tattwas have been descended from the fifth tattwa, the akasha-principle. Consequently akasha is the cause ultimate and to be regarded as the fifth power, the so called quintessence. In one of the following chapters, I shall inform the reader about this most subtle element "akasha" in detail. The specific qualities of each element, beginning with the highest planes right down to the grossly material level, will be mentioned in all the following chapters. By now the reader has surely realised that it is no easy task to analyze the great mystery of creation, and word it in such a way that everybody gets the chance of penetrating the topic to form a plastic picture of it all.

The analysis of the elements will also be discussed and the great practical value of them underlined, so that every scientist, whether he be a chemist, a physician, a magnetiser, an occultist, a magician, a mystic, a quabbalist or a yogi, etc. can derive his practical benefit from it. Should I succeed in teaching the reader so far that he is able to deal with the subject in the proper way and to find the practical key to the branch of knowledge most suitable for him, I will be glad to see that the purpose of my book has been fulfilled.

The Principle of Fire

As it has been said before, *akasha* or the etheric principle is the cause of the origin of the elements. According to the oriental scriptures, the first element born from akasha is believed to be TEJAS, the principle of fire. This element as well as all the others manifest their influence not only in our roughly material plane but in everything created. The basic qualities of the fiery principle are heat and expansion. In the beginning of all the things created must therefore have been fire and light and in the Bible we read: "Fiat lux—There shall be light". The origin of the light, of course, is to be sought in the fire. Each element and therefore that of fire, too, has two polarities i. e., the active and the passive one which means positive (+) and negative (—). Plus will always signify the constructive, the creative, the productive sources whereas minus stands for all that is destructive or dissecting. There are always two basic qualities which must be clearly distinguished in each element. Religions have always imputed the good to the active and the evil to the passive side. But fundamentally spoken, there are no such things as good or bad, they are nothing but human conceptions. In the Universe there is neither good nor evil, because everything has been created according to immutable rules, wherein the Divine principle is reflected and only by knowing these rules, we shall be able to come near to the Divinity.

As mentioned before, the fiery principle owns the expansion which I shall call electrical fluid for the sake of better comprehension. This definition does not just point to the roughly material electricity in spite of its having a certain analogy to it. Every one will realize at once, of course, that the quality of expansion is identical with extension. This elementary principle of fire is latent and active in all things created, this means, in the whole universe beginning from the tiniest grain of sand to the most sublime substance visible or invisible.

The Principle of Water

In the previous chapter we have studied the origin and the qualities of the positive element of fire. In this chapter I am going to describe the opposite principle, I say the water. It is also derived from *akasha,* the etheric principle. But in comparison with fire, it has quite contrasting qualities. These basic qualities are coldness and shrinkage. The point in question are also two poles, the active one being constructive, life-giving, nourishing and protective whereas the negative pole, similar to the one of fire, is destructive, dissecting, fermenting, and dividing. As this element owns the basic quality of shrinking and contraction, it has produced the magnetic fluid. Fire as well as water are operating in all regions. According to the rules of creation, the fiery principle would not be able to exist all by itself if it did not conceal inside as opposite pole the principle of water. These two elements, fire and water, are the basic elements with the help of which all has been created. In consequence of these facts, we have everywhere to reckon on two main elements, moreover with the electrical and magnetical fluids which represent the contrasting polarities.

The Principle of Air

Another element derived from *akasha* is that of air. Initiated people do not regard this principle as a real element, but they will grant it the role of a mediator between the fiery and the watery principles, so that the principle of air will, in a certain way, establish the neutral equilibrium, acting as a medium between the active and the passive activities of water and of fire. Through the interaction of the active and passive elements of fire and water the whole created life has become motion.

In its mediatorship the principle of air has assumed the quality of warmth from the fire and that of humidity from the water. Without these two qualities any life would be unconceivable. These two qualities will also grant two polarities to the airy principle which means in the positive outcome the life-giving polarity and in the negative aspect the destructive polarity.

In addition to that let me say that the mentioned elements are not to be regarded as ordinary fire, water and air which would solely represent aspects of the grossly-material plane, but in this case universal qualities of all elements are concerned.

The Principle of Earth

It has been said of the principle of air that it does not represent an element proper and this affirmation goes for the principle of earth likewise. Now this means that out of the interaction of the 3 foresaid elements the earthy principle has been born as the last element which by its specific quality, the solidification involves all the three elements. It is this quality in particular which has given a concrete shape to the three afore said elements. But at the same time the action of the 3 elements has been limited with the result of space, measure, weight, and time having been born. The reciprocal action of the three elements together with that of the earth, thus, has become tetrapolar so that the earthy principle may be labelled now as a four-pole magnet. The fluid in the polarity of the earthy element is electro-magnetic. All the life created can therefore be explained by the fact that all elements are active in the fourth i. e. the earthy element. Through realization in this element came out the FIAT *"it shall be"*.

Details concerning the specific influences of the elements in the various spheres and kingdoms, such as the kingdoms of nature, of animals and of human beings will be found in the following chapters. The main point is that the reader gets a general impression about the workshop and the effect of the elemental principles in the entire Universe.

The Light

Light is established on the principle of fire. Light without fire is unconceivable and for this particular reason it is an aspect of the fire. Each fiery element can be converted into light and the other way round. Therefore light involves all the specific qualities such as shining, penetrating, expanding.

The opposite of light is darkness which has come out of the principle of water. Darkness has the contrasting specific qualities of the light. Without darkness, light would not only remain quite unrecognizable, but without darkness there would never be any light at all. Evidently light and darkness must have been produced by the mutual play of two elements, consequently those of fire and water. Light in its outcome therefore has the positive quality whereas darkness has the negative one. This interplay evidently is working in all regions.

Akasha or the Ethereal Principle

Several times, while describing the elements, I have said that they proceed from the ethereal principle. Accordingly, the ethereal principle is the ultimate, the supreme, the most powerful thing, something unconceivable, the ultimate cause of all things existing and created. To put it in a nutshell, it is the causal sphere. Therefore *akasha* is spaceless and timeless. It is the non-created, the incomprehensible, the indefinable. The various religions have given it the name of God. It is the fifth power, the original power. Everything has been created by it and is kept in balance by it. It is the origin and the purity of all thoughts and intentions, it is the causal world wherein the whole creation is subsisting on, beginning from the highest spheres down to the lowest ones. It is the quintessence of the alchemists, it is *all in all.*

Karma, the Law of Cause and Effect

An immutable law which has its aspect especially in the *akasha-principle*, is the law of cause and effect. Each cause sets free a corresponding effect. This law works everywhere as the most sublime rule. Consequently every deed proceeds from a cause or is followed by any result. Therefore we should not only accept *Karma* as a rule for our good actions, as the oriental philosophy puts it, but its signification reaches farther and is a very deep one. Instinctively all men have the feeling that something good can bring good results only and again all the evil must end up with evil or in the words of a proverb: "whatsoever a man soweth that shall he also reap". Everybody is bound to know this law and to respect it. This law of cause and effect governs the elemental principles, too. I have no intention to enter into details of this law which could be expressed by a few words, as they are quite clear so that every reasonable man will understand them. Subject to this law of cause and effect is also the law of evolution or development. Thus development is an aspect of the *Karma*-law.

M A N

About the body

Man is the true image of God, he has been created in the likeness of the universe. Everything great to be found in the universe is reflected, in a small degree, in man. For this reason man is signified as a microcosm in contrast to the macrocosm of the universe. Strictly speaking, the entire nature manifests itself in man and it will be the task of this chapter to inform about these problems.

I do not intend to describe the physical occurrences in the body because everybody can find informations about it in any respective work. What I shall teach is to regard man from the hermetic standpoint and I shall enlighten interested people, how to use the fundamental key, the influence of the elements on man, in the right way.

A well-known maxim says: "A sound mind in a sound body". The genuine truth of this aphorism presents itself immediately to everybody dealing with the problem of man. There surely will arise the question, what health is from the hermetic point of view. Not every one is capable to answer this question at the first instant. Seen from the hermetic angle, health is the perfect harmony of all the forces operating inside the body with respect to the basic qualities of the elements. There need not prevail such a great disharmony of the element as to set free a visible effect which is called disease. For disharmony in the form of sickness is already an essential disturbance in the workshop of the elements inside the body. The main condition for the novice is to concentrate himself absolutely on his body. The outwardly visible expression of the body resembles that of a beautiful garment, and beauty, in all its aspects, is likewise an aspect of the divine nature. Beauty, properly speaking, is not only that which pleases us or appears to be sympathetic to our taste, because sympathy or antipathy are dependent on the interaction of the elements. Genuine health is rather a basic condition of our spiritual rising. If we like to live in beauty, we must form our house, our flat or, in this case, our body beautifully and fill it with harmony.

According to the universal law, the elements have to perform certain functions inside our body. These are mainly: building up the body, keep it alive and dissolve it. The positive part in the body, the upbuilding is therefore the business of the positive or active side of the elements. The preserving part is brought about by the linking or connecting part of the elements i. e. the neutral, whereas the destructive or dissolving part in the body is realized by the negative qualities of the elements.

It is obvious that the fiery principle in the active form with its electrical fluid will exert the active, expansive, building-up influence. The contrary will be the case in the negative form.

The watery principle, in its active form, will influence the building-up activity, in its negative form, it will produce the disintegrating, dissolving activity of all the fluids in the body.

With the principle of air rests the task of controlling the electrical fluid of the fire and the magnetic fluid of the water in the body, keeping them in balance. For this reason it has been characterized as the neutral or mediating element.

It has been said in the fundamental key about the forces of the principle of earth that it has the function inside the body to keep together the influences of all the three elements. In the active form of the earthy elemental principle, it has an animating, vivifying, invigorating influence and, in the negative form, it is the other way round. The earthy principle is responsible for the thriving as well as for the ageing of the body. We could mention quite a lot of analogies with respect to the influence of the elements inside the body, but let it be enough with the fore-going explanations.

Adepts of all periods never described the effects of the elements in particular, probably to avoid any misuse, but they did know very well all about it. They divided man in three basical conceptions, attributing the head to the fiery principle, the abdomen to that of water and the chest to the airy one as the mediating principle between fire and water. How very right they were with their dividing man, becomes obvious, at the first look, because all that is active or fiery takes place in the head. In the abdomen it must be the contrary, the watery, the secretion, the work of the saps, etc. The chest underlies the air and has a mediating part, because here breathing takes place quite mechanically. The earthy principle with its cohesive power or ability of holding together represents the whole of the human body with all its bones and flesh.

Now the question will arise where and how *akasha* or the etheric principle occurs in the grossly-material body. In doing some deeper thinking, everybody will be able to answer this question by himself, for the etheric principle is hidden in its most grossly-material form in the blood and in the seed and in the reciprocal action of these two substances in the vital matter or in the vitality.

As we have learned, the fiery element produces the electrical and the water-element the magnetic fluid. Each of these fluids has two-pole radiations, an active and a passive one and the mutual influences and interactions of all the radiations of four poles resemble a tetra-polar magnet which is identical to the secret of the Tetragrammaton, the Yod-He-Vau-He of the quabbalists. Therefore the electro-magnetic fluid in the human body, in its emanation, is the animal magnetism, the Od or whatever name it has been given. The right side of the human body is active-electric, providing the individual be a right-handed one. The left side is passive-magnetic. As for a left-handed person the contrary will take place. The emanative power of this electro-magnetic fluid is dependent on the capacitance i. e. the intensity of action of the elements inside the body. The more harmoniously this action of the elements is going on in the body, all the stronger and purer this emanation will be.

With the help of certain exercises as well as by a correct attitude and an exact observance of these rules, the capacitance, strength and influence of this electro-magnetic fluid or Od can be increased or diminished according to whatever necessity requires. The way of doing it will exhaustively be illustrated in the practical part of the present work.

The electrical as well as the magnetical fluid in the human body have directly nothing to do with the kind of electricity or magnetism we know although a certain analogy exists. This law of analogy is a very important factor in the hermetic science and the knowledge of it enables the adept to perform great miracles with the aid of this key.

The food contains the elements mingled with each other. The result of taking in food is a chemical process by which the elements are preserved in our body. From the medical point of view, the taking in of any kind of food, together with the breathing, causes a process of combustion. The hermetist sees far more in this process than just a simple chemical event. He regards this combustion as the mutual dissolving of food, just like the fire is kept burning by fuel. Therefore the whole life depends on the continuous supply of fuel that is the food and the breathing. To supply every element with the necessary preserving substances, a mixed food is advisable which contains the fundamental materials of the elements. If we were to restrict our whole life to a one-sided kind of food only, our body would, without any doubt, fall ill, that means such a kind of food would produce a disharmony in the body. By the disintegration of air and food, the elements are provided with the supporting substances and this way their activity is maintained. Such is man's natural mode of life. If any element is missing, as it were, the fuel, all the functions depending on it are immediately affected. If e. g. the fiery element in the body works excessively, we feel thirsty, the airy element makes us feel hungry, the element of water causes a feeling of cold and the earthy element produces tiredness. On the other hand every over-saturation of the elements causes reinforced effects in the body. A surplus of fiery element creates a yearning for movement and activity. If this be the case with the watery element, the secretive process will be stronger. Any over-saturation of the airy element indicates that we must be moderate in taking food at all. An over-saturation of the earthy element affects the aspects of sexual life, which must not necessarily find expression in the sexual instinct in the fleshly sense. It is quite possible and this will especially occur in the case of elderly people that they feel a longing for increased activity and for productive agility.

In their active and passive polarity the electric and the magnetic fluids have the task of forming acid combinations in all the organic and anorganic bodies, from the chemical point of view, eventually from the alchimistic standpoint, too. In the active sense they are constructive and in the negative sense they are destructive, dissolving and disintegrating. All this explains the biological functions in the body. The final result is the circulation of life, which is brought into existence, thrives, ripens and fades away. This is the sense of evolution of all things created.

Diet

A reasonable line of life maintains the harmony of the elements in the body. As soon as a disharmony in the effect of elements becomes manifest, the elements being extant in a weakened or a prevailing way, special measures have to be taken as far as food is concerned to carry the elements back to their normal course or at least to influence them favourably in this respect. Therefore the most varying diets are prescribed for specific cases. In times long passed, numerous observations led men to this opinion, of which they ignored, the exact reason.

If the disturbance of the elements is such as to render visible this disharmony, it is no longer solely a disharmony but we have to deal with an illness. This will mean that more drastical remedies will be necessary to re-establish the indispensable harmony, providing we desire to bring the body back to its normal function and complete recovery. All the curing methods known up to this day have been based on this fundament. I desist from particularizing such methods, as most of them are generally known. The natural therapy employs thermic effects such as bathings, poultices, herbs, massages, etc. The allopathist utilizes concentrated medicines which are causing the effects corresponding to the elements and destined to repair health. The homœopathist brings to life the contrasting element according to the device *Similia similibus curantur* to achieve the balance of all that is in danger in conformity with the polarity laws. The electro-homœopathist by the use of his remedies, influences the electrical and magnetical fluids directly to balance the disorderly elements, according to the kind of illness, by a suitable reinforcement of these fluids.

And so each curing method serves the purpose of restoring the disturbed equipoise of the elements. By studying these influences of the elements on our body, the magnetopathist or magnetizer has far more possibilities of influencing the body through his powers, especially if he is capable to awake the electrical or magnetical fluid consciously in himself, increasing and transferring it into that part of the body which has come to disharmony. I have dedicated a special head of this book to the practical side of this treatment.

So far the total functions of the body have been stated in detail. But each part of the body is also, in analogy with the effect of the elements in the body, influenced by a specific element which finds its expression in the polarity of the responsive part of the body. It happens to be a very interesting fact that in the workshop resp. in the clockwork or mechanism, I mean to say in the human organism, some organs, from the inside to the outside, reciprocally own the electrical fluid and from the outside to the inside they possess the magnetical fluid, which affects the functions in the entire organism in an analogous and harmonious way. In other organs the reverse process takes place, the electrical fluid operating from the outside to the inside, the magnetical one from the inside to the outside. This knowledge of the polar emanation is called in the hermetic art the *"occult anatomy of the body"*. And the knowledge of the effect of this occult anatomy is extremely important for every adept who wants to know his body, to influence and to control it.

I shall therefore describe this occult anatomy of the human body with respect to the electrical and the magnetical fluid that is to say in the positive and in the negative sphere of action.

These arguments will turn to a magnetopath's great advantage, because, according to the center of the disease, he will treat the sick part of the body either with the electrical or the magnetical fluid. But this knowledge will bring great profit to everybody else, too.

The Head

The forepart is electric, the back of the head is magnetic and so is the right side; the left side is electric and so is the inside.

The Eyes

The forepart is neutral and so is the background. The right side is electric and so it is with the left side. The inside is magnetical.

The Ears

Forepart neutral, back-part also. Right side magnetical, left side electrical, inside neutral.

Mouth and Tongue

Forepart neutral, back-part as well. Right side and left side both neutral, inside magnetical.

The neck

Forepart, back-part and right side magnetical, left side and inside electrical.

The chest

Forepart electromagnetical, back-part electrical, right side and inside neutral, left side electrical.

The abdomen

Forepart electrical, back-part and right side magnetical, left side electrical, the inside magnetical.

The hands

Forepart neutral, back-part also, right side magnetical, left side electrical, the inside neutral.

The fingers of the right hand

Fore- and back-part neutral, right side electrical, left side also, the inside neutral.

The fingers of the left hand

Fore- and back-part neutral, right side electrical, left side as well, the inside neutral.

The feet

Fore- and back-part neutral, right side magnetical, left side electrical, the inside neutral.

The male genitals

Forepart electrical, back-part neutral, right and left side also, the inside magnetical.

The female genitals

Forepart magnetical, back-part, right and left side neutral, the inside electrical.

The last vertebra together with the anus

Fore- and back-part neutral, right and left side as well, the inside magnetical.

With the help of this occult anatomy and the key of the tetrapolar magnet, the adept may compile further analogies if wanted. The alchemist will recognize that the human body represents a genuine *Athanor* in which the most perfect alchemistic process, the great work or the preparation of the *"philosophers' stone"* is visibly performed.

Herewith the chapter dealing with the body is finished. I do not assert that all has been regarded, but in any case, with respect to the elements, I mean to say, the four-pole magnet, I have treated the most important problems and revealed the secret of the tetragrammaton in view of the body.

The roughly material plane or the material world

In this chapter I will not describe the roughly material world, the kingdoms of minerals, vegetables and animals, nor will I deal with the physical processes in nature, because everybody has already learned at school that there are things such as the north- and the south-pole, how rain originates, how storms are brought about, etc. The incipient adept might not be so very interested in these occurrences, he will rather endeavour to know all about the material world by means of the elements and their polarities. It is needless to mention that on our planet, there are fire, water, air and earth, a fact absolutely clear to each reasonably thinking person. Notwithstanding, it will be very useful, if the adept becomes acquainted with the cause and the effect of the four elements and knows how to use them correctly, according to the corresponding analogies on the other planes. How it is possible to contact higher planes through knowing the grossly material elements, will be reserved to a further chapter dealing with the practical use of magic. At the moment, it is important to know that on our earth the working of elements in the most subtile form is evolving off in exactly the same manner as in the human body. By drawing analogies to the human body, one will certainly find out, how to draw the parallel to the elements, and state that the analogy with the human body seems justified. In the chapter relative to the body we have been dicussing the mode of life and the functions of the elements, with respect to the body and, if the adept succeeds in using the elements in the most subtile form, he will already be able to achieve wondrous things on his own body, and not only this, he can, in all conscience, affirm that nothing is impossible in this respect.

The earthy element implies the four-pole magnet with its polarity and the effect of the other elements. The fiery principle, in its active form, causes the vivifying principle in nature and in the negative form the destructive and disintegrating one. The principle of water, in its negative form, is operating the contrary effect. The principle of air, with its bipolar polarity, represents the neutral, the balancing and the preserving essence in nature. The earthy element, according to its peculiarity of cohesion, has as a basis the two great fundamental elements of fire and water together with the neutralization of the airy principle. Hence it must be regarded as the most grossly-material element. By the interaction of the fiery and the watery element, we have, as already mentioned in connection with the body, got the magnetic and the electric fluid, the two basic fluids originating, according to the same laws, in the body and having their mutual effects. Both these elements, with their fluids, are the cause of all that happens materially on our earth, they influence all the chemical processes inside and outside of the earth in the kingdoms of minerals, plants and animals. Hence you see that the electric fluid is to be found in the centre of the earth, whereas the magnetic one is on the surface of our earth. This magnetic fluid of the earth-surface, apart from the property of the principle of water or the cohesion, attracts and holds all material and compound things.

On the basis of the specific properties of an object, which depend on the composition of the elements, each object, with respect to the electric fluid, owns certain emanations, the so-called electronic vibrations which are attracted by the general magnetic fluid of the entire material world. This attraction is called the weight. Consequently, weight is an appearance of the attractive power of the earth. The well-known attractive power of iron and nickel is a little example resp. an imitation of that which is happening, in a big measure, on our whole earth. What we understand, on our earth, as magnetism and electricity, is nothing else but an appearance of the four-pole magnet. For, as we know already, by an arbitrary pole-changing, electricity can be obtained from magnetism and, in a mechanical way, we get magnetism through electricity. The transmutation of one power into another, properly-speaking, is already an alchemistic or magic process, which, however, in the course of time, has been generalized so much that it is no longer regarded as alchemy or magic, but is simply ascribed to physics. For this reason, it is obvious that the four-pole magnet can be used also here. According to the law concerning the problems of magnetism and electricity not only in the body—as mentioned in the foregoing chapter—but also in the grossly-material world, each hermeticist exactly knows that, what is above, is also that which is below. Each adept who knows, how to employ the powers of the element or the great secret of the tetragrammaton on all planes, is also capable to achieve great things in our material world, things which the outsider would regard as miracles. The adept, however, sees no miracles in them, for backed by the knowledge of the laws, he will be able to explain even the most remarkable curiosity.

Everything on our earth, all thriving, ripening, life and death depend on the statements made in these chapters. Hence the adept fully conceives that physic death does not mean disintegration, passing into nothingness, but what we consider as annihilation or death, is nothing else but the transition from one stage into another. The material world has emerged from the principle of *akasha* i. e. the known ether. The world is also controlled and kept by this same principle. Therefore it is understandable that it is the transmission of the electric or the magnetic fluid on which are based all the inventions connected with the communication at distance, through the ether, such as radio, telegraphy, telephony, television and all the other inventions to be achieved in the future, with the aid of the electric or magnetic fluid in the ether. But the fundamental principles and laws were, are and will be always the same.

A very extensive and exciting book could be written solely about the effects of the various magnetic and electric fluids on the grossly-material plane. But the interested reader who has decided to walk on to the path of initiation and will not be deterred by the study of the principles, will find out by himself all about the varieties of powers and properties. The fruits and the insights he earned, in the course of his studies, will indemnify him amply.

The Soul or the Astral Body

Through subtler vibrations of the elements, through the electric and the magnetic fluid of their polarity, the man proper, the soul has proceeded from the *akasha*-principle or the finer etheric vibrations. In the same way as the elements are functioning in the material body, the soul or the so-called astral body will behave. The four-pole magnet, with its specific qualities, connects or amalgamates the soul with the body. This amalgamation takes place, with analogy to the body, by the electro-magnetic influence of the elements. We, the adepts call astral matrix or life this active behaviour of the elements or the so-called electro-magnetic fluid of the soul. This astral matrix or the electric-magnetic fluid of the soul is not identical with the occultists' *aura* I shall speak of later. The astral matrix or the electro-magnetic fluid is the connecting link between body and soul. The fiery principle causes in the soul what is constructive, the principle of water causes the animating, the principle of air is balancing and the earthy principle causes what is thriving, compound and preserving in the soul. The astral body is performing exactly the same functions as the material body.

Man has been fitted out with five senses corresponding to the five elements, of which the astral body or the soul, with the help of the bodily senses, makes use to receive perceptions of the physical world. This receiving and operating of the five senses through the astral and the material body is realized by our immortal spirit. Why this spirit is immortal, this will be explained in a later chapter. Without any activity of the spirit in the soul, the astral body would be without life and dissolve itself into its components.

As the spirit would not be able to operate, without the intervention of the soul, the astral body is the seat of all the qualities the immortal spirit has. According to its development and maturity, spirit has a different electric or magnetic fluid vibration, which becomes patent, in soul, in the four temperaments outwardly. In accordance to the predominant elements, we distinguish the choleric, the sanguine, the melancholic, and the phlegmatic temper. The choleric temper comes from the fiery element, the sanguine temper is due to the element of air, the melancholic temper is born from the watery element and the phlegmatic one is ascribed to the earthy element. To the strength and vibration of the respective element, correspond, in the various properties, the strength, vigour and expansion of the respective fluid vibrations.

Each of these four elements which determine man's temper, in the active form, owns the good or good properties, and in its passive form, the contrary or the bad qualities. It would be too prolix to inform, here, about the effects of the elements, and it is better for the incipient adept to find out himself further effects by his own meditation. This manner also has a very special reason, on the path to initiation. Here I shall cite a few examples only:

The choleric temper, in its active polarity, has the following good qualities: activity, enthusiasm, eagerness, resolution, courage, productivity, etc. In the negative form these qualities are: gluttony, jealousy, passion, irritability, intemperance, bent to destruction, etc.

The sanguine temper in its active form shows: capacity of penetrating, diligence, joy, adroitness, kindness, clearness, lack of grief, cheerfulness, optimism, eagerness, independence, familiarity, etc. In the negative form: continual feeling of being affronted, contempt, propensity to gossipping, lack of endurance, slyness, garrulosity, dishonesty, fickleness, etc.

The melancholic temper in its active form: respectability, modesty, compassion, devotion, seriousness, docility, fervour, cordiality, comprehension, meditation, calmness, quick to give one's confidence, forgiveness, tenderness a. s. o. In the negative form: indifference, depression, apathy, shyness, laziness, etc.

The phlegmatic temper in its active form: respectability, reputation, endurance, consideration, resolution, firmness, seriousness, scrupulousness, thoroughness, concentration, sobriety, punctuality, reservedness, objectivity, infallibility, responsibility, reliability, circumspection, resistance, self-assurance and so on. In the negative form: insipidity, unscrupulousness, misanthropy, dullness, tardiness, laziness, unreliability, laconism and so on.

The qualities of the temperaments, according to the preponderant quality, form the basis of the human character. The intensity of these qualities shown outwardly, depends on the polarity, the electric or the magnetic fluid. The total influence of the effects of the temperaments results in an emanation professionally called *aura*. Therefore this kind of aura is not to be compared with the astral matrix, because between these two conceptions there is a thumping difference. The astral matrix is the connecting substance between body and soul, whilst the aura is the emanation of the action of the elements in the various qualities, having its origin either in the active or in the passive form. This emanation in the whole soul, produces a certain vibration corresponding to a certain colour. On the grounds of this colour, the adept can exactly recognise his own aura or that of an other being with the astral eyes. Backed by this aura, the seer can establish not only a man's basic character, but he also can perceive the action or the polarity of the soul's vibration, and influence it eventually. I shall speak of these problems, in a more detailed way, in a separate chapter relating to introspection. Hence, a man's temperament influences his character, and both together, in their effect as total result, are creating the emanation of the soul or the aura. This is also the reason for high adepts or saints always being represented, in the images, with a halo identical to the aura we have described.

Besides the character, the temperament and the activity of the electro-magnetic fluid, the astral body still has two centres in the brain, the cerebrum being the seat of normal consciousness, whilst in the cerebellum, there is the opposite to the normal consciousness, the sub-consciousness. As to their functions, see chapter concerning the "Spirit".

As it has been said before, according to the elements, the soul is divided in exactly the same way as the body. The psychic functions, powers and properties also have their seat resp. in the soul and certain centers analogous to all the elements which the Indian philosophy designates as lotuses. The awakening of these lotuses is named *Kundalini-yoga* in the Indian doctrine. I desist, however, from a comment on these lotuses or centers, because the student interested in this problem will find all the necessary enlightment in the respective literature. Only slightly I will touch it and say that the lowest center is the so-called *muladhara* or earthy center, having its seat in the lowest part of the soul. The next center is that of the water, with its seat in the region of the sexual organs and designated in the Indian terminology as *swadhistana*. The center of the fire, as center of the soul, is in the umbilical region and is named *manipura*. The center of the air as compensatory element, is in the region of the heart and is termed *anahata*. The center of the ether or principle of akasha is found in the region of the neck and is named *visudha*. Another center, that of volition and intellect is between the eyebrows and is called *ajna*. As the supreme and most divine center is regarded the thousand-leaved lotus, named *sahasrara* from which derive and are influenced all the other powers of the centers. Beginning at the top, from the supreme center, along the back, down to the lowest earthy center, like a channel, runs the so-called *susumna* or the akasha-principle already known to us, liable for the connection and control of the entire centers. Later-on, I shall come back to the problem of the evocation of the snake-power in the single centers. In describing the soul, the principal task will be to establish the connection of the elements with their positive and negative polarities in the soul, and give a neat idea of it. One will see that the body, as well as the soul, with their effects are alive and working, that their preservation and destruction are subject to the immutable laws of the four-pole magnet i. e. the secret of the tetragrammaton, and governed by them. If he who is to be initiated will attentively meditate about it, he will win a clear idea not only of the bodily functions, but also of those of the soul, and come to a sound notion of the mutual interaction according to the original laws.

The Astral Plane

The astral plane often designated as the fourth dimension, has not been created out of the four elements, but it is a density-degree of the akasha-principle, consequently of all that up to now, in the material world occurred, is actually occurring and will occur, and has its origin, regulation and existence. As said before, akasha, in its subtlest form, is the ether well known to all of us in which, amongst other vibrations, electric as well as magnetic ones are propagating. Consequently this vibration-sphere is the origin of light, sound, colour, rhythm, and life in all things created. As akasha is the origin of all existing things, all that ever was produced, is being produced and will be produced in the future, is reflected in it. Therefore, in the astral plane, there is to be seen the emanation of the eternal, having neither a beginning nor an end, as it is timeless and spaceless. The adept who sees his way about this plane, may find every thing here, no matter the point in question be in the past, the present or the future. How far this perception will reach, depends on the degree of his perfection.

Occultists and spiritualists and most of religions name the astral plane the World Beyond. However, the adept knows very well that there is no such thing as Hence and Beyond and feels no fear of death, which concept is quite strange to him. If, by the disintegrating work of the elements or a sudden break-up, the astral matrix which is the connecting matter between the grossly material body and the astral body, has got loose, then will happen what we commonly call death which, however, in reality is nothing else but a passage from the terrestrial world to the astral world. Backed-up by this law, the adept knows no fear of death, being convinced that he will not approach uncertainty. Through his control of the elements, besides many other things, he also can achieve a slackening of the astral matrix, which will result in a spontaneous separation of the astral body from the mortal frame. Thus he will be able to visit the remotest regions, transfer himself into various planes in the form of his astral body. This is the positive explanation of so many tales in which saints have been seen, at the same time, in different places and have even been working there.

The astral plane has various kinds of inhabitants. First of all, there are the deceased ones who having left the earth are abiding in the corresponding density-degree, according to their spiritual maturity, which is designated by the various religions as heaven or hell, the adepts seeing only symbols therein. The nobler, purer and the more perfect an entity happens to be, all the purer and finer will be the density-degree of the inhabited astral plane. Little by little, the astral body is dissolving, until it has become suitable to the degree of vibrations of the respective step of the astral level, or identical with it. As you see, this identification depends on the maturity and the spiritual perfection the entity concerned achieved on this earth.

Besides, the astral plane is inhabited by many other beings of which I am mentioning only some species here. There are e. g. the so-called elementaries, entities with one or only very few qualities, according to the dominant vibrations of the elements. They are living on the similar vibrations proper to man and transmitted by him into the astral plane. Among them, there are some which have already reached a certain degree of intelligence, and some magicians are using these low-powered beings for their selfish purposes. Another kind of beings are the *larvae* which have been brought into life consciously or unconsciously, by intense sensorial thinking, through the astral matrix. They are not real beings, but only forms thriving on the passions of the animal world, on the lowest step of the astral level. Their instinct of self-preservation carries them into the sphere of those men whose passions are responsive to them. They will try, directly or indirectly, to raise and kindle the passions slumbering in man. If these forms are succeeding in seducing men to give in to their suitable passion, they are feeding and thriving on the emanation of this passion produced in man. Man laden with many passions will attract a host of such larvae in the lowest sphere of his astral plane. A great fight takes place and, in the problem of magic, this fact plays an important role. More about it is to be found in the chapter dealing with introspection. There are also other elementaries and larvae which can be produced in the artificial magic way. As to further details, see in the practical part of this book.

Another kind of beings the adept often has to deal with, in the astral plane, must not be overlooked namely the beings of the four pure elements. In the element of fire, their name is salamander, in the airy element they are the sylphides, in the water-element, they are called mermaids or undines and in the element of earth there are the gnomes or goblins. These beings represent, as it were, the connection between the astral plane and the earthly elements. How to establish the connection with these beings, how to control them, what can be achieved with their help, all this will be reserved to the practical part of the present book to which I shall dedicate the special chapter "magic of the elements".

Furthermore, there is a host of other beings such as satyres, woodmaidens, watergoblins, etc. who could be specified. Even if all this sounds like a fairy-tale, on the astral plane, the previously described beings are the very same realities as all the other earthly beings. The adept's clairvoyant eyes can see all of them, if he desires so, and is able to establish the connection with them, so excluding any doubt of the existence of these beings right from the beginning. That is why the adept has to ripen first and learn to examine, before being able to judge.

The Spirit

It has been said before that man has been created in the image of God and consists of body, soul and spirit. The preceding chapters have made it evident that body and soul serve only as a veil or garment for the spirit. The spirit is the immortal part and the image of God. It is not easy to define something divine, immortal, imperishable, and to put it into the correct terms. But here, as well as with any other problem, the key of the four-pole magnet will be a great help for us.

From the supreme prototype (akasha), original source of all beings, has proceeded the spirit, the spiritual EGO with the four specific elemental qualities, proper to the immortal spirit which was created in God's image.

The fiery principle, the impulsive part, means the will (volition). The airy principle shows up in the intellect (mind), the watery principle resp. in the life and the feeling, and the earthy principle is representing the union of all the three elements in the consciousness of the *ego*.

All the other qualities of the spirit are based upon these four original principles. The typical part of the fifth, say, the etheric principle (akasha) manifests itself, in the highest aspect, in the faith and, in the lowest form, in the instinct of self-preservation. Each of these mentioned four elemental principles has many other aspects corresponding to the law of analogy of the polarity or the positive and negative elements. All of them together form the "*ego*" or the spirit. For this reason, we can make responsible the fiery principle for strength, power and passion; memory, power of discrimination and judgement are ascribed to the airy principle, conscience and intuition to the principle of water, egotism and the instincts of self-preservation and propagation to the earthy part of the spirit.

It would be too long to quote all the properties of the spirit with regard to the elements. The incipient adept can enlarge these qualities by serious studies and deep meditation, with respect to the analogous laws of the four-pole magnet. This happens to be a very meritorious work which never ought to be neglected, because it will lead to great success and secure results.

These three chapters relating to body, soul and spirit have represented man in his most perfect form. By now, the disciple ought to have realised how very important it is to know one's own microcosm for the initiation and especially for the magic and the mystic practice, as a matter of fact, for the whole of the secrets. Most of the authors, from sheer ignorance or for other cogent reasons, have omitted this extremely important part, the foundation.

The Mental Plane

As the body has its earthly plane, and the astral body or the soul owns the astral plane, the spirit, too, has its own plane, the so-called mental plane or mental sphere. This is the mental sphere with all its virtues.

Both these spheres, the material as well as the astral one have been born from the akasha or original principle of the respective sphere, through the four elements, and also the mental sphere is built upon the same foundation, and therefore likewise a product of the akasha principle of the spirit. Similar to the spirit, developing in a four-pole magnet by corresponding work and showing an electro-magnetic fluid analogous to the astral body, on account of the effect of the elements, as a secondary phenomenon of the polarity on the outside, the mental body develops in the mental or spiritual sphere. Just in the same way as the astral body, through the electro-magnetic fluid of the astral world, forms an astral matrix, the so-called astral *od,* the electro-magnetic fluid of the mental world forms a mental matrix linking the mental body to the astral body. This mental matrix or the mental od, the so-called mental substance is the subtlest form of *akasha* which controls and preserves the spiritual activity in the astral body.

At the same time, this mental substance is electro-magnetic and is regarded as leader of the ideas to the consciousness of the spirit, from where it is put into activity through the astral and the roughly material body. So this mental matrix or the mental od, with its double-pole fluid, is the subtlest substance we can imagine in the human body.

Simultaneously, the mental sphere is the sphere of thoughts which have their origin in the world of ideas, consequently in the spiritual *akasha*. Each thought is preceded by a basic idea which, according to its property, accepts a definite form, and arrives to the consciousness of the ego through the etheric principle, consequently the mental matrix, as expression of the thought in the shape of a plastic picture. Therefore Man himself is not the founder of the thoughts, but the origin of each thought is to be sought in the supreme *akasha* sphere or the mental plane. Man's spirit, as it were, is the receiver, the antenna of thoughts from the world of ideas, according to the situation in which Man happens to be. The world of ideas being all in all, each new idea, new invention, in short, all Man believes to have created by himself, has been brought out of this world of ideas. This production of new ideas depends on the maturity and attitude of the spirit. Each thought involves an absolutely pure element especially if the thought implies abstract ideas. If the thought is based on several combinations of the ideal world, different elements are effective in their form as well as in their mutual emanation. Only abstract ideas have pure elements and pure polar emanations, as they descend directly from the causal world of an idea.

From this cognition we may draw the conclusion that there are pure electric, pure magnetic, indifferent and neutral ideas from the standpoint of their effect. According to the idea, each thought in the mental sphere has its own form, colour and vibration. Through the tetra-polar magnet of the spirit, the thought arrives at the consciousness, from where it is forwarded to realisation. Each thing created in the material world consequently has its cause in the ideal world through the thought and the spiritual consciousness, and is reflected therein. If the point in question is not exactly an abstract idea, several forms of ideas can be expressed. Such thoughts are electric or magnetic or electro-magnetic, according to the elemental property of the idea.

The material plane is bound to time and space. The astral plane, sphere of the perishable or mutable spirit, is bound to space, the mental sphere being timeless and spaceless. The very same thing happens with all the mental properties. The reception of a thought in the mental body, through the link of the astral and mental matrix bound to space and time in the total form, needs a certain amount of time to become fully conscious of this thought. According to the mental maturity, the train of thoughts is different in each individual. The more advanced, the more cultured man is, the faster thoughts will develop in mind.

Likewise as the astral plane is inhabited, so is the mental plane, too. Besides the ideal forms, there are principally the deceased ones whose astral bodies have been dissolved by the elements in the course of their ripening, and alotted, according to the degree of perfection, to regions corresponding to their mental sphere.

Besides the mental sphere is the sphere of the so-called elementals, beings created consciously or unconsciously by Man as a result of repeated and intense thinking. An elemental being is not yet so much condensed to form or to assume any astral shape for itself. Its influence is therefore limited to the mental sphere. The difference between an ideal form and an elemental lies in the fact that the ideal form is based on one or several ideas. On the other hand, the elemental is equipped with a certain quantity of consciousness and therefore with the instinct of preservation, but otherwise it does not much distinguish from other mental living beings, it can even take the same shape as the ideal form. The adept often resorts to these elemental beings. How to create such an elemental, how to preserve it and how to to utilize it for certain purposes, this problem will be approached in the practical part of this book.

There would be still quite a lot to be said about the particular, specific properties of some beings. But all that we have pointed out previously should be sufficient to stimulate the work and contribute to a succint enlightenment about the mental plane.

Truth

Let us now leave the microcosm, I mean to say, Man with his earthly, astral and mental body, and turn to other problems which also are imminent to be solved by the incipient adept. First of all, there is the problem of truth. A great many philosophers have often already paid a serious attention to this problem, and we also will have to approach this task.

We shall deal here only with such kinds of truth we must be informed about thoronghly. Truth depends on the insight of each individual. And as we cannot, all of us, have the same insight or perception, it is impossible to generalize the problem of truth. Therefore from his standpoint and in conformity with the degree of his maturity, each one will have his own truth, providing he sees it quite honestly. Only he who knows and masters the absolute laws of the microcosm and the macrocosm is entitled to speak of an absolute truth. Certain aspects of the absolute truth will be surely acknowledged by everyone. Nobody, indeed, will doubt that there is life, volition, memory and intellect, and will refrain from arguing about these facts. No sincere adept will impose his truth to anyone who is not yet ripe for it. The person concerned would do nothing else but regard it again from his own standpoint. Therefore it would be useless to argue with non professionals on higher kinds of truth, excepting people eager to search the heights of truth and beginning to ripen for it. Anything else would be a profanation and, from the magic point of view, absolutely incorrect. At this point, all of us will have to remember the words of the great Master of Christianity: "neither cast ye your pearls before swine, lest they trample them under their feet."

To truth belongs also the capacity of correctly differentiating among knowledge and wisdom. Knowledge depends, in all domains of the human existence, on the maturity, receptivity and understanding of the mind, and the memory without regard to whether or not we have heen able to enrich our knowledge by reading, transmitting or other experiences.

There is a wide difference between knowledge and wisdom and it is much easier to win knowledge than wisdom. Wisdom depends, not in the least, on knowledge although both are identical up to a certain degree. The source of wisdom is in God that is to say in the causal principle (the *akasha)* on all planes of the grossly-material, astral and mental world. Therefore wisdom does not depend on mind and memory but on the maturity, purity and perfection of the individual personality. Wisdom could also be considered as a developmental stage of the "ego". Therefore insights are not passed on through the mind, but—and this particularly—through intuition or inspiration. The degree of wisdom is therefore determined by the state of development of the individual.

This will not mean, of course, that we ought to neglect knowledge, on the contrary, knowledge and wisdom must go hand in hand. The adept will therefore endeavour to get on in knowledge as well as in wisdom for none of the two must lag behind in development.

If knowledge and wisdom keep the same pace in the development, the adept is enabled to grasp all the laws of the microcosm and the macrocosm, not only from the point of wisdom, but also from the intellectual side that is to say in a bipolar way, namely to perceive and utilize them for his own development.

In all the planes, we have already learned to know one of the numerous laws, the first main key, the secret of the tetragrammaton or the four-pole magnet. Being a universal key it can be used to solve all problems, all laws, all kinds of truth, in short, everything, provided the adept knows how to use it properly. As time goes on and his development unfolds and he is advancing in hermetics, he will be acquainted with many an aspect more of this key, and be forced to accept it as an unchangeable law. He will no more wander in darkness and uncertainty, but he will carry a torch in his hand, the light of which will penetrate the night of ignorance.

This brief summary will suffice for the adept to instruct him how to deal with the problem of truth.

Religion

The incipient magician will confess his faith to a universal religion. He will find out that every religion has good points as well as bad ones. He will therefore keep the best of it for himself and ignore the weak points, which does not mean necessarily that he must profess a religion but he shall express awe to each form of worship, for each religion has its proper principle of God, whether the point in question be Christianity, Buddhism, Islam or any other kind of religion. Fundamemtally he may be faithful to his own religion. But he will not be satisfied with the official doctrines of his Church and try to penetrate deeper into God's workshop. And such is the purpose of our initiation. According to the universal laws, the magician will form his own point of view about the universe which henceforth will be his true religion. He will state that, apart from the deficiencies, each defender of religion will endeavour to represent his own religion as the best of all. Each religious truth is relative and the comprehension of it depends on the maturity of the person concerned. Therefore the adept does not interfere with anybody in this respect, nor will he try to sidetrack anyone from his truth, criticize him, to say nothing of condemning him. At the bottom of his heart he may feel sorry for fanatics or atheists without showing it outwardly. Let everybody hold on to what he is believing and makes him happy and content.

Should everybody stick to this maxim, there would be neither hatred nor religious dissensions on this earth. There would be no reason for disputes and all turns of mind could exist happily side by side.

Quite a different thing is, if a seeker, dissatisfied by materialism and doctrines, and longing for spiritual support, will ask advice and information of an adept. In such a case the adept is obliged to supply the seeker with spiritual light and insight, according to his mental powers. Then the magician should spare neither time nor pains to communicate his spiritual treasures and lead the seeker to the light.

God

Since the remotest ages, Mankind has always believed in something beyond human understanding, something transcendental he idolized, no matter, whether there was question of personified or unpersonified conceptions of God. Anything man was unable to understand or to comprehend was imputed to the powers above such as his intuitive virtue admitted them. In this way, all the deities of mankind, good and evil ones (demons) have been born. As time went on, gods, angels, demiurges, demons and ghosts have been worshipped irrespective of their having ever been alive in reality or their having existed in fancy only. With the development of mankind, the idea of God was shrinking especially at the time when, with the aid of the sciences, were explained phenomena ascribed before to the gods. A lot of books would have to be written if one wished to enter into details of the various ideas of God in the history of the nations.

Let us approach the idea of God from a magician's standpoint. To the ordinary man the idea of God serves as support for his spirit so as not to entangle himself in uncertainty, or to loose his spiritual balance. Therefore his God remains always something unconceivable, intangible and incomprehensible for him. It is quite otherwise with the magician who knows his God in all aspects. He holds his God in awe as he knows himself to have been created in his image, consequently to be a part of God. He sees his lofty ideal, his first duty and his sacred objective in the union with the Godhead, in becoming the God-man. The rise to this sublime goal shall be described further on. The synthesis of this mystic union with God consists in developing the divine ideas, from the lowest up to the highest steps, in such a degree as to attain the union with the universal. Everyone is at liberty to abandon his individuality or to retain it. Such genii usually return to earth entrusted with a definite sacred task or mission.

In this rise, the initiated magician is a mystic at the same time. Only performing this union and giving up his individuality, he voluntarily enters into dissolution which in the mystic wording is called mystic death.

It is evident that true initiation knows neither a mystic nor a magic path. There is only one initiation linking both conceptions, in opposition to most of the mystic and spiritual schools which are dealing with the very highest problems, through meditation or other spiritual exercisis, without having gone through the first steps at first. This would be similar to somebody starting with the university studies, without going through the elementary classes first. The results of such a one-sided training, in some cases, are disastrous, sometimes even drastic, according to the individual talents. The error is generally to be found in the fact that most of the matter comes from the Orient, where the material as well as the astral world is regarded as *maya* (illusion) and, consequently, paid little attention to. It is impossible to point out details, for this would overstep the frame of this book. Sticking to a carefully planned, step-by-step development, there will be neither a mishap nor a failure or bad consequences, for the simple reason that ripening takes place slowly, but surely. It is quite an individual matter, whether the adept will choose, as his idea of God, Christ, Buddha, Brahma, Allah or someone else. All depends on the idea, in the initiation. The pure mystic wishes to approach his God only in the all-embracing love. The *yogi*, too, walks towards one single aspect of God. The *bhakti yogi* keeps to the road of love and devotion, the RAJA and *hatha yogi* choose the path of self-control or volition, the *jnana yogi* will follow that of wisdom and cognition.

Let us regard the idea of God, now, from the magic standpoint, according to the four elements, the so-called *tetragrammaton,* the unspeakable, the supreme: the fiery principle involves the almightiness and the omnipotence, the airy original principle owns the wisdom, purity and clearness, from the aspect of which proceeds the universal lawfulness. Love and eternal life are attributed to the watery principle, and omnipresence, immortality and consequently eternity belong to the earthy principle. These four aspects together represent the supreme Godhead. Let us tread upon this path to this supreme Godhead practically and step by step, beginning from the lowest sphere, arrive at the true realisation of God in ourselves. Let us praise the happy man who will reach this still in his earthly existence. Let us banish fear of the pains, for all of us will once reach this aim.

Asceticism

From the remotest times, all religions, sects, turns of mind and training systems have regarded asceticism as a very important problem. Various systems of the Orient turned asceticism into fanaticism, causing great damages by exaggeration and wild excesses which were unnatural and unlawful. The mortification of the flesh, generally speaking, is just as one-sided as developing one part of the body only, neglecting all the other parts. If asceticism serves the human body, say, in the pattern of a diet, to get rid of slags and other impurities, or save the body from illness and compensate disharmonies, ascetic measures may reasonably be employed, but beware of any exaggeration.

Somebody doing hard physical work would, indeed, be very foolish to deprive the body of substances absolutely necessary for its preservation, just because he is privately interested in yoga or mysticism. Such extremes would, doubtlessly, end up with serious and dangerous injuries to the health.

Vegetarianism is not implicitly important for the mental progress or the intellectual development, unless it is supposed to be a remedy to clean the body from slags. A temporary abstinence from meat or animal food is indicated only for very specific magic operations as a sort of preparation, and even then only for a certain period. All this is to be considered with respect to sexual life.

The idea that, by eating the meat of an animal, the animal powers or faculties could be conveyed to oneself is nonsense and originates in a mentality ignoring the perfect and genuine primitive laws. The magician does not pay any attention to such misconception.

In the interest of his mago-mystic development, the magician must be moderate in eating and drinking, and observe a reasonable mode of life. It is impossible to fix precise rules or prescriptions, the magic way of life being quite individual. Each and all must know best what agrees or disagrees with them. It is a sacred duty to keep the balance everywhere. There are three kinds of asceticism: 1. intellectual or mental asceticism 2. psychic or astral asceticism 3. physical or material asceticism. The first kind has to do with the discipline of thoughts, the second kind is engaged in ennobling the soul through control of passions and instincts, and the third kind is concerned with harmonizing the body through a moderate and natural way of life. Without these three kinds of asceticism which must be developed at the same time and parallel to each other, a correct magical rise is unthinkable. None of the three kinds may be neglected, none of them may prevail to avoid any one-sided development. Further information about how to accomplish this task will be given in the practical training course of this book.

Before bringing the theoretic part to an end which has illustrated the theoretic principles, I advise everybody that this part should not only be read, but must become the mental possession of the concerned person by means of intense reflection and meditation. He who is going to be a magician will recognize that life is dependent on the work of the elements in the various planes and spheres. It is to be seen in great and in small things, in the microcosm as well as in the macrocosm, temporally and eternally, everywhere there are powers in action. Starting from this point of cognition, you will find out that there is no death at all, in the true sense of the word, but everything goes on living, transmuting and becoming perfect according to primitive laws. Therefore a magician is not afraid of death, for he believes the physical death to be only a transition to a subtler sphere, the astral plane, and from there to the spiritual level and so on. Consequently he will neither believe in heaven nor in hell. The priests of the various religions stick to these fancies solely to keep their kids to the point. Their moralizing serves only to provoke fear of the hell or the purgatory and to promise heaven to morally good people. Average people, as far as they are religiously inclined, are favourably influenced by such a point of view, for, from fear of hell, they will try to be good.

But as to the magician, he sees the purpose of the moral laws in ennobling the mind and the soul, for it is in an ennobled soul only that the universal powers can do their work, especially if body, soul and mind have been equally trained and developed.

PART II

PRACTICE

STEP I

Let us now turn to the practical side of the initiation. We must always be aware of the fact that body, soul and mind are to be trained simultaneously, for, otherwise, it would be impossible to gain and maintain the magic equipoise. In the theoretic part I already called the attention to the dangers possibly arising from a one-sided training. It is not advisable to hasten development, because everything needs time. Patience, perseverance and tenacity are fundamental conditions of the development. The pains taken in one's development will amply be rewarded. Whosoever is willing to enter the magic path, should regard it his sacred duty to practise regular exercises. He ought to be kind, generous and tolerant with his fellow-men but relentless and hard with himself. Only such a behaviour will be followed by success in magic. Refrain from condemning or criticizing and sweep first before the own doorsteps. Do not permit anyone to look into your sanctuary. The magician will always keep silence with respect to his way, rise and success. This silence grants the highest powers and the more this commandment is obeyed, the more easily accessible will these powers be. Do manage it so that you spend as much time as possible in your rise or advance. It is quite unnecessary to waste time with sitting, for hours, drinking beer and passing time in a trivial company. Time is running away like water never to come back again. A certain amount of time ought to be provided for, but it is very necessary to stick to it. Exceptions ought to be allowed only in quite inevitable cases. Man is subject to habits and once accustomed to a definite time-table for his exercises, he will feel compelled to do his exercises. In the same way as there is a want for the necessities of life such as eating, drinking and sleeping, it ought to happen in regard of the exercises which must become, as it were, a habit. This is the sole way to attain a sure and full success. There is no prize without diligence. It is my ambition to arrange for the instructions as if they were meant for the busiest man. He who has plenty of time on hand, may be able to be occupied with two or more exercises at the same time.

Magic Mental Training (I)

Thought-control, discipline of thoughts, subordination of thoughts

Take a seat in a comfortable chair or lie down on a settee. Relax the whole body, close your eyes and observe the train of your thoughts for five minutes trying to retain it. At first, you will find that there are rushing up to you thoughts concerning every-day affairs, professional worries and such like. Take the behaviour of a silent observer towards these trains of thoughts, freely and independently. According to the mentality and the mental situation, you happen to be in at this moment, this exercise will be more or less easy for you. The main point then is not to forget yourself, not to loose the train of thoughts, but pursue it attentively. Be aware of falling asleep while doing this exercise. If you begin feeling tired, stop instantly and postpone the exercise to another time, when you intend not to give in to tiredness. The Indians e. g. sprinkle cold water in their faces or rub it down the face and the upper part of their bodies to remain brisk and not to waste precious time. Some deep breathings before you begin, will also do to prevent and keep from tiredness and sleepiness. As time goes on, every disciple will find out such little tricks by himself. This exercise of controlling thoughts has to be undertaken in the morning and at night. It is to be extended each day by one minute to allow the own train of thoughts to be pursued and controlled without the slightest digression for a time of 10 minutes at least after a week's training.

This space of time is destined to the average-man. If it should not suffice, everyone can extend it, according to his own apperception. At all events, it is advisable to go ahead very consciously, because it is no use to hurry, development being quite individual in men. On no account go further, before the preceding exercise is perfectly under control.

The attentive disciple will realize how, at the beginning, thoughts rush on to him, how rapidly they pass before him so that he will have difficulties to recollect the lot of manifold thoughts. But from one exercise to the next, he will state that thoughts come up less chaotic, moderating little by little, until at last only few thoughts emerge in his consciousness arriving, as it were, from a far distance.

To this work of thought-control the keenest attention ought to be given as it is very important, for the magic development, a fact everybody will realise later on himself.

Providing the mentioned exercise has been thoroughly worked through and everyone has a complete command of it in the practice, let us pass over to the mental training.

Up to now, we have learned to control our thoughts. The next exercise will consist in not giving way in our mind to thoughts obtruding themselves on our mind, unwanted and obstinate. For instance, we must be able not to occupy ourself any longer with the tasks and worries of our profession when we come home from it and return to the family circle and the privacy. All thoughts not belonging to our privacy must be set aside, and we ought to manage to become quite a different personality instantly. And just the other way round: in our job, all our thoughts have to be concentrated in it exclusively, and we must not allow them to digress or wander, say, home, to private affairs or somewhere else. This has to be practised time and again, until it has developed a habit. One ought to accustom oneself, above all, to achieve whatever one does, whether in professional work or in privacy, with full consciousness, regardless of the point being a big or a trifle one. This exercise should be kept for a lifetime, because it is sharpening the mind and strengthening the consciousness and the memory.

Having obtained a certain skill in this exercise, you may turn to the following one. The purpose will now be to hold on to a single thought or idea for a longer while, and suppress any other thoughts associating and obtruding with force on the mind. Choose for this purpose any train of thoughts or ideation or a suitable presentation according to your personal taste. Hold on to this presentation with all your strength. Refuse all the other thoughts vigorously which have nothing to do with the thoughts exercising. At first, you will probably succeed only for a few seconds, later on for minutes. You must manage to concentrate on one single thought and follow it for 10 minutes at least.

If you succeed in doing so, you will be fit for a new exercise. Let us then learn how to produce an absolute vacancy of mind. Lie comfortably down on a bed or settee or sit in an armchair and relax your whole body. Close your eyes. Dismiss energetically any thought coming upon you. Nothing at all is allowed to happen in your mind, there must reign an absolute vacancy. Now hold on to this stage of vacancy without digressing or forgetting. At first, you will manage to do so a few seconds only, but when practising it oftener, you will surely succeed better in it. The purpose of the exercise will be attained if you succeed in remaining in this state for full 10 minutes without losing your self-control or even falling asleep.

Enter your success, failure, duration of your exercises and eventual disturbances carefully into a magic note-book, (see details under the heading "Magic Soul Training"). Such a diary will be useful to check your progress. The greater the scrupulousness you use in doing so, the more easily you will undergo all the other exercises. Prepare a working schedule for the coming day or week and, most of all, indulge in self-criticism.

Magic Psychic Training (I)

Introspection or self-knowledge

In our own mansion, meaning our body and our soul, we must, at every moment, find our way about. Therefore our first task will be to know ourselves. Each initiation system, no matter which kind it be, will put this condition in the first place. Without self-knowledge there will be no real development on a higher level.

In the first days of psychic training, let us deal with the practical part of introspection or self-knowledge. Arrange for a magic diary and enter all the bad sides of your soul into it. This diary is for your own use only, and must not be shown to anybody else. It represents the so-called control-book for you. In the self-control of your failures, habits, passions, instincts and other ugly character traits, you have to observe a hard and severe attitude towards yourself. Be merciless towards yourself and do not embellish any of your failures and deficiencies. Think about yourself in quiet meditation, put yourself back into different situations of your past, remember how you did behave then and which mistakes or failures occurred in the various situations. Make notes of all your weaknesses, down to the finest nuances and variations. The more you are discovering, all the better for you. Nothing must remain hidden, nothing unrevealed, however insignificant or great your faults or frailties may be. Some especially endowed disciples have been able to discover hundreds of failures in the finest shades. Disciples like these possessed a good meditation and a deep penetration into their own souls. Wash your soul perfectly clean, sweep all the dust out of it.

This self-analysis is one of the most important magic preliminaries. Many of the occult systems have neglected it, and that is why they did not achieve good results. This psychic preliminary work is indispensable to obtain the magic equilibrium, and without it, there is no regular progress of the development to be thought of. You therefore ought to vow some minutes' time to self-criticism in the morning and at night. If you have got the chance of some free moments during the day, avail yourself of them and do some intensive thinking, whether there are still some faults hidden anywhere and if you discover them, reeord them on the spot not to forget a single one. Whenever you happen to find out any deficiency, do not delay to note it immediately.

If you do not succeed, within a weeck, in discovering all your faults, spend another week on these inquiries until you have definitely established your list of offences. Having achieved this problem within one or two weeks, you have reached the point to begin with a further exercise. Now by intensive thinking, try to assign each fault to one of the four elements. Appoint a rubric in your diary to each element and enter your faults into it. About some of the faults you will not feel sure which of the elements they are to be assigned to. Record them under the heading of "indifferent". In the progressing development you will be able to determine the element corresponding to your deficiency.

For instance, you will ascribe jealousy, hatred, vindictiveness, irrascibility, anger to the fiery element; frivolity, self-presumption, boasting, squandering, gossiping to the element of air; indifference, laziness, frigidity, compliance, negligence, shyness, insolence, instability to the watery element; laziness, conscienceless, melancholy, irregularity, anomaly and dullness to the element of earth.

In the following week you will meditate on each single rubric dividing it in three groups. In the first group you will enter the biggest failures, especially those which influence you strongest or happen at the slightest opportunity. The second group will embrace faults occurring less frequently and in a slighter degree. In the last group you are recording those faults which happen only now and again. Go on doing so with the indifferent faults, too. Work conscientiously at all times, it is worth while!

Repeat the whole procedure with your good psychical qualities, entering them into the respective categories of the elements. Do not forget the three columns here as well. So e. g. you will assign activity, enthusiasm, firmness, courage, daring to the fiery element; diligence, joy, dexterity, kindness, lust, optimism to the air element; modesty, abstemiousness, fervency, compassion, tranquillity, tenderness, forgiveness to the watery element; respect, endurance, conscientiousness, thoroughness, sobriety, punctuality, responsibility to the earthy element.

By doing so, you will get two so-called astral psycho-mirrors, a black one, with the evil psychic qualities, and a white one, with the good and noble character traits. These two magic mirrors are correct occult mirrors, and none but the owner has any rights to look into them at all. Let me repeat once more that the owner must endeavour to elaborate his magic mirrors precisely and conscientiously. If, in the course of the development, he should remember any good or bad quality, he can still record it under the respective heading. These two magic mirrors will allow the magician to recognise rather exactly which of the elements is prevailing in his black or white mirror. This recognition is absolutely necessary to attain the magic equipoise, and the further development depends on it.

Magic Physical Training (I)

The material or carnal body

Hand in hand with the development of spirit and soul has to go that of the outwards, I mean the body also. No part of our EGO must lag behind or be neglected. Right in the morning, after getting up, you will brush your body with a soft brush, until your skin turns faintly reddish. By doing so, your pores will open and be able to breathe more freely. Besides, the kidneys are exonerated for the most part. Then wash your whole body or the upper part of it, at least, with cold water and rub it with a rough towel, until you feel quite warm. Sensitive people may use luke-warm water, especially in the cold season. This procedure ought to become a day's routine and be kept for life-time. It is so refreshing and removes tiredness.

In addition to this, you should practise morning gymnastics, at least for some minutes a day, to keep your body flexible. I shall not put up a special programme of such gymnastic exercise as everybody can draw it up, according to his age and personal liking. What matters chiefly, is to get your body elastic.

Mystery of Breathing

Breathing is to be given your very careful consideration. Normally each living creature is bound to breathe. There is no life at all, without breathing. It is obvious that a magician ought to know more than the mere fact of inhaling oxygen together with nitrogen which the lungs absorb and exhale as nitrogen. The lungs cannot exist without breathing and food. All we need for our life, and what preserves our life, say, breathing and food is tetrapolar, four elemental plus the fifth, the vital element or akasha principle as we have said in the theoretical part about the elements. But the air we are inhaling has a finer degree of density than the grossly material food has. But according to the universal laws, both of them have the same nature, being tetrapolar and serving to keep the body alive. Let us therefore turn to breathing.

Oxygen is subject to the fiery element and nitrogen to the element of water. The airy element is the mediating element and the earth element is that which holds together the oxygen and the nitrogen. The akasha or etheric element is the lawful causal or divine principle. Just as in the great universe, the nature, here the elements, too, have their polarity, the electric as well as the magnetic fluid. By normal or unconscious breathing, the body is supplied only with as much elemental substance as is necessary for its normal preservation. Here also the supply depends on the consumption of elemental substance. Quite different it is with conscious breathing.

If we put a thought, an idea or an image, no matter whether it be concrete or abstract, in the air to be inhaled, it will take in the akasha principle of the air concerned, and convey it, through the electric and magnetic fluids, to the air substance. This impregnate air substance when conveyed to the lungs, through the blood-vessels, will play a double role. In the first place, the material parts of the elements are destined to preserve the body, secondly the electro-magnetic fluid, charged with the idea or the image, will lead the electro-magnetic air coloured with the idea, from the blood-stream through the astral matrix, to the astral body, and from there to the immortal spirit through the reflective mental matrix.

And this is the solution of the secret of breathing from the magic point of view. Many theologies utilize conscious breathing for instructive purposes, as for example the *hatha-yoga-system*, without knowing the right process. Several people have suffered severe damages of their health, a fact only to blame on the extreme breathing exercises asked for by this system, especially, when such practices have been realized without the guidance of an experienced leader *(guru)*. In most of the cases, the unexperienced reader has been persuaded to do these practise, because they were promising a quick acquiring of occult powers. If he wants, the magician will reach this aim much more easily and sooner with the aid of the universal initiating system described so thoroughly and in all details in the present book.

Consequently, it is quite evident that it is not the quantity of the inhaled air that matters, but the quality resp. the idea impregnating the air substance. Therefore it is not necessary nor even advisable to pump the lungs full with a lot af air, putting a needless strain on them. Consequently, you will do your breathing exercises slowly and calmly, without any haste.

Sit down comfortably, relax the whole body and breathe in through the nose. Imagine that, with the inhaled air, health, tranquillity, peace, success or everything you are aiming at, will pass into your body through the lungs and the blood. The eidetic image of your idea must be so intense that the air you are inspiring is so strongly impregnated with your desire that it has already become reality. You should not allow the slightest doubt about this fact. To avoid weakening, it will be enough to start with seven inhalings in the morning as well as at night. Increase the number of breathings gradually to one more in the morning and at night. Do not hurry or exaggerate, for everything needs time. In any case you should not proceed to the imagination of another desire different before the chosen one has not been completety accomplished. In a pupil endowed with talents of a high order, success will manifest itself, at the earliest, after seven days, all depending on the degree of imagination and aptitude. Some one, for the realisation of his desires will need weeks, even months, because the kind of desires will also play an important role. It is therefore advisable not to form egoistic wishes to begin with, but confine them to the above mentioned ones, such as tranquillity, health, peace and success. Do not extend breathing exercises to over more than ½ hour. Later on, a 10 minutes' standard will do for you.

Conscious Reception of Food

What has been said about breathing, applies in the same way to taking nourishment. Here also the same elemental processes are going on, as they happened to do in the air to be inhaled, but the effect of the elements is stronger and more material. Desires impressed on food have a considerable influence on the material plane where they are exposed to the most material emanations of the elements. The magician, therefore, will do best to consider this aspect, if he wants to achieve anything concerning his body or other material desires.

Now sit down in front of your dish of food which you are going to eat, and with the intensest possible imagination, concentrate on your desire being embodied in the food and as effective as if it had, indeed, been realized already. If you happen to be alone, undisturbed and not watched by anyone, hold your hands in a blessing manner above your food. Not having this opportunity, at least, impress your desire on the food you are taking in or close your eyes. You may give the impression of saying a prayer before eating your meal, a gesture which, as a matter of fact, is quite true. Then eat your food slowly but consciously with the intrinsic conviction that, factually, together with the food, your desire is passing into your whole body, down to the finest nerves. The taking of food ought to be to you something similar to the communion of Christians, as it were, a sacred act.

For the magic constitution it is not advisable to eat in a hurry. All kinds of food and beverages are suitable for the magic impregnation with desires. Yet all the impregnate foods and drinks have to be consumed entirely and nothing should be left over. Do not read during a meal. Unfortunately a great deal of people are in this bad habit. Any kind of conversation is also undesirable. One should eat only with the maintenance of one's desire. It is to be noted that no opposite desire should associate. For instance, if you are aspiring after health through conscious or magic breathing, you must not concentrate on success during your meal. It is most advantageous to foster the same desire in breathing as well as in eating to avoid any opposite vibration or emanations in your body. Remember the proverb: "He who chases two hares at the same time, will never catch one."

Who, in conscious reception of food, takes example in the eucharistic mystery, will find an analogy to it here, and remembering the words of our Lord Jesus Christ: "Take and eat, for this is my flesh, take and drink, for this is my blood", he will seize their true and primary meaning.

The Magic of Water

Water plays one of the most important parts, not only in daily life, being absolutely indispensable for drinking, preparing food, washing, producing steam in factories, etc., but also, in our magic development, the watery element may prove to be a great factor. As we have already stated in the theoretical part, the watery element rules magnetism or the attractive force, and it is just this property we shall utilize in the development of our faculties. All the books dealing with animal magnetism, emanation of od and so on are acquainted with the fact that water can be magnetized or od-ized. But far less it is known how to enlarge this quality or use it in a different way. Not only water but every kind of liquid has the specific property of attracting, and according to the contraction, holding fast, no matter whether good or bad influences be concerned. Therefore we may consider the watery element, especially the material kind of it, as an accumulator. The colder water is, the greater is its accumulative capacity. With its full specific weight, namely at $39°$ F ($4°$ C) (above zero), it is most responsive. This notion is not so decisive, for the difference of receptivity of water (or other liquids) up to $43°$ F ($6°$ C) (above zero) is so insignificant and so faintly visible that only a thoroughly trained magician can recognise these differences. If by increase of heat, water grows luke-warm, its receptivity is rapidly diminishing. Between $97—99°$ F ($36—37°$ C) it becomes neutral to magnetism. Attention! Here, our concern is only with the specific properties of the attractive power and its practical value with respect to magnetism which results from the interaction of the elements as an undeniable matter of fact.

The impregnation (through the *akasha* principle present in each substance, consequently, in physical water, too) with a desire can be operated in any object and at any temperature whichsoever. A piece of bread as well as a hot soup or a cup of coffee or tea might be loaded or charged magically. But this charge does not depend on the accumulative capacity of the watery element, but takes place through the causal principle of the fifth power of the elements, and is brought about by the electro-magnetic fluid of the elements concerned. It is important to pay attention to this difference to avoid errors. For instance, it is quite impossible to magnetize a dish of hot soup, because the accumulating power of the watery element, by the expansion of the heat present in the water, is balanced, or increased, if it rises above 99° F (37° C). The soup, however, can be impregnated with the corresponding desire.

Now let us regard the magic of water from the practical side.

Every time you are washing your hands, think intensively that, by washing, you wipe the dirt off your body not only, but also the uncleanliness of your soul. Think of failure, trouble, dissatisfaction, illness being, likewise, respectively washed off and turned over to the water. Wash yourself, if possible, under the tap, so that the dirty water can run off immediately, and think, at this moment, that your weaknesses, too, are flowing off together with this water. If you have nothing else but a wash-bowl at your disposal, do not forget to throw the water you were using away immediately, so that nobody else can contact it afterwards. You can also dip your hands into cold water, for a little while, and concentrate on the magneto-astral attractive force drawing all weaknesses out of your body and your soul. Be firmly convinced that all failures are passing into the water. You will be surprised at the success of this exercise after a short time. This water also is to be thrown away at once. Extraordinarily effective is this exercise if you can manage it, in summer, while taking a bath in the river, when the whole body (except for the head, of course) is beneath the water.

You can do this exercise also the other way round, by magnetizing the water you are willing to use, or by impregnating it with your desire, remaining firmly convinced that, through washing, the power will pass into your body, and the desire be realized. He who has time to spare, can combine both exercises by stripping off all evil in one water (say under the tap or in a separate basin), and then washing himself in another basin with the water impregnated with his desire. In this case, namely the first exercise, when you are washing off the evil, you have to utilize a soap. Female adepts, besides the two possibilities afore-mentioned, have a third opportunity: they will concentrate their magnetism on the fact that water makes the face and skin look much younger, more elastic and thus more attractive. It is therefore advisable not only to wash the face, but dip the whole face into the water for some seconds. This procedure is to be repeated at least seven times in one turn. A bit of borax may be added to the water for this purpose.

There is a further opportunity given to the magician which ought not to be overlooked, I mean the magnetic eye-bath. In the morning, the magician dips his face into a water which has been boiled on the previous day (using a half-filled washing-basin) and opens his eyes in this water. He rolls the eyes in all directions, repeating this exercise equally seven times. At first, he will have the sensation of a slight stinging in his eyes, but this will disappear as soon as the eyes get accustomed to the exercise. Anyone suffering from a weak eyesight, may add a thin decoction of eyebright euphray (Herba Euphrasia) to the water. This eyebath makes the eyes resistant against changes of weather and, consequently, strengthens the visual faculty, makes good the weakness of sight and the eyes become clear and shining. Do not forget respectively to magnetize the water destined to this purpose and to impregnate it with your concentrated wish. Advanced pupils who are training for clairvoyance, are offered the opportunity here of promoting their clairvoyant faculties.

That is all, for the moment, about the material development and training of the body.

Summary of all exercises of Step I

I. *Magic Mental Training:*

   1. Thought control.
   2. Discipline of thoughts.
   3. Subordination of thoughts.
      to 1. Control of thoughts twice a day from 1—10 minutes.
      to 2. Suppression of certain thoughts. Holding on to a self-chosen thought. Provoking vacancy of mind.
      to 3. Magical diarizing. Self-criticism. Planning of thought-trains for the day or the week ahead.

II. *Magic Psychic Training:*

   1. Introspection of self-knowledge.
   2. Making of the (black and white) mirrors of the soul with respect to the elements, in three spheres of activity.

III. *Magic Physical Training:*

   1. Habituation to normal and reasonable mode of life.
   2. Setting-up exercises.
   3. Conscious breathing.
   4. Conscious eating (Eucharistic mystery).
   5. Magic of water.

The time limit for the completion of these exercises is fixed from a fortnight up to one month and is meant for people of average aptitudes. Those who have already practised concentrating and meditating should get along with this space of time. Such as are not yet experienced at all, will, of course, have to extend their training period, success depending chiefly on the individuality of the pupil. For the practice, it would be useless for him to pass from one step to the next, without having completed the foregoing one, in such a way that he has complete control over it.

End of the first Step

STEP II

Autosuggestion or the Secret of Subconsiousness

Before proceeding to describe the exercises of the second step, let me explain the secret of the subconscious and its practical consequences. In the same way as normal consciousness has its seat in the soul, and is activated by the cerebrum in the body, consequently the head, subconsciousness is a property of the soul, residing in the cerebellum i. e. the back part of the head. With respect to the magical practice, let us deal with the study of the psychologic function of the cerebellum, consequently the subconscious.

In every individual that is in his right senses, the normal sphere of consciousness is intact i. e. he, always and at any time, is capable of making use of the functions of normal consciousness. As it results from our investigations, there is no power in the universe, nor in man either which does not vary between opposites. Hence, we may consider subconsciousness as opposite to normal consciousness. That which, in normal consciousness, we subsume by the concepts of thinking, feeling, willing, memory, reason, intellect is reflected in our subconsciousness in a contrary way. Practically speaking, we can regard our subconsciousness as our opponent. The incentive or the impulse to all that is undesirable, such as our passions, our failures and weaknesses, is originating just in this very sphere of consciousness. Now, to the pupil, in the introspection, falls the task of disclosing the work of this subconsciousness, according to the key of the elements or the tetrapolar magnet. This is a satisfactory task in as much as the pupil will acquire self-reliance by his own reflection or meditation.

Hence, subconsciousness is the incentive of all we do not wish for. Let us learn how to transmute this, so-to-speak, antagonistic aspect of our *ego*, so that it not only does no harm but, on the contrary, will help to realise our desires. Subconsciousness needs time and space in the material world for its realisation, two basic principles valid for all things that have to be transmuted into reality from the causal world. Withdrawing time and space from the subconscious, the opposite polarity will cease to bring its influence to bear upon us, and we shall be able to realise our wishes through the subconscious. This sudden elimination of the subconscious offers the key for the practical use of autosuggestion. If e. g. we inculcate in the subconsciousness the wish of not giving in to-morrow or any other time, to any of our passions, say, smoking or drinking (alcohol), subconsciousness will have time enough to put some hindrance, directly or indirectly, in our way. In most of these cases, mainly, in presence of feeble or under-developed willpower, subconsciousness will nearly always succeed in taking us by surprise or causing failures. On the other hand, if we exclude the concepts of time and space from subconsciousness, while impregnating it with a desire, only the positive pole of subconsciousness will affect us, normal consciousness being equated, and our impregnate desire must have the success we are expecting. This knowledge and the possibilities related to it, are of the greatest importance for the magical development and have, therefore, to be considered as far as self-suggestion is concerned.

The phrasing to choose for autosuggestion must always be expressed in the present and imperative form. You should not say: "I shall stop drinking or smoking or so." The correct form is: "I do not smoke, I do not drink" or else "I do not like smoking or drinking" and so on and so forth, according to whatever you wish to suggest in a positive or a negative sense. The key or clew to self-suggestion is to be found in the form of the phrasing. It is that which, always and in every respect, has to be considered, if you wish to do auto-suggestion through subconsciousness.

Subconsciousness is acting in the most effective and penetrating way during the night, when man is asleep. In the state of sleep, the activity of normal consciousness is suspended, subconsciousness working in its place. The most appropriate time for autosuggestion receptivity, therefore, is the moment when the body is resting drowsily in bed i. e. immediately before falling asleep as well as immediately after waking up, when we remain still in a sort of being half-awake. That does not mean that a different time would be quite unsuitable for self-suggestion, but these two moments are most promising, subconsciousness being most responsive then. That is why the magician will never go to sleep in an emotional attitude such as anger, depression, worries which would have an unfavourable influence in his subconsciousness, going on in the same train of thoughts he had fallen asleep with. Look here: always go to sleep with peaceful and harmonious thoughts or ideas about success, health and pleasant feelings.

Before you are deciding for autosuggestion practice, make up a small chain of wooden or glass-pearls, about 30—40. If you have difficulties in procuring such a string of pearls, a piece of ordinary string will do fine. Tie 30—40 knots in it and the little expedient for self-suggestion is completed. It is only meant to avoid counting, when you are reiterating the suggestive formula over and over, and not to divert your attention. This little gadget will also serve to make sure, how many disturbances happened, during a certain time, when you were practising concentration and meditation exercises. All you have to do is to move a bead or a knot, at every interruption.

The practical use of autosuggestion is very simple. If you have worded that which you want to achieve, in a precise sentence respecting the present and imperative form, such as: "I feel better and better every day" or "I do not like smoking" or "drinking" or "I am healthy, content, happy", then you may pass to the real practice. Immediately before falling asleep, take your string of pearls or knots and, whether in an undertone, softly or in your mind only, according to your surroundings, repeat the phrase you have chosen, and move one bead or knot, at every repetition, until you arrive at the end of the string. Now you know for sure that you did repeat the formula forty times. The main point is that you do imagine your wish as being realised already and having actual existence. Should you not yet feel sleepy, after the repetition of the entire string of beads, engage yourself for a longer time with the idea that your wish has been accomplished, and keep on doing so, until you fall, at last, asleep with your desire still in mind. You must try to transfer your desire to the sleep. Should you fall asleep, while reiterating the formula, and without having reached the end of the string for a second time, the purpose will, nevertheless, be achieved.

In the morning, when you are not yet quite up, and have some time to spare, you ought to reach for the string of pearls, once more, and repeat the exercise. Some people get up, several times, during the night, for discharging urine or for some other reasons. If so, they can repeat this exercise as well, and all the sooner they will attain their desired aim.

Now the question is arising: what kind of wishes can be accomplished by self-suggestion? Principally, every wish can be fulfilled as far as mind, soul and body are concerned, for example refining of the character, repression of ugly qualities, weaknesses, disorders, recovery of health, removal and promotion of various aptitudes, development of faculties and so on. Certainly, desires having nothing to do with the personality such as lottery prices and such like can never be fulfilled.

You should never pass on to choose a new wish formula, before you are not absolutely satisfied with the result of the first one. Who is starting seriously and systematically in these exercises, will soon be amazed at the favourable influence of auto-suggestion, and hold on to this method all his life.

Magic Mental Training (II)

On the first step of our magical mental training, we have learned how to control and master our thoughts. Now let us go on to teach you how to raise the capacity of mental concentration in order to strengthen the will-power.

Put some objects in front of you, say, a knife, a fork, a cigarette-case, a pencil, a box of matches, and fix your eyes on one of these objects for a while. Try to remember their shapes and colours exactly. Then close your eyes and endeavour to imagine a certain object plastically, in exactly the same form, as it is in reality. Should the object vanish from your imagination, try to recall it again. In the beginning, you will be successful, in this experiment, for a few seconds only, but when persevering and repeating this exercise, the object will become more distinct, and reappearance and disappearance will take place more rarely, from one exercise to the next one. Do not be frightened by initial failures, and if you feel tired, change to the next object. At the beginning, do not exercise longer than 10 minutes, but, after a while, you may extend the exercise up to half an hour, little by little. In order to check disturbances, use the string of beads or knots described in the chapter about auto-suggestion. Move one bead at every disturbance or interruption. So you will be able, later on, to state how many disorders happened in the course of an exercise. The purpose of the exercise is accomplished, if you can hold on to one object, without any interruption, for five minutes.

If you have got to this point, you may pass on imagining the objects with your eyes open. Now the objects ought to make the impression of hanging in the air and be visible, before your eyes, in such a plastic shape as to, seemingly, be tangible. Apart from the one object you imagined, nothing else of its surroundings must be noticed. Check eventual disturbances with the aid of the string of beads here also. If you have succeeded in holding on to any object hanging plastically in the air for five minutes, without the least incident, the task of the exercise has been fulfilled.

After the *visual* concentration, let us make an inquiry about the *auditory* concentration. At the beginning, the creative imagination has to perform a certain role. It is, as it were, impossible to say: imagine the ticking of a clock or something like that, because the concept of "imagination" generally involves a pictorial representation, which cannot be said about auditory concentration exercises. For the sake of a better understanding, we ought so say: imagine you hear the ticking of a clock. Therefore let us employ this kind of expression. Now do imagine you are hearing the ticking of a clock on the wall. You will succeed in doing so, only for a few seconds, at the beginning, exactly as in the foregoing exercise. But persisting in your exercise, you will hear the sound more and more distinctly, without any disturbance. The string of beads or knots will benefit, here also, for checking the disturbances. Afterward, try to listen to the ticking of a pocket-watch or a wrist-watch, or the chime of bells tuned in various harmony. You may also practise other auditory concentration experiments such as the sounding of a gong, the different noises of hammering, knocking, scratching, shuffling, thunder-claps, the soft rustling of the wind increasing to the howling of the storm, the tunes of a violine or a piano and other instruments. When doing these exercises, it is most important to keep within the limits of auditory concentration, not allowing for pictorial imagination. Should such an imagination emerge, you must banish it immediately. Never must the chiming of the bell provoke the imagination of the bell itself. This exercise is completed, as soon as you are able to keep this auditory imagination for five minutes.

Another exercise is the *sensory* concentration. Try to produce the sensations of cold, warmth, gravity, lightness, hunger, thirst, tiredness and hold on to this feeling for, at least, five minutes, without the slightest visual or auditory imagination. If you have acquired the faculty of concentration in such a degree as to be able to produce any sensation you like, and hold it fast, you may pass on to the next exercise.

Now let us throw some light upon the *olfactory* concentration. Imagine you are smelling the scent of various flowers such as roses, lilacs, violets or other perfumes, and hold on to this imagination, without allowing an pictorial image of the respective flower to emerge. Try to practise the same with disagreeable smells of different kinds. Exercise this kind of concentration, until you will be able to, imaginarily, bring about any scent, at will, and keep it for five minutes, at least.

Our last exercise will deal with the *taste* concentration. Without thinking of any food or drink or without imagining the same, you have to concentrate on taste. Choose the thumping sensations of taste such as sweet, bitter, salt and acid to begin with. Having got a certain skill herein, you may carry out an experiment on the taste of divers spices, at the discretion of the novice. If he has succeeded in producing any sensation of the taste chosen and holding on to it for, at least, five minutes, the purpose of this exercise is fulfilled.

You will state that one or the other of the trainees will meet with smaller or greater difficulties in practising these concentration exercises. This means that the cerebral function, with respect to the concerned sense, has been neglected or imperfectly developed. Most of the teaching systems only pay attention to one or two, at best, to three functions. Concentration exercises performed, with all the five senses, strengthen your mind, your will-power, and you learn not only how to control all senses, but also to develop and finally master them perfectly. A magician's senses must all be developed equally, and he must be able to control them. These exercises are of paramount importance for the magical development, and should therefore never be omitted.

Magic Psychic Training (II)

In the first phase, the pupil has learned how to practise introspection. He has recorded his good and bad properties in accordance with the four elements, and has divided them in three groups. This way, he has made two soul mirrors, a good (white) one and a bad (black) one. These two soul mirrors represent his psychic character. Now he must find out from these records which elemental powers, on the good as well as the evil side, are prevailing in him, and endeavour to establish the balance of these elemental influences, at all events. Without a balance of the elements in the astral body or in the soul, there is no possible magical progress or rise. Consequently, we must next turn, on this step, to establish this psychic equipoise. If the magician novice disposes of a sufficient amount of will-power, he may pass on to master the passions or qualities which exercise the greatest influence on him. Should he not own a sufficiently strong volition, he may start from the opposite side by balancing the small weaknesses first, and fighting against greater faults and weaknesses, bit by bit, until he has brought them under control. For mastering the passions, the scholar is offered three possibilities:

1. Systematical utilization of auto-suggestion in the way we described previously.
2. Transmutation of passions into the opposite good qualities attainable through auto-suggestion or respectively through repeated meditations on, and continuous assurance of the good qualities.
3. Attention and volition. By using this method you will not allow for any outbreak of the passion, fighting it right in the bud. Evidently, this method is the most difficult and appropriate for people only, disposing of a good deal of volition, or willing to achieve a strong will-power by fighting against their passions.

If the novice has time enough on hand and wishes to advance as fast as possible in his development, he may use all the three methods. The most profitable way is to orientate all methods towards one single direction, for example conscious eating, magic of water and so forth. Then success will not be far off.

The purpose of this step is the balancing of the elements in the soul. The scholar ought, therefore, to endeavour quickly and surely to get rid of those passions which most hinder him from being successful in the magic art. Under no circumstances should he start with exercises belonging to the steps ahead before having absolutely mastered the exercises of the second step and having booked a sweeping success especially in balancing the elements, too. The refinement of character should be aspired after, during the entire course, but as early as on this level, faults rapidly gaining ground and bad qualities handicapping development in a higher order, ought to be eradicated.

Magic Physical Training (II)

The tasks of the magical training of the body according to step I must be retained and ought to become a daily habit such as washing with cold water, rubbing the body from head to toe, athletic exercises in the morning, magic of water, conscious breathing and so on and so forth. The second step training of the body orders a change of the breathing exercises. In the previous step, we have learned how to breathe consciously and convey the desire inhaled together with the air (through the akasha-principle) to the blood stream via the lungs. In this chapter I am going to describe the conscious pore-breathing.

Our skin has a double function i. e. the breathing and the secretion. Therefore we may consider the skin as a second piece of lungs and as a second kidney of the body. Everybody will understand now, for which important reason, we have recommended dry-brushing, rubbing, washing with cold water and all the other directions. First of all, this was intended to exonerating our lungs completely and our kidneys partially, and secondly to stimulate the pores to a greater activity. It is certainly superfluous to explain how very profitable all this is for the health. From the magic point of view, conscious pore breathing is of the utmost interest for us and, therefore, we shall pass on to practice instantly.

Sit down comfortably in an arm-chair or lie down on a sofa, and relax all your muscles. Try to think that, with each inspiration, not only your lungs are breathing i. e. inhaling air, but the whole body is doing so. Be firmly convinced that, together with your lungs, simultaneously each single pore of your body receives vital power and conveys it to the body. You ought to feel like a dry sponge which, when dipped into water, sucks it in greedily. You must have the same feeling when breathing in. This way the vital power will pass from the etheric principle and your surroundings to yourself. According to his character, each individual will feel this entering of vital power, through the pores, in a different manner. When, after a certain amount of time and repeated exercises, you are skilled in inhaling, through the lungs and with the whole body simultaneously, connect the two breathing methods to your desire-inhaling i. e. breathing in health, success, peace, mastering of passions, or whatever you need most urgently. The fulfillment of your desire (imparted in the present and commandement moods) is to be realized not only through the lungs and the blood-stream but through your whole body. If you have attained a certain skill in this experiment, you may also influence exhaling magically by imagining that, at each breathing out, you are secreting the opposite to your desire such as weakness, failure, trouble and so on. If you have succeeded in exhaling and inhaling, through your lungs and your whole body, this exercise is completed.

The next exercise will deal with the control of your body. It needs a great skill to sit quietly and comfortably, and therefore it is necessary to learn how to do it. Sit down on a chair, in such a way, that your spine remains straight. At the beginning, you are allowed to lean on the back of the chair. Hold the feet together so that they form a right angle with the knees. Sit relaxed, without any strain of the muscles, both your hands resting lightly on your thighs. Set an alarm-clock to run off after five minutes. Now close your eyes and watch your whole body. At first, you will notice that the muscles are becoming restless in consequence of the nervous stimulus. Force yourself, as energetically as you can, to persevere to sit quietly. However easy this exercise seems to be, as a matter of fact, it is rather difficult for a beginner. If the knees tend to separate constantly, you may tie the feet together with a towel or a string to begin with. If you are able to sit, without jerking and any special effort, for five minutes, each new exercise has to be extended one minute longer. If you have managed to sit, at least, for half an hour quietly, comfortably and without any trouble, this exercise will be finished. When you have arrived at this point, you will state that there is no better position for the body to relax and to rest.

Should anyone wish to use these exercises of physic carriage for the purpose of developing the will-power, he may make out various carriages, at his own discretion, provided he be able to sit relaxed and comfortable, without any disturbance at all, for a full hour. The Indian *yoga*-system recommends and describes quite a lot of such positions, in the chapter of *asanas*, asserting that one may win various occult powers by mastering them. It must be left undecided, whether it is on the strength of these positions of the body (asanas) that such powers are set free. We need a certain position for our magic development, no matter which one, the simplest being that which we described above. It is meant to reassure the body and strengthen the will-power. The main point will always be that mind and soul are in need of an undisturbed action of the body, a problem to be discussed in special exercises further on. Those scholars who become very tired, mentally as well as psychically, in performing the exercises of the first and second steps, and fall regularly asleep during the concentration and meditation exercises, will do best practising them in the afore-mentioned position.

The beginner ought to practise this sort of body-control in his every-day life. He will find a great deal of opportunity by observation and attention. For example, if you feel tired, force yourself to do something else, in spite of your tiredness, irrespective of this being any hobby or a short walk. If you feel hungry, put off the meal for half an hour, if you feel thirsty, do not drink on the spot, but wait for a while. Being used to hurry all the time, try to act slowly and the other way round. Anyone being Peter slow coach, should make a point of working fast. It is entirely up to the scholar to control and force body and nerves by will-power. This is the end of the second step exercises.

Summary of all exercises of Step II

I. *Magic Mental Training:*

1. Auto-suggestion or the unveiled enigmas of the Unconscious.
2. Concentration exercises:
   a) visual (optical),
   b) auditory,
   c) sensory,
   d) olfactory,
   e) taste.

Exercises concerning the elimination of thoughts (negative state) are continued and deepened here.

II. *Magic Psychic Training:*

Mago-astral balance with respect to the elements, transmutation or refinement of character:
a) by fight or control,
b) by auto-suggestion,
c) by transmutation or transforming into the opposite quality.

III. *Magic Physical Training:*

a) conscious pore breathing,
b) conscious position of the body (carriage),
c) body control in every-day life, at will.

Before falling asleep, the most beautiful and purest ideas are to be taken along into the sleep.

End of the second Step

STEP III

Knowledge, daring, volition, silence, these are the four pillars of Solomon's temple i. e. the microcosm and the macrocosm upon which the sacred science of magic is built. According to the four elements, they are the fundamental qualities which must be inherent in each magician, if he aspires to the highest perfection in science.

Everyone can acquire magic *knowledge* by diligence and assiduity, and mastery of the laws will lead him, step by step, to the *supreme wisdom.*

Volition is the aspect of will-power which can be obtained by toughness, patience and perseverance in the holy science and, chiefly, in its practical use. He who does not intend to satisfy his sheer curiosity only, but is, in earnest, willing to enter the path leading to the lofty hights of wisdom, must possess an unshakeable will.

Daring: He who is not afraid of sacrifices nor hindrances, indifferent to other people's opinions, who keeps his objective firmly in his mind, no matter whether he meet with success or with failure, the highest mystery will be disclosed to him.

Silence: The braggart who is talking big and exhibiting his wisdom will never be a genuine magician. The true magician will never make himself conspicuous with his authority, on the contrary will he do anything not to give himself away. Silence is power. The more reticent he is about his knowledge and experience, without segregating from other people, the more he will be awarded by the Supreme Source.

Who aims at acquiring knowledge and wisdom may do his utmost to obtain the afore-said four fundamental qualities, for nothing at all will be achieved in holy magic, without these requirements.

Now will follow the third step exercises.

Magic Mental Training (III)

In the second grade course, we have learned how to practise sensorial concentration by training each sense. On this step, we shall widen our concentration power, expanding from one sense to two or three senses at once. I shall quote some examples, with the help of which the skilled student will be able to arrange his own sphere of action. Imagine plastically a clock hanging on the wall with its pendulum swinging to and fro. Your imagination must be so perfect and so constructive as if there were, indeed and factually, a clock hanging on the wall. Try to perceive it and to hear its ticking on the wall. Hold on to this double imagination of seeing and hearing for five minutes. In the beginning, you will succeed in doing so for seconds only, but, by means of frequent repetition, you will be able to hold on to your imagination for a longer while. Practice makes perfect. Repeat this experiment with a similar object such as a gong, of which you must hear not only the sound but also see the person sounding it. Or try to imagine you see a brook and hear the rustling of the water. Or a cornfield stirred by the wind and you are listening to the whispering of the breeze. Now try for a change and look for similar experiments, arranging them so that two or more senses are affected. Other experiments with optical and acoustic imageries may be composed, where e. g. the eyes and tactual sensations (sense of touch) are engaged. All your senses have to be quickened and trained for concentration. You should make a special point of seeing, hearing and feeling, all of which is indispensable for progress in magic. I cannot emphasize enough the high significance these exercises have for your development as a magician. Practise such exercises carefully and daily. If you will be able to hold on to two or three sense-concentrations, at the same time, for, at least, five minutes, your task will be accomplished. If you begin to feel tired during the concentration exercises, stop and cease to go on. Postpone the exercises till a more favourable moment when you feel mentally and physically fitter. Beware of falling asleep during an exercise. Experience has evidenced early morning hours to be most suitable for concentration work.

As soon as you have attained a certain skill in the preceding concentration exercises and if, consequently, you are capable to engage two or three senses at one time for, at least, five minutes, you may go on.

Choose a comfortable position again which for all concentration work is absolutely necessary. Close your eyes and form an imaginary picture in full plasticity of a well-known country part, village, place, house, garden, meadow, heath, wood, etc. Hold on to this imagery. Every trifle detail such as colour, light and form is to be kept exactly in mind. All that you are imagining ought to be modelled in such plastic forms as to allow you to touch them, as if you were present there factually. You must not let anything slip, nothing should escape your observation. If the image becomes blurred or is about to vanish at all, recall it again and all the more distinctly. If you have managed to hold the plasticity of the picture fast for, at least, five minutes, the task is achieved. Next let us try to apply the auditory concentration to the same imagery. Perhaps you were imagining a wonderful forest, listen then, at the same time, to the warblings of the birds, the murmuring of the brook, the rustling of the wind, the humming of the bees and so on. If you did succeed in one imagery, try a similar one you have arranged yourself. This exercise will be fulfilled as soon as you are able to imagine any region, place or spot you like, and engage two or three senses, at once, for as long as five minutes. If you have reached this degree of concentration, try to do the same exercises, with your eyes open, whether fixing your look at one definite point, or staring into vacancy. The physical surroundings, then, must no longer exist for you, and the imagery you chose is to appear before your eyes floating in the air like a fata-morgana. When you are able to hold such an imagery fast, for five minutes, exactly, you may choose another one. The exercise is to be regarded as fully completed, if you will be able to produce any imagery you like, with your eyes open, and keep it, with one or several senses, for five minutes. In all of your further concentration exercises, you ought to proceed, in the same way, as after reading a novel, when you unfold the images of the single events in your mind.

We have learned how to form representations of places and localities we know, and have seen before already. Now let us try to imagine localities we never saw before in our life. At first, we shall do it, with our eyes closed, and if we succeed in doing so, with two or three senses, at once, for five minutes, let us reopen them. The exercise is fully completed, if we have, indeed, managed to keep this imagination, for five minutes, with our eyes open.

Now let us pass over from inanimate objects such as places, villages, houses, woods to living creatures. We shall imagine various animals such as dogs, cats, birds, horses, cows, calves, chickens, etc. as plastically as we did before, with our objects of concentration. Begin with your eyes closed, for five minutes and, later on, with your eyes open. Mastering this exercise, imagine the animals in their movements as much as a kitten washing itself, or catching a mouse, drinking milk, or a dog barking, running about; a bird flying or picking food and so forth. The scholar may choose such or similar scenes, at his own liking, first, with his eyes closed and, later on, opening them. If you manage doing it, for five minutes, without any disturbance, the purpose is fulfilled and you may go on to the next exercise.

Now concentrate on men in the same kind of way. Start with friends, relatives, acquaintances, deceased people, later imagine strangers you never saw before, first their features only, then the whole head and finally the fully dressed body, always beginning with your eyes closed and opening them after a while. You must have reached a minimum of five minutes, before you pass over to the next exercise dealing with men in their movements such as walking, working, talking, etc. If you have noticed a success with one sense, say, visually, add an other sense e. g. trying auditory imagination so that you can hear the individual talking, and imagine his voice. Endeavour to adapt imagination always to the reality e. g. the modulation of the voice, slow or fast speech, just as the person of your imagination actually does or did. First with closed eyes, then with the eyes open.

If you have booked any success in this field, too, concentrate your imagination on quite strange people, retaining their different features and voices. They may be people of both sexes and of any age whichsoever. After that, imagine people of other races, women, men, young and old, children e. g. negroes, Indians, Chinese, Japanese. Make shift with books or magazines. Visits to a museum can also do for this purpose. Having managed all this and keeping the imagination, for five minutes, with the eyes closed as well as open, your magic mental training of the third step will be complete. All these exercises have required perseverance, patience, persistence and toughness to cope with the enormous difficulties of the task. But those of our scholars who will master them, will be much satisfied with the powers they won through these concentration exercises. The next step will teach them how to deepen these powers. Such concentration exercises do not only strengthen the will-power and the concentrative faculty, but all the intellectual and mental forces, lifting the magic capacities of the mind on a higher level and besides, they are indispensable, as a preliminary practice, for thought-transference, telepathy, mental wandering, television and clairvoyance and other things more. Without these faculties, the magic disciple would never get on. You ought, therefore, to make every effort to work carefully and conscientiously.

Magic Psychic Training (III)

Before starting on the training for this step, the astral equipoise of the elements in the soul has to be established by introspection and self-control unless you wish to do mischief to yourself. If it is absolutely sure, that none of the elements is prevailing, you ought to keep working on the refinement of the character, in the course of the development, but you might as well go on to work with the elements in the astral body.

The task of this step will be to acquire the basic qualities of the elements, producing and dissolving them in the body at will. We are already acquainted with the theory of the action of the elements. Let us deal with the practice:

Fire, with its expansion or extendibility in all directions, has the specific quality of heat and, therefore, is spherical. Let us then, first of all, acquire this quality and produce it, at will, in the body as well as in the soul. In body-control, we chose an attitude allowing us to remain in a comfortable position, free of any disturbance. Indians call this position *asana*. For the sake of better understanding, we shall also use this expression henceforth. Take in the asana-position and imagine yourself in the center of the fiery element which, in the shape of a ball, envelops the whole universe. Imagine all around you, even the entire universe being fiery. Now inhale the fire element with your nose and, at the same time, with your whole body, (pore-breathing). Draw deep breaths regularly, without pressing air or straining the lungs. The material and the astral body ought to resemble to an empty vessel into which the element is being inhaled, better to say, sucked in, with each breath. The heat of the element has to be increased and pressed into the body with each breath. This heat ought to grow more and more intense, with every breath. The heat and the expansion-power must become stronger, the fiery pressure higher and higher, until you feel yourself, at last, fiery, red-hot. This whole process of inhaling the fiery element, through the body, is, of course, a purely imaginary occurrence and should be exercised with the utmost plastic imagination of the element. Start on seven times inhaling the fire-element and increase each exercise by one breath more. An average of 20—30 breaths will do. Only physically strong pupils of a great will-power are allowed to exceed this number at discretion.

Use the string of beads or knots again to spare counting the breaths by moving one pearl or knot with each inhaling. In the beginning, the imaginary heat will be perceived psychically only, but with every repeated experiment, the heat will become psychically as well as physically more perceptible. From a rise of temperature, (outbreak of perspiration) it can actually increase to a fever. Once the scholar has managed to establish the balance of the elements in the soul, such an accumulation of elements in his body can do him no harm.

Having finished the exercise of imaginary accumulation of the fiery element, you will, through imagination, feel the heat and the expansion of the fire, and now you may start on the exercise in the opposite succession, inhaling normally through the mouth and exhaling, through it and through the whole body (pore-breathing), the fiery element, successively, into the entire universe again. The number of breaths done, when exhaling the element, has to correspond exactly to those of inhaling the fiery element. For example, if you began inhaling with seven breaths, you also must exhale seven breaths. This is very important, because after finishing the exercise, the scholar should have the impression that not the smallest particle of this element has remained in him, and the sensation of heat produced in him, must disappear again. Therefore it is advisable to use the string of pearls or knots for breathing in as well as for breathing out. Do the exercises with eyes closed, at first, and then with open eyes. The Tibet explorer and traveller Alexandra-David-Neel described in her books a similar experiment, pretending it to be practised by the *lamas* under the name of *tumo* which is, however, very imperfect for practical purposes, chiefly for Europeans and not at all suitable for any student of magic.

In the Orient, there are adepts who perform this exercise (called *sadhana*) for years, and are able to condense the fire-element to such a degree that they walk about naked and barefeet even in the coldest season, without being affected by the cold, they can, indeed, dry wet towels which they are wrapping around their bodies, in no time. By accumulating the fire-element, they affect even their environs, which directly means the surrounding nature as well, so that they succeed in melting snow and ice not only around themselves, but at a distance of kilometers. Such and similar phenomena can be produced by a European also, if he can afford the necessary time for it.

For our progress in magic, we need, however, master not only one, but all the elements, a fact which is absolutely correct from the magic standpoint. So much for this.

Let us pass now to the exercises concerning the airy element. What has been said about the fiery element, applies, in the same way, to the airy element but for the fact that a different imagination of the senses has to be considered. Take up the same comfortable position, close your eyes and imagine yourself to be in the middle of the mass of air which is filling the whole universe. You must not perceive anything of your surroundings, and nothing should exist for you but the air-filled space embracing the whole universe. You are inhaling the aerial element into your empty vessel of the soul, and the material body through the whole-body-breathing (with the lungs and the pores). Every breath is filling the whole body to an increasing extent and with more air. You have got to hold fast the imagination of your body being filled, by each breath, with air, in such a way that it resembles to a balloon. Combine it, at the same time, with the imagination that your body is becoming constantly lighter, as light as air itself. The sensation of lightness should be so intense that finally you do not feel your body at all. In the same way you did begin with the fiery element, start now also with seven times inhaling and exhaling. This exercise done, you should again have the positive feeling that not the smallest particle of the air-element has remained in your body and, consequently, you should feel in the same normal condition as before. To avoid any counting, take the string of beads again. Increase the number of breaths (inspiration and expiration) from one exercise to the next, but do not overstep the number of forty. By constant practice of this experiment, adepts will succeed in producing phenomena of levitation such as walking on the surface of the water, floating in the air, displacement of the body and many more, especially if one concentrates on a single element only. But a magician is not satisfied by one-sided phenomena, because this would not agree with his aims. He wants to penetrate far deeper into the cognition and the mastery, and achieve more.

Now follows the description of the practice concerning the water-element. Take up your position you are accustomed to, by now, close your eyes and forget all around you. Imagine the whole universe is like an enormous ocean and you happen to be in the center of it. Through each whole-body-breath your body is filled with this element. You should feel the cold of the water in your whole body. If you have filled up your body with this element completely by inhaling seven times, breathe out, equally, seven times again. With each breathing out, you withdraw the water-element from your body so that not the smallest particle will remain in it at the last exhaling. Here again the string of beads may be a great help for you. With each new exercise, take one more breath. The oftener you will practise this exercise, the more distinctly you will feel the cold properties of the water-element. You ought to feel, as it were, like a lump of ice. Each of the exercises should not extend over more than twenty minutes. As time goes on, you ought to be able to keep your body as cold as ice, even in the hottest summer-time.

Oriental adepts master this element in such a degree that they can perform the most astonishing phenomena straight away. For example they produce rain during the hot or dry season, and stop it again at will. They can ban thunderstorms, calm down the roaring ocean, control all the animals below the water and so on. Such and similar phenomena are no miracles for a real magician who understands them perfectly.

All that is left to me is to describe the last element, say, that of the earth. Take up your routine position as you did before. This time, imagine the whole universe being the earth with yourself sitting in the middle of it. But do not imagine the earth as a lump of clay, but being a dense earthy material. The specific property of this earthy material is density and gravity. Now you ought to fill your body with this heavy material. Begin again with seven breaths and increase one breath more with each new exercise. You must manage to concentrate so much of the earthy material into yourself that your body seems as heavy as a lump of lead and almost paralyzed by the weight. Breathing out happens in the same way as it did with the other elements. At the end of this exercise, you ought to feel as normal as before the beginning. The duration of this exercise is also limited to 20 minutes at the utmost.

This (sadhana-) exercise is practised by a great deal of Tibetan lamas mostly in such a way that they begin meditating on a lump of clay, dissecting it and going on to meditate again on it. The genuine magician knows better how to approach this element, in a much simpler way, and master it without the help of such a difficult meditation process.

The colour of the different elements may serve as a useful resort to imagination, as far as fire is red, the air blue, water is greenish blue and the earth yellow, grey or black. Colour vision or sensation is quite individual, but not absolutely necessary. Anyone believing it to favour his work, may make use of it, in the beginning. What chiefly matters in our exercises is the sensory imagination. After a longer spell of exercises, everybody should be able, for example, to produce heat with the fire-element, in such a degree that it can be demonstrated with a thermometer as a fever-heat. This preliminary exercise of element-mastery is irremissible and needs to be given the utmost attention.

Manifold is the kind of phenomena an adept can produce, say, in controlling the earth-element, and it is left to everybody to meditate on this problem for himself. Mastery of the elements is the darkest chapter of magic about which very little has been said up to date, because the greatest arcanum is hidden in it. At the same time, it is, however, the most important magical domain and he who does not rule over the elements will scarcely get on in magic science.

Magic Physical Training (III)

The first step of this training course ought to have become second nature with you by now. Let us, therefore, go into greater details here. The position of repose of the body is to be kept during half an hour. The pore-breathing of the whole body shall now be limited to certain single organs. The beginner must be enabled to allow any part of his body to breathe, at will, through the pores. One begins with the feet and finishes with the head. The practice is as follows:

Sit in your usual position and close your eyes. Transfer yourself, with your consciousness into one of your legs. It will not matter, whether you start with the right or the left leg. Imagine your leg, like the lungs, inhaling and exhaling the vital force together with your pulmonary breath from the universe. Consequently, the vital power is inhaled (sucked in) from the whole universe, and exhaled (secreted) back again into the universe. If you have succeeded in doing so, after seven breaths, turn to the other leg. Now do breathe through both the legs at once. Having been successful herein as well, start with your hands, take one first, then the other hand in order to breathe, later, with both hands at the same time. If you achieved the desired result, let us step up to the next organs such as genitals, bowels, stomach, liver, lungs, heart, larynx and head.

The purpose of this exercise will be accomplished, if you have got each organ of your body, even the smallest to do breathing. This exercise is all the more important as it gives us the opportunity of controlling each part of the body, charging it with vital power, healing and restoring it to life. If we have managed to do all this on our own person, it is not difficult to act on other bodies, by transference of consciousness, which fact plays an important part in the magnetic power-transference, consequently, in the magic art of healing. Pay, please, the greatest attention to this exercise.

Another exercise of magic body-training is the accumulation of vital power. We have already learned how to inhale to, and to exhale from, the universe vital power through the whole-body-pore-breathing. Now let us pass to the accumulation of vital power. Its practice is as follows: Sit in your customary position and inhale the vital force, out of the universe, into your body, through the lungs and the pores of your whole body. But this time, do not give back the vital power to the universe, do keep it back in your body. When breathing out, do not think about anything at all, and breathe out the consumed air quite regularly and evenly. With each new breath you feel how you are inhaling more and more vital power, accumulating, as it were, storing it in your body. You need to feel the pressure of the vital force like compressed steam in yourself, and imagine the compressed vital power coming out of your body like heat-waves from a radiator. With every breath, the forces of pressure and radiation increase, spreading and strengthening by meters. After repeated exercises, you must be able to emit your penetrating vital power even for miles. You must actually feel the pressure and penetration of your rays. Practice makes perfect! Begin, equally, inhaling seven times and increase to one inspiration more every day. Each single exercise should be limited to twenty minutes at the most. These exercises have to be practised mainly in such tasks and experiments as require a great and intense expenditure of vital force, say, the treatment of sick people, telepathy, magnetizing of objects and so on. If the vital power is no longer wanted, in this accumulated form, the body must be brought back again to its original tension, because it is not advisable to walk about, in every-day-life, in an overdimensioned tension. It would over-strain the nerves and cause nervous irritation, exhaustion and other bad side-effects.

The experiment is broken off by giving the accumulated force back to the universe, through imagination, while breathing out. By doing so, you will inhale pure air only, and breathe out the tension of the vital force until attaining the sensation of equipoise. After a longer practice, the magician will succeed in rendering the vital force at once, as it were, in an explosive manner, to the universe, similar to a bursting tyre. This abrupt elimination should not be practised, before your body has got a certain resisting power. Having acquired a certain skill, you may go on to achieve the same experiment with the single parts of the body slowly, as it were, step-by-step. Mainly specialize on your hands. Adepts do the same with their eyes, too, and thus they can fascinate and get under the spell of their will not only one individual, but a great number of them, sometimes even crowds of people. A magician who can manage all this with his hands is known, then, for having blessing hands. That's on which the mystery of blessing, or of putting hands on sick people depends.

The exercise of this stage will have answered to its purpose, if you have learned how to accumulate vital power not only in the whole body, but in each single part of it, and emit the rays of this accumulated force directly to the outside. When you master this exercise, the third stage of the magic physical training will be at and end.

Appendix to Step III

The scholar who has arrived at this point of his magic development will already observe a general transmutation of his individuality. His magic faculties will increase in all the spheres.

As to the mental sphere, he will have attained a stronger will-power, greater resistance, a better memory, a keener observation and a clear intellect.

In the astral sphere, he will notice that he has become calmer and steadier and, according to his aptitudes, he will farther develop the faculties still slumbering in him.

In the material world, he will persuade himself that he feels healthier, fitter and a sort of rejuvenated. His vital force will by far surpass that of his fellow-men and he will achieve a great deal in every-day-life by means of his emissive power.

For example, he will be able to free any room he is living in from unfavourable influences, and fill it with his vital power, instead. He will be able to treat sick persons successfully, even at remote distances, because he can emit his rays for miles. Besides, his emissive force allows him to charge objects with his desire. The scholar, then, will find out for himself, when and where he can best utilize his magical faculties. But never ought he to forget that magic powers can be used for good as well as for egoistic purposes. Remember the quotation: "Thou shalt reap what thou hast sown." Let always be your final goal to do noble things and to make man better.

The technique of magnetism presents all possible variations of which we are going to show you some.

Space Impregnation

Through pulmonary and pore breathing of your entire body, you inhale vital force, pressing it with all your imagination into your whole body, so that it, as it were, becomes dynamically radiant. Your body is something like the radiant energy, the focus or let me say, an individual sun. With every inhaling you enforce the compressed vital power as well as the radiant energy, and fill the room you live in. With the aid of this radiant power, the room must be literally sunlit. With repeated and persistent exercises, it is even possible to illuminate the room in darkness or at night, too, to such a degree that objects can be perceived not only by the experimenter himself but also by laymen, because it is possible, in such a way, to materialize the light of the vital force in the form of real daylight, which, properly speaking, is a simple imagination exercise.

This phenomenon alone will, of course, not satisfy the magician who knows very well that vital force has a universal character, being not only the carrier of his ideas, thoughts and desires, but also the realizer of his imagination, and that he can attain all things through this vital power. As for realization, it depends on the plastic imagination.

If the experimenter has filled his work room with his radiant energy, he ought to imagine what he wishes to attain e. g. all astral or magic influences existent in the room shall disappear and dissolve, or the magician himself shall feel sound and safe in the room as well as all people coming in. Besides, the magician may impregnate his rooms with the desire of being benefitted in all his works by inspiration, success, etc. Advanced magicians screen their rooms from unwelcome people by rendering them restless and uncomfortable as soon as they enter the room so that they turn unwilling to remain in, there. Such a room, then, is loaded or impregnated with protective or alarming ideas.

But it is possible to load any room, in a more subtle way, so that anyone who should enter the room without a special permission, will feel sort of paralyzed and thrown back.

You see, a magician is offered a lot of possibilities and, with the help of these instructions, you can find out other methods more.

The magician can give back the accumulated vital virtue to the universe, when breathing out, leaving the radiant or illuminating force in the room only with the aid of his imagination. But through this same imagination, he also can suggest the vital force from the universe, directly, to the room, without accumulating it before, by his physical power, especially, if he has got some practice in accumulating vital force. This way, he can impregnate a room even with his own desires. Imagination combined with willpower and faith and firm conviction knows no bounds. These experiments of the magician do not depend on one definite room, he may impregnate two or more rooms, at the same time, and load or charge an entire house with his vital force and radiant energy, according to the aforesaid method. As imagination knows neither time nor space, he can do all this, at the remotest distance. As time goes on and his technique is improving, he will be able to load any room whatever and wherever. But with regard to his ethical development, he will never make wrong use of his faculties, but do noble things only, and his power will be unlimited. For practice makes perfect.

Appendix to Step III

Biomagnetism

Let us deal with another specific property of the vital energy which is of particular relevance for the magic work. As we have already seen, each object, each animal, each human being, each form of ideas can be charged with vital force and the corresponding desire of realization. The vital force, however, has the property of accepting any—also strangers'—ideas and feelings, influencing or combining them. The concentrated vital force, therefore, would soon mingle with other ideas, a fact which would reduce the effect of the impregnated thought or even scuttle it, if the magician did not provoke a reinforced tension by frequent repetition, thus reviving the desire or the idea. But this often means loss of time and is not very favourable to the final success. The desired influence will persist only as far as the tension is effective in the desired direction. Then the vital force will dissolve, mingle with other vibrations, and the effect is fading away, by and by. To prevent this, a magician ought to be well acquainted with the laws of bio-magnetism. The vital force accepts not only an idea, a concept, a thought or a feeling, but also involves time-ideas. This law resp. this specific property of the vital virtue must be considered when working with it or, later on, with the elements. Therefore, when impregnating desires with the aid of vital energy, remember time and space. In magic work you have, above all, to consider the following rules:

Working in the akasha-principle is timeless and spaceless.

In the mental sphere, you operate with the time.

In the astral sphere, you work with the space (shape, colour).

In the material world, you work with time and space simultaneously.

In the light of some examples, I am going to explain the functions of bio-magnetism. With the help of your vital force, charge a room with the desire that you feel well in it. Enthral this force with the desire that, as long as you live in the room, the influence should persist, continue renewing, and keep doing so, even when you left the room, and are absent for some time. Should anyone else enter your room ignoring that there is an accumulation of vital force, he will feel very comfortable in your dwelling. Now and again, you can reinforce the density and power of your radiant energy in your room by repeating the desire. If you live in a room influenced, in such a favourable way, the stored vital force will always exert a good influence on your health, consequently, your body. The vital force in this room has the desire-vibration of the health. If, however, you intend to do occult exercises in this room which have nothing at all to do with health, following another thought-vibration, you will not book the same good results as in an unloaded room or in a room you have charged with a desire responsive to your idea. Therefore, it is always advisable to load the room with the thought-vibrations corresponding to your respective works and experiments.

So for instance, you might charge a ring, a stone or any other object with the wish that the person wearing it should be favoured by fortune and success. Now there are two possibilities of fixing and timing. The first method consists in fixing the vital virtue on the stone or the metal with your imagination and your concentrated wish, timing it so, that the force shall remain for ever in it, drawing even further force from the universe to bring fortune and success to the person concerned, as soon as she will wear the object. You may, of course, load the object you chose, for a short time only, if you like, so that the influence is broken off, as soon as the purpose aimed at is attained. The second possibility is called the universal loading which is operated in the same way, including, however, the concentrated wish that, as long time as the object (ring, stone, jewelry) exists, the bearer of it should be benefited by fortune, success, etc. Such universal loadings performed by an adept will keep their virtues and their effects for centuries. As we have learned from the history of the Egyptian mummies, such fixed forces continue acting for thousands of years. If a talisman or an object destined and loaded for a definite person, individually, falls into the hands of someone else, he will not experience the least influence. But if this object returns to the true owner, this influence will go on acting.

Now let me describe another field where vital force is active, namely that of healing magnetism. If a magician treats a sick person, no matter whether personally by magnetic strokes or by putting on hands, or at distance i. e. by imagination and will-power, he must exactly observe the law of time, if he wants to be successful.

The routine manner of magnetizing is as follows:

The magnetizer, with the aid of imagination, makes his vital force flow out of his body, mostly from his hands into the sick person. This method supposes the magnetizer to be positively sound and to have a surplus of vital force, unless he will bring into danger his own health. I am sorry to say that I have seen bad cases where the magnetizer, by excessive transfer of his own vital force, suffered so heavy damages of his health that he faced nearly a complete nervous break-down, apart from the other side-effects such as diseases of the heart and so on. Such consequences are unavoidable if the magnetizer spends more force than he is able to restore, especially, if he is treating several patients at once.

This method presents another disadvantage namely the magnetizer, with his own force, transfers his own psychic vibrations and character traits onto the patient, influencing him, indirectly, in a psychic way, too. Therefore, every magnetizer is supposed and required to be of a noble character. Yet if a magnetizer has a patient whose character properties are worse than his own, he, indirectly, will draw the evil influences of the patient on himself which is disadvantageous for the magnetizer at all events. The magnetizer, however, who has been trained in occultism does give the patient not all the vital force of his own body, but draws it from the universe and makes it stream into the patient's body, directly, through his hands, together with the concentrated desire of health. With both methods, magnetizing has to be often repeated, if one wants a quicker success, for disharmony or diseases suck in and consume the transferred force very rapidly and are, as it were, greedy of a further supply of force, so that the treatment has to be repeated soon to avoid the state growing worse.

It is otherwise with the magician. The patient feels relieved only when the magician has been psychically opened i. e. if he has accomplished a dynamic accumulation of vital force in his own body and emits lightrays of vital force. The magician can employ many methods successfully, but always must he maintain the imagination combined with the desire concentration, wishing that the patient be better and better, hour by hour, from day to day. Some methods will follow, the use of which will help a magician in the treatment of diseases.

Above all, he must be well versed in the diagnosis of diseases and their symptoms. He will gain this knowledge through a careful study of the respective literature. Anatomical knowledge is absolutely indispensable. He will not be so careless as to treat diseases necessitating a rapid chirurgical intervention or infectious diseases. But in such cases he will be able to accelerate the healing process and contribute to soothe the pains, beside the medical treatment. He can manage doing so even at a distance. Very serviceable it would be, if physicians specialized themselves on this field and, besides the allopathic art, learned to employ the magic practice. Therefore the magician should only treat such sick persons as are recommended for this kind of treatment directly by a physician or work together with a physician to avoid to be regarded as a quack or a charlatan. He should follow his calling from pure love of his neighbours and not for the purpose of earning money or as a means of enriching himself. Do not climb upwards on credulities of mankind. Hold on to the ideal of goodness, and blessing will not fail. Ideally coloured magicians will help sick persons without them knowing anything. This kind of help is the most blissful. Let me add some of the most conventional methods a magician can make use of, without risking to endanger his health and nervous system.

Before approaching a sick person's bed, do seven breaths, at least, through the lungs and pores, accumulate an enormous amount of vital force, drawing it from the universe into your body, and let this vital force shine, like a sun, in the brightest light. Try, by repeated inhaling of the vital force, to produce a radiant energy of ten yards, at least, around your body which corresponds approximately to a vital force of ten normal persons. You ought to feel, as if your accumulated vital force were lighting up like a sun. If, in such a radiance, you happen to be close to a patient, we will instantly experience a relief, a sensation of ease, and if not afflicted by an ill too painful, he will feel an immediate alleviation. You transfer the accumulated radiant energy quite individually to the patient and it is left to you to act as you like. A skilled magician need no magic strokes nor put up hands, all that being only auxiliary manipulations, supports, as it were, of the utterance of his will. It will suffice completely, if the magician seizes the patient by one, eventually, by both hands and begins to work with imagination. He may keep his eyes open or closed during this operation. If he wants, he may look straight at the patient, but he need not do it directly. Here it is exclusively the imagination which is working. But during the whole act of power-transference, the magician may also sit by the patient, without contacting him personally. Imagine that the radiant energy surrounding you will stream forth into the patient's body, and, with your imagination, as it were, be pressed into it, penetrating and illumining all the pores of the sick person. Let your will-power order the compressed radiant energy to bring about the recovery of the patient.

All the time you have to be absolutely convinced that the patient is feeling better from one hour to the next one, that he does look better every day, and you must also order the radiant energy not to escape from the body before the patient has fully recovered. Loading the body of a patient quantitatively with the radiant energy which, in a sound person, means a radiance range of one yard (1 m), you will be able to bring about recovery in a surprisingly short time in proportion to the kind of illness. Do repeat the loading after a while, reinforce the tension of the concentrated radiant energy and you will be very surprised, indeed, at noticing the wonderful success you have accomplished. First of all, the radiant energy cannot escape, because you did fix it, ordering it to renew itself continually. Secondly, you did fix the time so that the body should feel better from hour to hour, from day to day and thirdly, you have proportioned to the power the space corresponding to the circumference of the body. At this point, it should be recommended to fix the power of radiation about 1 yard (1 m) outside the body, which is equal to the radiation of a normal human being. With this method you have now fulfilled the main condition of the material law of time and space.

While using this method, the magician will notice, that his radiant energy which he transferred to the patient does not diminish, but keeps on lighting up in the same intensive manner as before. This is to impute to the fact, that the vital power accumulated in the body renews itself automatically, similar to communicating pipes, instantly replacing the radiated power. It is, therefore, quite obvious that a magician is able to treat hundreds of patients without ruining his mental strength or his nerves.

A different method has to be used if the magician is pressing the vital power directly into the patient's body or into the sick part of the body, only by way of the pores, together with the imagination of renewing itself constantly from the universe, till the moment of complete recovery is reached. Here, the imagined desire of completing recovery is limited to time and space as well. But this method is only practised with patients whose nervous system is not yet wholly exhausted, and can consequently bear a certain pressure of the accumulated vital power. With a well-trained magician, of course, the accumulated vital force is, as it were, materialised already, that means it is condensed material power which can be compared to electricity. This method, in comparison with the others, is the most popular, because it is very simple and exceedingly effective.

A very peculiar method is to let the patient inhale one's own radiant power emanation with the help of the imagination. Presuming the patient to be able to concentrate, he can do so by himself, otherwise the magician has to perform the imagination instead of the patient. In practice, the occurence is as follows:

Your radiant energy is emitting up to a range of 10 yards (10 m). As you happen to be near the patient, he is actually swimming in the light of your radiation which has been impregnated with the desire of recovery. The patient on whom this power has been concentrated will be firmly convinced that he is inhaling your radiant energy with every breath, and will get well. He must imagine intensively that the healing power will remain in him and that he will go on feeling better and better, even when the magician will no longer be near him. Presuming the patient to be unable to concentrate or, in the case of sick children, you imagine yourself that the patient, with every inhaling, accepts your own radiation of vital power, conveys it to the blood and will bring about a complete recovery. Here also, you will have to concentrate on the wish, that the force inhaled by the patient should keep on working positively in him. This has been an example of vital force transference from the magician's to another body, by breathing.

We can rely here on the word of the Bible, when our Lord Jesus Christ was touched by a sick woman in the hope of recovery. Our Lord did feel the diminution of his vital power and he remarked to his disciples: "I have been touched"! —

Working with vital power and magnetism, one has to consider time and space. With a view to this fact, I have quoted several examples concerning the treatment of diseases and I could still mention quite a number of methods for treating sick people from the magnetic standpoint. The magician, for example, is capable to take up a connection with the mind of a sleeping patient and to realize various methods of treatment in the patient's body. Apart from treating the sick with vital power, he can also cure them magically with the help of the elements, magnetism and electricity. The detailed description of all the methods and possibilities of treatments would certainly fill a very voluminous book. In this work I am only going to point out single procedures of treatment, with regard to time and space, that is magnetism. High adepts and Saints who have trained their imagination to such a perfection that all their imageries are realised immediately in all planes, do not need methods any more. Such people have only to express any kind of desire and it will be realised the very same moment.

Summary of all exercises of Step III

I. *Magic Mental Training:*

    1. Concentration of thoughts with two or three senses at once.
    2. Concentration on objects, landscapes, places.
    3. Concentration on animals and human beings.

II. *Magic Psychic Training:*

    1. Inhaling of the elements in the whole body:
        a) Fire   — Warmth;
        b) Air   — Lightness;
        c) Water   — Coolness;
        d) Earth   — Gravity.

III. *Magic Physical Training:*

    1. Retaining of Step I which has to become a habit.
    2. Accumulation of vital power:
        a) by breathing through the lungs and pores in the whole body;
        b) in the different parts of the body.

Appendix to Step III:

    3. Impregnation of space for reasons of health, success, etc.
    4. Bio-magnetism.

End of Step III

STEP IV

Before describing the difficult exercises of the following step, I wish to point out again that the scholar is not allowed to hurry in his development. He ought to take sufficient time for this purpose, if he wants to achieve a real success on the road to magic. He must be absolutely firm in all the exercises of the previous steps before turning to the following ones.

Magic Mental Training (IV)

I shall describe here how to transplant our consciousness outwards. We must understand how to transplant our consciousness optionally into every object, animal and human being. Similar to the concentration on objects, put some objects which you are using every day in front of you. Sitting, in your habitual position, fix your eyes, for a short while, on one of the objects, and inculcate the shape, colour and size of it firmly into your mind. Now imagine yourself being transmuted in this object. You must feel, in a way, as the object itself and adopt all its properties. You have to be quite certain of the fact that you are fastened to the spot you have been put, unable to abandon it, but through an outside influence. You have also to consider the purpose of the object after being transmuted into it imaginarily. You should even be capable, by intense concentration, to regard your surroundings from the point of this object, and to grasp its relationship to other objects. For example: supposing the object happens to be on the table, you feel the relationship to this table as well as to all the other things on the table, including the room in which the objects happen to be. Having managed this exercise with one object, you can gradually turn to the other things. The exercise is fulfilled, if you have managed to connect each object you did select, to your consciousness so that you have adopted the shape, size and quality of the object, and that you can remain in it for, at least, five minutes, without any interruption. It must be possible for you to overlook and forget your body completely. Having managed this task, you can choose bigger objects like flowers, plants, shrubs, trees, etc. for your concentrative transmutation of consciousness. Consciousness knows neither time nor space, it is consequently an akasha-principle.

Nobody should be deterred by the unusual kind of the exercises and by eventual failures at the beginning; patience, perseverance and tenacity will soon lead to the success aimed at. The scholar will learn later what significance these preliminary exercises have for the further magical work. As soon as one is able to manage trans-planting consciousness into inanimated objects, the exercises with living objects will follow. It has been said before that consciousness is timeless and spaceless, and it is not necessary, while doing the exercises with living creatures, to have the object concerned directly before our eyes. By now, the scholar should be trained so far as to be able to imagine any creature he likes to. Let him therefore transplant his consciousness in the imagination of a cat, a dog, a horse, a cow, a goat, etc. The kind of the experimental object does not matter, it might as well be an ant, a bird or an elefant. At first one begins with the imagination of the animal in the motionless condition, later on walking, running, creeping, flying or swimming corresponding to the kind of object in question. The scholar must be capable to transmute his consciousness in any form he likes to, and be active in it as well. He must endure, at least, for five minutes, without interruption, if he wishes to regard this exercise as being mastered. Adepts who have been practising this exercise, for years, are capable to understand any animal, and handle it by their willpower.

In connection with this fact, all we need is to remember the legend of werewolves and other tales, in which wizards transmuted themselves into animals. But fairy tales and legends have a far deeper significance to the magician. There is no doubt that these are cases of the so-called black magicians, who adopt all sorts of animal shapes in the invisible world not to be recognised, while doing their wicked work. The good magician will always condemn such actions, and his spiritual faculties allow him to see through such creatures and to recognise the real figure of the artificer. Our preliminary exercises do not serve to induce the scholar to wicked deeds, but to prepare him for the higher magic, where he will have to adopt higher divine forms into which he will transplant his self-consciousness. If one has been trained, during the exercise, to the point to be capable of adopting any kind of animal shape with the consciousness, and if one can manage to maintain this imagination for five minutes without interruption, the same exercise has to be practised on human beings. For the beginning, select acquaintances, friends, members of the family, whose imagination you are able to keep in mind, without discrimination of sex and age. One has always to be very sure about how to transplant the consciousness into the body, so that one feels and thinks oneself as being the imaginary person. From well-known people one may turn to strangers never seen before and, therefore, to be imagined. Finally you may choose people of different races and colours as experimental objects. The exercise is ended, if you manage to transplant your own consciousness, for at least five minutes, into one of the imaginary bodies. The longer the spell of this achievement is, the more profitable it will become.

This particular exercise gives the magician the power to connect himself with every human being, not only to know his ideas and feelings developing in the consciousness of the imaginary person, his past and his presence, his way of thinking and acting, but even to influence him according to his own liking, but still with the proverb in mind: "What man is sowing he will harvest"! So the magician will never use his influence for anything bad or force people to act against their own will. He will use the great power over every human being given him through these exercises for the good only, and the blessing will never fail. The magician will learn from these facts, why the Oriental scholar bestows the highest worship to his master. By worshipping the master, he connects himself instinctively with the master's consciousness, and so being influenced indirectly, his progress will be far more certain and faster as well. It is quite obvious that the oriental training methods regard a master *(guru)* as absolutely necessary for the development of the scholar. The well-known Tibetan ankhur is based on the same fundament, but in the inverted order: the master connects himself with the scholar's consciousness and transplants power and enlightenment to him. The same thing happens in the case of the mystics, the point in question being the so-called pneuma-transfer.

Magic Psychic Training (IV)

In this chapter we shall amplify the work concerning the elements. We have learned to take in the element, by breathing through lungs and pores, and to perceive its specific qualities in our whole body. Now we shall charge single parts of the body with any element we like, which can be executed in two different ways. The magician should manage both methods. The first one is as follows:

In the same way as described in Step III, through inhaling with lungs and pores, you are breathing the element into the whole body, and accumulate it there, that means you are breathing out thoroughly without any imagination at all. While inhaling, connect your imagination of feelings with the specific quality of the element: fire forming the idea of heat, water that of cold, air of lightness and the earth of gravity. You have to begin with inhaling seven times. Instead of dissolving the accumulated element, giving it back to the universe through imagination, lead it to that part of the body you chose, by compressing the specific quality of the element, and fill the concerned part of the body with it. You should feel the compressed element, with its specific quality, much stronger in the single part of the body than in the whole body. Similar to the steam producing a higher pressure, when being compressed, the flesh, the bones and the skin of the single part of the body have to be penetrated with the element. Consequently, if you are feeling the specific quality of the element enormously strong, in the loaded part of the body, let it be dissolved with the help of your imagination throughout the whole body, and by breathing out (as described in Step III), let is stream forth and back to the Universe. This exercise has to be done with each of the elements, alternately with every external and internal organ, with the exception of the brain and the heart. Do never accumulate any element in these two organs at all, neither in your own case, nor in the case of other people, to avoid damages. Only a master who is perfectly experienced in managing elements, may allow himself a certain accumulation in the heart and brain, without ruining himself. He knows his body and has got it well in hand. Every organ, the heart and brain as well are suited for the supply of elements with their specific qualities, but, of course, without any accumulation. The beginner should always avoid to accumulate elements or vital power, neither in the heart nor in the brain, especially, if he is not yet able to observe the functions of the different organs with the help of clairvoyance. By performing an accumulation of elements or vital power in the whole body, the brain and the heart are getting used to the general accumulation, because, in this case, the tension is not related to one organ only, but is expanding over the whole body. It is very important, indeed, to manage the accumulation of elements and vital power in the hands and feet very well, because this will be of manifold use in the practical application of magic. The keenest attention should be paid to the fingers.

A further possibility of withdrawing an element from an organ of the body is, not to lead back the accumulated element into the body and to deliver it, through the pore-breathing, to the universe, but with the help of the imagination, one can return, through the pores, the whole element to the universe at once from the organ. This process is quicker. A magician naturally must be capable to manage both methods and must understand how to handle them quite at will.

The second method of element-accumulation in any part of the body is, to transfer one's own personality, with the consciousness, into one part of the body and allow it—similar to the breathing through the pores—to inhale and to breathe out. The element which is inhaled with every breath, stays there, while you are breathing out thoroughly. As soon as you are feeling that a sufficient amount of the element has been accumulated in the inhaling part of the body, do set it free again while you are breathing out, that means, give it back to the universe from where you have drawn it. This process is quite simple and quick, but it requires a perfect transplantation of the consciousness. On the other hand, the accumulation of vital power, in a certain part of the body, has to be managed very skilfully indeed. When perfectly acquainted with this practice, you can proceed to a further step.

We all know that the human body is divided in four principal regions, corresponding to the elements. For the sake of a better understanding we shall repeat it: The feet up to the thighs, rumpbone including the genitals correspond to the earth; the abdominal region with all the internal organs such as bowels, milt, gall, liver, stomach to the midriff correspond to the water-element. the chest, the lungs and the heart to the neck correspond to the air-element and the head with all its organs to the fire-element. The task of the next exercise is to load the different regions of the body with the corresponding element. The practice is as follows:

Take up your favourite position (asana). By breathing through the lungs and pores, inhale the earth-element with its specific property of gravity into the earth-region of the body—from the feet along the genitals to the rump bone. Inhale the earth-element seven times, breathe out thoroughly, filling the earth-region thus with the element influencing it. Keep the earth-element in the earth-region and inhale the water-element seven times into the water-region, that is the abdomen, without breathing it out, so that this region remains equally filled with its own element. Then, turn to the next element and fill the chest by inhaling the air-element seven times and leaving this element, without breathing it out, in its own region. Now it is the turn of the head-region, which you are also filling by inhaling the fire-element seven times; exhale the empty breath and the head-region will remain also filled with the fire-element. All the regions being loaded with the corresponding elements, remain, about two to five minutes, in this position and then begin with the dissolving of the elements. One begins where one did finish, in our case evidently from the head with the fire-element by empty inhaling seven times, and (altogether seven times) breathing out the fire-element into the universe. The head-region, being disengaged from the element, the next region, we have to look at, is the one of the air, after that the region of the water and finally the one of the earth, until the whole body is free from the accumulation of elements. If you did achieve a certain skill with this exercise, you may still extend it, by not only filling the different body-regions with the elements, but accumulating the elements in these regions. The process is the same as just described, that is, you begin again with the earth-element and finish with the fire-element. The procedure of dissolving is equal to the one of the previous experiment.

These exercises are of great importance, because they are establishing the harmony between the material, as well as the astral body and the universal rules of the elements. If the magician should ever get into disharmonies, through any peculiar circumstances, all he has to do is practising these exercises, and he will immediately redress the harmony. He will experience the comforting influence of the entire universal harmony not only for a few hours but for days, which is creating and keeping in him the feeling of peace and happiness. The harmony of the elements in the body offers other more advantages, of which I shall mention only a few. First of all, the scholar is protected against the pernicious influences of the negative side of the elements. The very moment the scholar has achieved the magical equipoise, he is standing in the centre of all events, and will be aware of all the laws, all the constitutive moments and processes taking place in the universe, in the true perspective. The scholar is spared from many illnesses producing an effect of balance on his own Karma and thus on his fate; he becomes more resistant against any dangerous influence. He is cleaning his mental and astral *aura,* strengthening his mental and astral matrix, he is reviving his magical faculties and his intuition will become of universal character. His astral senses will be refined and his intellectual capacities will rise.

Magic Physical Training (IV)

The exercises of the first step should have become a habit by now. Those of the second step have to be enforced and deepened according to time and opportunity. One ought to have the capacity of sticking firmly to any asceticism one has imposed upon oneself without having to fight temptations or even to succumb to any of them. The exercises of the third step are to be deepened as well. One has to manage the position of the body so far as to endure the asana-seat for hours, without feeling the slightest disturbance, nervousness, tension or convulsion. The power of radiation has to be enforced, deepened and must become more expansive that means more dynamic, which has to be accomplished by imagination and deep meditation. The magician has to learn the practical use of the radiant power for any purpose and in any situation. He must reach such a degree of perfection that any desire which he is transplanting into the radiant power is realised instantly. In this manner, he will be enabled to help suffering people in cases of illness and accidents, and thus bring great blessing to himself.

Now we shall go on to a further chapter, also rather unknown up to date, concerning positions of the body, gestures and positions of the fingers, generally known as ritual. The fundamental principle of rituals is based on confirming an idea, a train of thoughts by an external mode of expression or the other way round, producing a train of thoughts by a gesture or an action, which we shall designate "evocation" in hermetics. This maxim is standing for the entire magic ritual. It is stated hereby, that not only any idea can be expressed by an action, but can also be bound to a certain task. This refers to any creature as well. Anything not receiving and bearing a special name, symbol or external mark is without significance. All the magical processes and rituals are based on this primordial thesis, every religious system has its special cults, since the remotest times. The only difference is that nothing but a very small part has been accessible to the masses, whilst most of it has been kept strictly secret and reserved only to Highpriests and adepts. Every ritual answers a certain purpose, regardless whether the point in question be the ban-witchcraft of Tibet or, the gestures of fingers performed by the Bali priests at their cults, in the Orient, or the exorcism ritual of magicians. The synthesis will always remain the same. At a trial, the hand with three fingers risen for the oath as confirmation of a truthful statement, may also be regarded as a magical gesture. From the Christian point of view the risen fingers are symbolising the Trinity. Each of the numerous lodges and sects has its own rites. The lodges of the freemasons, for example, are all bound to a fixed sign, word and touch. A lot could be said about this problem from the historical point of view. For practical magic resp. the magical training, however, studies like these would be absolutely useless.

It is of no importance at all to the genuine magician, if he reads books about the particular way in which any other magician is drawing his magical circle, regarding it as a symbol of infinity, Divinity and purity, planting his genii and angels in it for the sake of protection, or else, how a Lama is painting his Mandala and sets up his Thatagatos as a symbol of protective deity. He does not need such strange directions, because he knows very well, they are only a mental support for the mind. In this fourth step the magician will learn how to produce his own rituals, cults, gestures and manipulations of the fingers. All this depends a great deal on his individuality and perception. Many a magician has achieved more with the most primitive rituals than a philosophic speculator with all his complicated performances of his cult. It is not possible to give an exact direction in this matter and the scholar will have to act intuitively and must understand how to express the ideas, trains of thoughts and everything he would like to be realised by a suitable gesture, position of fingers or by a ritual. He will certainly not try to express a blessing gesture by a clenched fist, ready to attack. He will compose his individual, unceremonious ritual according to his situation and position, which he is using when nobody is watching him. There are magicians who are performing rituals unnoticed, being in the middle of the biggest crowd, by movements of their fingers in the pocket of their coat. In conformity with the elements, they are using the analogy of the five fingers by imputing the forefinger to the fire, the thumb to the water, the middle-finger to the akasha, the ring-finger to the earth and the little finger to the air. The right hand represents the positive elements and the left one the negative elements. May this small example be sufficient.

Do learn to give quite individual signs to different ideas. But keep silent about them, because if anybody else should use the same sign for the same idea, he would weaken it by the derivation of its strength. Bind and fix your personal desire which you wish most eagerly to be realised to your own small ritual or gesticulation, best of all, gesticulations of the fingers, and imagine, that your desire is being realised by this gesture, or that it has been realised already. The rule of the present-imperative formula is valid here as well. The imaginary realisation, in connection with the gesture or the rite, has to be performed, at the beginning, with the feeling of assurance, self-confidence and self-reliance and with the un-shakeable faith in success.

At first, the ritual as well as the imagination have to be used. Later on, dealing with only the imagination of the desire and its realisation, you will be induced, without even noticing it auto-matically to use the gesture or the ritual. Having arrived at this point, that a desire has become an automatic function of your imagination, the process will go on in inverted order: you perform the ritual or the gesture, and the imagination or the power in ques-tion will automatically release their effect. This is the real purpose of the ritual, the position or the gestures of the limbs and the fingers. As soon as the ritual has become self-acting with the imagination, it will be sufficient to perform the ritual only, to achieve the effect or influence you have been wishing for. A comparison very near to the point is offered by a fully charged battery which needs nothing else but the correct contact to produce the current at any time. By repeating the imagination with the selected gesture or ritual, a power reserve is formed in the causal sphere of the akasha-principle which will adopt the necessary vibration (electro-magnetic fluid), colour, sound and all the analogies corresponding to the desire or purpose. We can rightly assert that they are blood-particles of its entire condition. If this power-reservoir has been loaded by frequent repetition, the mere ritual will produce the discharge of one part of this reservoir, bringing about the necessary effect in this way. It is therefore profitable not to talk about; otherwise somebody else could easily draw up the power by the same ritual and accomplish the effect, naturally, at the sacrifice of the originator.

Certain lodges let their beginners perform rituals by which such a power-reservoir is loaded automatically. The higher adepts would get, in this case, a cheap additional allowance and could work with it effortless. But as soon as the scholar is making progress and is capable to obtain it by himself already, he will be advised to use this ritual as little as possible.

Evidently some people will come to the conclusion that several of the political movements or parties are performing an indirect magical action with the gesture of salute, and supply, in this manner, the general reservoir with more, however small parts of the vital power, by the constant repetition. We all shall remember the salute of the German NSDAP, consisting in a lifting of the hand and certainly representing a certain gesture of power. But if such an increased collective power reservoir is misused for greedy and questionable purposes, this mentally strained power is turning against the founders, because of its polarity, decay and destruction will follow, apart from the fact that the curses of the numerous absolutely innocent victims partly pining in dungeons, partly sentenced to death or sent to hopeless battles in the field, will invisibly produce an opposite polarity which will also contribute to the decomposition of the power reservoir.

The same law works in all the rest of cult-practices, no matter, whether they happen in religions, sects or lodges. The miraculous healings in places of pilgrimage have the same fundamental base. The devoted believer is drawing up the spiritual power from the akasha-principle, accumulated there by the worshippers as a result of their firm faith and unshakable confidence, and the miraculous effect is carried out in this manner. The well trained magician will always find the sole true explanation for such and similar phenomenona by this knowledge of the universal laws. Using his knowledge of the polarity laws he could, without any doubt, grasp all the power from the cult-reservoir by force and produce healings or other ostensible miracles, at any time, he wanted to. The magician, on a high ethical level, would regard such deeds as a sort of stealing, and therefore will always refuse to lower himself to do it, because he has many other possibilities at hand. This shall be mentioned only by the way and we shall turn back again to the rituals.

It has been said before, that any idea, every desire and every imagination can be realised by a ritual, no matter which of the planes, material, astral or mental be concerned. Only the time of realisation depends, first, on the mental maturity and, secondly, on the diligence of using the rituals. The magician will best choose such rites as he can use for a lifetime, that means rituals of a universal character. The fewer desires he has, all the sooner he can book the success. Supposing the rituals he chose do not function at first effectively enough, he should not subjoin with others. In the beginning he ought to be satisfied with one, at most three, rituals. Having arrived at this step of development, the magician will understand perfectly to check on the right measure and he will also know how much he is capable to load.

Summary of all exercises of Step IV

I. *Magic Mental Training:*

Transplantation of consciousness:
a) into objects,
b) into animals,
c) into human beings.

II. *Magic Psychic Training:*

1. Accumulation of elements:
   a) in the whole body,
   b) in single parts of the body with the help of two methods.
2. Production of element-harmony in the appropriate regions of the body:
   a) Fire   — head,
   b) Air   — chest,
   c) Water   — abdomen,
   d) Earth   — rump-bone, genitals, feet.

III. *Magic Physical Training:*

Rituals and their practical applicability:
a) gesticulations (gestures),
b) bearings,
c) postures of the fingers.

End of the fourth Step

STEP V

The wise Archimedes once said: "Show me one point in the Universe and I shall lift the globe off its hinges"!

Very few people probably know that this sentence is concealing a great occult mystery, namely the secret of the fourth dimension. As we all remember from our schooldays, every thing having a shape—a stone, a plant, animal, man,—in short, every body owns length, width and height, definitions familiar to us. If in the middle of a form, for example, a spherical form we imagine a double-crossing, on the crossing spot we get a point, the so-called depth-point. And Archimedes certainly did have this point in mind, because it is actually the point of beginning, the starting point, the nucleus of every form. Regarded from this point, every form is symmetrically objective, that means, it happens to be in its true equilibrium. This is the base of the mystery of the fourth dimension, hence the concept of time and space, of timelessness and spacelessness, and therefore also the secret of space-magic. The scholar is advised to meditate very intensively about this problem, and he will be able to open up profundities he never dreamed of and a high intuition will be his reward. In association with the magical mental training of the fifth Step, we shall speak about the space-magic.

Magic Mental Training (V)

With all the previous exercises the scholar has achieved a certain capacity of concentration and he has learned to transform his consciousness, at will, or to adjust it to any form, and he will be capable to see farther and deeper. The instructions of the fifth step shall show us how to transplant the consciousness into the centre of any form, beginning with the tiniest atom to the highest universe. In this manner, the scholar does not only learn to understand and interpret every form from its centre, he will also be taught to master it from the centre. The faculties acquired by means of the following exercises are of a very great importance for the magic, because, in this manner only, the mental balance can be established at any time. This mental balance is the specific fundamental property of the akasha or causal principle of the mind. Let us therefore turn immediately to the practical exercises:

Take up your customary position. Now put some larger objects in front of you, perhaps a solid ball, a die, a cube, etc. It will be profitable to select first objects with full contents. Do fix your eyes, for a short time, on one of these objects, close your eyes and transfer your consciousness to the depth-point, that is to the centre. Imagine yourself being and feeling right in the centre of the object. The transplantation of your consciousness has to be so close that you forget your body entirely. This exercise is very difficult, indeed, but practice will make perfect! Nobody should be scared away by failures in the beginning, but keep on working diligently. Man being accustomed to three dimensions only, some difficulties will occur at first, but they will diminish from one exercise to the other, and gradually one gets accustomed to concentrate on being in the depth-point of any object. If you have been successful to stay, for at least, five minutes with your consciousness in the centre of the object you chose, you may go on to the next object. After achieving the same good result, select different objects for exercising, but this time unsymmetrical ones. Each time you must go so far that you transfer your consciousness in the centre of any object, and feel yourself as small as a poppy-seed, even as an atom. If you can manage this without any disturbance, go ahead to the next exercise, seizing the dimension and shape of the object from your depth-point. The smaller you feel yourself and the more your consciousness is shrinking, all the bigger the circumference or the width of the object will appear to you. From your point of view, the selected object represents a whole universe, and you must hold on to this feeling as long as possible. Once you have managed this exercise, free from disturbances, with a symmetrical object as well as with an unsymmetrical one, you can turn to another object. You may believe this exercise well performed, if you can book the same good success with any object whichever. After numerous exercises of the depth-point-transference you will attain the capacity to look through any object, and you will intuitively recognise the material as well as the mental structure of such an object. At the same time, you will obtain the faculty to influence every object from the nucleus, to load it magically at will, and thus to impregnate the mental sphere of every object with your desire. We have learned in the fourth step to master this problem through the accumulation of vital power, from outwards to inwards, and this step will teach us to do the same, but in a manner far more impressive, from inwards to outwards.

A magician has to obtain the same effect with animals and human beings. He must also manage it with objects which are not directly before his eyes. Consciousness knows of no bounds at all, therefore he can practise transference to the farthest distance. As soon as the scholar has reached this point, he can start on transferring consciousness into the fourth dimension of his own body, the microcosm, that means into the akasha-principle of his own being. The practice is as follows:

You are sitting quietly in your familiar position with your eyes closed. Transfer your consciousness exactly into the middle of your body, I mean the pit of your stomach, the solar plexus. You must feel yourself as a mere dot, as an atom in the centre between the outer spine and the frontal pit of the stomach. This centre is the lowest point of your body. Try to stay there with your consciousness, at least, for five minutes; you may use an alarm-clock to check the time. Regard your body from this point. The more diminutive you imagine yourself, the bigger you will perceive the circumference of your body which will appear to you as a big universe. At this point, meditate as follows: "I am the centre of my body, I am the determining power therein"! Difficulties, in the beginning, should not discourage the scholar. Even if he does manage it, at first, for a few seconds only, by constant exercises, the seconds will become minutes. The limit for staying in this depth-point is five minutes. Working through this step, the scholar should be able to transfer himself, at any hour and in every situation, into this depth-point, that means into the akasha-principle, from there perceiving and influencing all that concerns his being. This consciousness transference into the own akasha-principle is the genuine magical state of trance and represents the preliminary stage of the connection with the cosmic consciousness. I shall describe the practice relating to this linking up to the cosmic consciousness in a further chapter.

The magical trance should not be mixed up with the state produced by spiritualistic mediums, provided we have to do with genuine psychical phenomena and mediums of integrity. Mostly a lot of mischief is done, in this line, to mislead credulous people. The real spiritualistic mediums bring about their trance whether with the help of a prayer, a hymn or some other meditation, or, conversely through a sort of passivity (emptiness) of the mind, conjuring up by this a spontaneous displacement (shifting) of the consciousness. In this state, it is possible for "elementals," deceased people and certain low beings to induce the astral body together with the material body to manifestations and other undertakings. Such experiments are to be regarded as a sort of obsession, from the hermetic point of view, even then, if the beings in question should be good ones. The true magician naturally does not doubt the performance of such experiments—if they are to be taken very seriously—but he will feel very sorry, indeed, about these mediums. For the magician himself can consciously form connexions with beings, in quite a different way, being fully aware of what he is doing. Particulars will be given in a special chapter.

Magic Psychic Training (V)

The practical instructions of the fourth step have taught us to draw the four elements from the universe into our body, to accumulate these elements, first, in the whole body and, afterwards, in every single part of it, thus producing a tension of elements which let us call *dynamide*. The body became more elastic, with respect to the tension of elements from one exercise to the next one, and more capable of resistance against the effect of pressure. This lesson will bring us farther step by step and teach us to project and manage the elements outwards, because without the outward projection of elements, any work in practical magic is inconceivable. We have to give our keenest attention to practical work.

Sit down in your usual position. Inhale through lungs and pores, and, with the help of the imagination, press the element of fire into your whole body. You are inhaling the fire-element with the specifical property of heat and you are exhaling empty breaths. If the warmth in your body seems to be very strong, consequently, if there is a sufficient accumulation of this element, let escape the element through imagination from the solar-plexus and fill the entire room you are in, at this moment, with the fire element.

While you empty the element from your body, you should have the feeling that your body is completely delivered from it, and the accumulated element has diffused itself in the whole room, similar to the procedure you followed in the impregnation of a room with vital power. Repeat the accumulation and evacuation several times, and by each emptying, you will accumulate the fiery element all the more in the room. As soon as you are free from the element yourself, you ought to feel how the element is amassing in the room, and get the sensation of the room becoming very warm. After some exercising, the warmth in the room will become not only a subjective, but a real matter of fact and any person—magically trained or not—entering this room is actually bound to feel the warmth. A thermometer does indicate, how far we are capable to condense our imagination with respect to the fire, so that factually a materially perceptible warmth can be produced in the room. The success of this exercise depends entirely on the will-power and the plastic imaginative faculty. It is not absolutely necessary, in this step, to bring about such an amount of physical warmth that it can be measured with a thermometer. But supposing a magician takes a keen interest in working in this more spectacular way, he can specialise himself in this problem with the help of these instructions. The genuine magician, however, will not be satisfied with such an insignificant phenomenon, and rather prefer to further his own development, because he is firmly convinced that he can obtain much more, as time goes on.

The exercise of the outward space-projection of the element is fulfilled as soon as the magician can distinctly feel the warmth in the room. Once he has got so far, he has to set free, and pour out, the accumulated fire-element into the infinity, that is the universe again, where it is dissolving spherically in all directions.

The magician can now leave the room any time he likes to, without dissolving the element, once it has been loaded with it. He can also confine the element to the room, for any period of time, just as he did before with the impregnation of a room. All the success depends on his willpower and imagination. On the other hand, it is not exactly advisable to leave a room filled with a certain element for a very long time, because beings belonging to the element in question like to do their pranks in such an atmosphere, usually at the cost of the master. You will find more about this in the chapter concerning the work with element-ghosts.

Something different should be mentioned at this point. Supposing the magician to do his exercise in the open air, that is in an unlimited space, he will have to proportion a certain space, no matter how big, for himself, with the help of the imagination. There are no bounds for the imagination, neither here nor there. In the same way as the scholar did his exercises with the fire-element, he has to work with the other three elements, and next to the fire, he should take up the air, after that, the water and finally the earth. The termination of the exercises belongs to the scholar himself, and depends on his time and opportunities. He can deal with one element one day, with the next one the following day and so on; or he can accumulate the first element in the morning, the second at midday, the third in the evening and the fourth element next morning. Scholars who have plenty of time at their disposal and also sufficient willpower can go through all the four exercises by turns. These scholars, of course, will make an enormous progress in mastering the elements. A scholar who does control all the four elements in this direction may continue.

The previous exercise has taught the magician how to condense the inhaled element outwards into a space through the solar-plexus. In the following exercise he will learn how to emit an element accumulated, through breathing with lungs and pores, into the space not only through the solar-plexus, but through the whole body pore breathing thus producing an accumulation of elements in space. This has to be practised with all the elements. The dissolving and scattering into the universe has to be performed in exactly the same manner as described in the previous exercise. As soon as the scholar masters this exercise as well, he will proceed to performing this exercise, not with the whole body, but with some limbs or parts of the body only. Hands and fingers are usually engaged in magic, consequently, the scholar ought to devote his full attention to them. He must accumulate the element, by pore-breathing in one hand or both of them in such a manner that through a sheer motion of his hand, as by flash, he emits the element from his hand into the selected space impregnating it instantly. Repeated practice makes perfect here as well. The scholar should practise this exercise on all the elements and master it. Then he may continue.

Sit, like you always do, in your customary position. Inhale the fire-element through the lungs and pores of your whole body and accumulate it there, until you get the sensation of heat again. Now imagine the accumulated fire-element forming a fiery ball of a diameter of 4—8 in. (10—20 cm) in the solar-plexus. This compressed ball must be so fiery and shining as to be very similar to the sun. Now imagine this ball moving out of its sun-network and floating free in the air. Thus floating in the space, the ball ought to be imagined white-hot and radiating heat. Stick to this ball imagery as long as you possibly can. If you happen to come near it with your hands, you must feel the heat radiating. Conclude this exercise by dissolving the ball slowly in the universe or by blowing it by a sudden explosion into the nothingness. Both methods should become familiar to you. You have to deal in the same way with the elements of air, water and finally with the earth-element. For the sake of a clearer imagination while dealing with the air-element, give the ball, while compressing it, a sky-blue colour. The imagination of water will prove much easier for you. Should you, however, have difficulties with doing so, imagine it, in the beginning, as a spherical lump of ice. You will certainly have no troubles at all to think the earth-element a ball of clay. When you have practised this exercise with all the four element balls, and are sure to master it, turn to form different shapes of the elements according to the same method. At first, choose simple forms like cubes, pyramides, cones, etc. The exercise is fulfilled as soon as you manage to condense any element you have accumulated in your body, in any form and to project it outwards.

Only if the previous exercise can be managed perfectly, the next one can be taken up, an exercise which is dealing with the projection of elements directly from the universe. The practice is as follows: You are sitting in your asana position breathing calmly and without any effort. Do imagine that you are drawing the fire-element out of the endless space, the universe, and fill with it the room you are living in. Imagine the universe in the shape of an enormous ball from which you are drawing the fiery element in all directions right to your room. Remember that the fire-element coming from the primary source is the most etheric and subtile, and the more you are pulling it down to you, the more it will become dense, material and hot. You are bound to feel the heat on your own body during this exercise. The more the compressed and accumulated element is being condensed in the room, the stronger will the heat grow. You should actually have the sensation of being in a baking oven. Now dissolve the element again by your will-power and imagination into the infinite.

Repeat the same procedure with the air-element, drawing it, out of the ball-shaped universe, down to you from all directions, filling and condensing your room with it. Performing this exercise correctly, you ought to have the sensation of floating in an endless ocean of air, free from any gravity and attractive power. In a room filled in the just described manner, you should feel as light as a balloon. Afterwards you may dissolve the condensed air-element again in its primary substance, in exactly the same way as you did with the fire-element. Do likewise with the water-element. Imagine you are drawing this element down to you out of an endless ocean, at first, in a sort of cold vapour which you are condensing more and more, the nearer you are bringing it to your body and your room. Fill the whole exercise-room with this cold vapour and try to imagine yourself to be right in the centre of this illusory water-element. You must feel icy-cold, a sort of cold which causes, as it were, goose-pimples on your material body. The moment you are feeling this cold, dissolve the water-element again in its original form and let it stream away into nothingness. In this manner, the magician is capable to cool and refresh his room, in a few moments, even in the hottest summer-days. Now try the same experiment with the earth-element. Draw out of the universe a grey mass which, similar to clay, is becoming browner and browner the nearer you are bringing it down to yourself. Fill your room entirely with this heavy mass. By doing so, you ought to experience the heaviness and cohesive power as well as its pressure on your own body. Having got the earth-element under control, through this feeling, dissolve it again into its original material, as you did with the other elements.

By now, it is quite evident that the drawing down, and materialising of, the elements is happening exactly there, where we concentrated it, without the element we are just working with, passing through the body; everything is evidently occurring outside our body. The magician is supposed to master both methods perfectly, because in some special magical tasks, he will need an element which has been materialised through his body, for example in cases of healing sick people, or creating subservient ghosts and "elementals", on the other hand, he will, now and again, need the direct, universally-condensed element. Mastering this practice, too, he is qualified to go ahead.

The next exercise will be to draw an element out of the universe, however, not to fill a space as described in the previous exercise, but to condense a self-selected form, similar to these exercises, where forms of the element had been condensed in, (Solar-Plexus) and kept outside, the body, sort of floating in the air, but with the difference, that the forming of the shape does not take place inside of the body, but immediately during its floating in the air. Consequently the magician must know exactly how to produce a fireball, a ball of air, such a one of water and an earth ball. If he has achieved this performance faultlessly, he has to shape different forms from the elements floating in the space and let these forms dissolve again in the universe after some time. All the time he ought to feel the specific property of the element he is working with quite distinctly; he should be able to induce even a layman or ignorant people to see and feel the element in question. These are high achievements, indeed, results of great effort in this line. In short, during the course of these exercises, the scholar should have learned to condense every element of the universe and understand to compress it into any form he likes to.

Magicians trained in this line, can condense an element to such a degree that it becomes a material power. That's why you can lighten a fire with the help of the fiery element at the greatest distance. At first, practise imaginary drawing a fiery ball down from the universe directly, without having it passed through the body, and compress it to a small bead so much as to grow a glowing spark. Put this spark in a cotton plug which has been soaked in easily imflammable liquids like ether, petrol or alcohol. A second spark is to be prepared, in the same way, with the air-element and, the very moment both sparks are touching the cotton plug, it will catch fire and begin to burn. Having succeeded in this little trick, the magician can make an attempt with the wick of an ordinary candle, and later on with a paraffin-lamp. He can do this near and far. Apart from it, he can also confine a spark to, and enclose in, a normal tumbler or a bottle, and fling a water-spark into this container as quick as a flash. As soon as these two sparks are touching each other, both elements will explode and the glass or the bottle will break off in a thousand chips. The magician can compose such artifices by himself, because he knows and masters the rules. The genuine magician will not waste his time with such dallying. He does know very well that he could produce as well as stop phenomena such as lightnings, thunder, rain, heavy thunderstorms by means of the elements. All these forces which strike the layman as wondrous manifestations are for the magician things that go without saying and it is entirely up to himself, whether he likes to specialise in the line of phenomena or prefers to continue with his magical development. It is also a wellknown fact to him that the oriental fakirs only by mastering the elements accomplish their genuine mango-tree miracle from seed to fruit within one hour's time.

Besides, the learner has the possibility of controlling the material condensation of an element physically by throwing the condensed form of an element into a glass of clean or even better, sterilized water and repeating this action several times. He will state that with fire the taste of the water will appear sort of acidulous, with air sweetish, with water astringent dry and, with earth, musty. This occurence can be tested chemically by dipping a small stripe of litmus paper into the prepared water. If the water has been impregnated very thoroughly, one will notice that an acid reaction will occur on the litmus paper when the active elements namely fire and air are concerned, while, in the case of water and earth, the reaction will be an alcaline one.

Who would not be reminded of the wedding at Kanaa where our Lord did transform the water into wine? Only such a high adept as Jesus Christ did accomplish this miracle, not by the influence of elements from the outside, but by mastering the akasha-principle of the water being transformed from the inside.

At this point I shall finish the mastering of elements as far as the magical training of the soul in Step IV is concerned. Nobody is expected to advance, before he has not been working thoroughly through all the exercises and tasks. The exercises are all going hand in hand, inter-depending on each other. I take it for granted that it will not enter anybody's mind to stick to single exercises and methods only. The result would be fateful to the health of the person and the success would never come. These facts have to be considered very carefully. But he who does perform one exercise after the other scrupulously, can proceed with a clear conscience and can work on the magical development at full blast.

Magic Physical Training (V)

In this step I shall quote some exercises which render possible a deliberate passive communication with the invisible ones from the magical point of view. In a certain way the methods resemble the spiritualistic ones, but the magician will soon notice that he is not training himself to become a person without any will of his own, called a medium by the spiritualists. The magician may not become a plaything of uncontrollable powers, on the contrary, he directs his powers consciously and also learns to use them deliberately. In this respect, he considers the laws of the invisible world as well as those of the physical world. To further the passive communication with invisible beings, there are recommended mainly the levitation exercises with the purpose to magically prepare any part of the body in such a manner, that such beings can manifest themselves with the help of levitation. Let us begin with the practice at once:

Do sit comfortably in front of a table and put your hands on it. Perform an accumulation of vital power in your right hand and concentrate on the fact that you are able to manage your hand and your fingers solely with your mere willpower, i. e., not with the help of the muscles. Let the accumulated vital power diffuse in the universe, afterwards, by the way of the imagination. Now begin with the proper levitation exercise. Accumulate the airy element in the forefinger of the right hand, and concentrate on the forefinger becoming as light as the air. Next try to imagine that you are lifting the forefinger with the help of your willpower, leaving the hand with the other fingers quiet and motionless on the table. You must have the feeling that it is not your muscles are lifting the finger, but that your willpower is doing so. As soon as you have managed to get the finger upward, let it drop again by your willpower. Should you stop to concentrate, while the finger is still aloft, it would drop instantly. One could try this, only to establish, how far the willpower or the muscles are intervening in it. If you are capable to "levitate" the forefinger of the right hand, optionally, with the own willpower, you can proceed in the same manner with the other fingers. The levitation exercise is fulfilled as soon as you can lift and drop all the fingers of the right hand at your own will. Now proceed in the same way with your left hand and its fingers. Having managed this as well, try to lift the whole hand this way, first the right hand and afterwards the left one. Provided you can notice a success after several exercises, go ahead by lifting the hand at will not only up to the elbow, but right to the upper-arm. You can extend these exercises and lift both hands at once with the help of your willpower. Should the magician decide to extend these exercises over the whole body, he would succeed after a while, without any doubt, in raising his whole body by his willpower. He would be capable to walk upon the water without sinking down, he could even ascend into the air with his whole body and accomplish numerous other similar actions just as it pleases him. It is obvious, of course, that he would have to practise these exercises for many years in order to gain the aforesaid success. Grand adepts do manage, without any difficulties, to produce such phenomena without being forced to do such exercises for years, because it all depends again on the magical maturity and development. Never will any magician of a high standard perform phenomena of that kind, without an urgent reason, and least of all, to satisfy the curiosity of other people. At our stage of development, we shall be content to move the hands and fingers according to our own will. Having reached this point, we shall turn to a different preparatory exercise which is absolutely necessary for the passive communication with the invisible ones and I shall demonstrate the practice as follows:

Sit down again in front of a table on which your hands are resting calmly. Now try to imagine plastically that your spiritual right hand is protruding from the physical one. Put the psychical hand close by the physical one or let it glide through the table on your knees. You have to regard the imaginary spiritual hand as your real one. In the carnal hand, there is now occurring a mental vacuum which has the shape of the external hand. Do think, at this moment, that the carnal hand is quite harmless, being thus in the fourth dimension, the akasha-principle. If you did manage this for a short while, go back again with your mental hand into the carnal one and finish the exercise. Repeat this several times, until you succeed in exteriorising the hand, as described, for at least, five minutes. You can work on the other hand, in the same manner. As soon as you have managed this very well, you are prepared to take up the communication with the invisible ones.

We can see by now that the magic preparation is very different from the one of the spiritualists who behave passively in so far as they take a pencil in their hands and write or paint. Whether the messages which are asked for by the medial writing or painting of the spiritualists, are actually coming out of the fourth dimension—or the way they call it: from the world beyond—or whether they originate only in the subconsciousness of the medium in question, is entirely left to the judgement of the magician.

A hand which has been exteriorised according to our method, has really been transplanted in the fourth dimension and can be seen by any being of that sphere, which wants to use it to send messages to our material world. As soon as the beginner has done these exercises, he is enabled to communicate with the beings of the fourth dimension. The magician will first of all try to come into contact with his guardian genius, his spiritual guide to whom he has the closest relationship. Every scholar of magics is fully aware of the fact that the Divine Providence, at the hour of his birth, has given him a being with the purpose to watch over its protégé, to guide and to inspire him. In accordance with the development and the karma, this being can be a deceased person or else an intellectual entity not yet embodied on this planet. This being takes care of the spiritual comfort of the protégé mostly up to the puberty period. The more man is maturing intellectually, the less attention does the spiritual leader pay to him, especially in cases of people who do not even remember their guide. The contact is loosened more and more. A lot could be said about the ranks of such guardians and their activity as well, but this would overstep the frame of this work. The magician, certainly, has got the faculty to communicate with his guide, to learn all he wants to know and to receive everything he is in need of. He may be quite sure, provided he be honestly interested in the whole problem, ennobling his character and working hard on his magical development, that his guide will try first to make himself known to him. Therefore the scholar should aspire to come into contact with his guardian genius. Here follows now the necessary practice:

Take a sidereal pendulum. It does not have to be a special pendulum, a ring or a small object will do likewise, even a nail if nothing else is conveniently near which is to be tied to a silk thread. Twist the end of the thread several times around your forefinger. The pendulum is swinging ca. 8—12 in. (20—30 cm) free in the air. Sit down in front of a table and put both your hands on it. The elbow of the hand holding the pendulum is to prop on the table. The pendulum is swinging free above the table-top ca. 0.8—1.2 in. (2—3 cm). The elbow remains propped up, the hand is to keep upright. Put a glass of water, a vase or any tinkling object ca. 2—2.8 in. (5—7 cm) sideways of the pendulum or behind it. As soon as you have finished all the preparations, according to these instructions, exteriorise your mental hand from the one holding the pendulum and put the mental hand close by the carnal one. Having done so, develop a state of trance in yourself for a few moments, the way you have been instructed in the chapter about mental training by recognising yourself with your consciousness in the centre of the navel; therefore you are now in the fourth dimension. In this condition, do call your guide and ask him, in your mind, he might manifest himself to you with the help of your magically prepared hand. Keep silent and observe the pendulum, beseeching the guide, at the same time, to indicate with one stroke of the pendulum on the glass a "no," with two strokes "perhaps" and with three strokes a "yes". You will be very astonished, indeed, to notice that the pendulum is beginning to move giving the requested strokes. Sensitive people will even notice that the hand holding the pendulum has been moved by a strange hand. You will probably have the feeling as if your own hand had become a glove with a strange hand in it which is moving the pendulum. Other persons again will not notice anything at all, but have the sensation instead, that the desire is guiding the mind indirectly, moving the muscles of the hand and hence causing the pendulum to sway to and fro. This outcome is absolutely individual and depends on the aptitudes. Supposing the first attempt to produce the communication with the spiritual leader should fail, there is no need of being discouraged. After a few more attemps, every scholar will certainly succeed in bringing about the communication. Once the connexion has been established, one can ask questions to the leader whether mentally or aloud, which will be answered with yes or no or with perhaps. The questions ought mainly to concern the leader himself, for example if he is willing to manifest himself or if he was already embodied on this planet and such like.

As soon as the contact, with the help of the pendulum, has been brought about, one can use a "planchette" instead of waiting for the strokes on the glass. This gadget is a circular disk which one has to divide in sections, marking each of them with a letter of the alphabet; a small circular blank is left in the centre of it. The pendulum will point out single letters and by spelling the letters, one will receive messages from the leader in detail. After achieving a good result, one can arrange for a bigger planchette, containing the entire alphabet, numbers, sections with yes, no and uncertain (perhaps), days and hours. In the centre remains again a blank to start from. For performances with this planchette, the pendulum will be replaced by a small liqueur glass. With ink, water-colour or indelible pencil trace an arrow serving as a pointer on the leg of the glass. Now take the lower part of the glass between your forefinger and middlefinger and allow the glass to be moved on the letters by the leader's hand. The peak of the arrow will then indicate the respective letter. To operate an easier gliding motion of the glass, one can set the planchette underneath glass, because the small liqueur glass will naturally move about much more smoothly on the glass base. The scholar may find out for himself such and similar appliances. He will also find many constructive observations in the spiritualistic literature. All that matters is satisfaction of the most urgent needs of the moment.

A further method is to beseech the leader to lift the forefinger of the magically prepared hand. Do ask him to lift the finger once, if the answer is no, twice in the case of uncertain and three times, if the answer is yes. Noticing a success with the forefinger, try it with the other fingers, too. One will notice that there is always a certain finger that is particularly easy to get on with. One scholar might be more efficient in lifting the forefinger, another using the middlefinger or the ringfinger. One ought to stick to that finger which is moving best. This, of course, depends on the flexibility.

The magician will appreciate this method very much, because it will enable him to operate a passive connexion with the invisible world, either with his leader or with a deceased person even in a situation where a planchette or a pencil cannot be used, for example in a party, out-of-doors and so on. He can even hold this hand in his pocket and get replies of yes or no, being in a vast crowd, especially, if he has acquired a certain skill in this matter. Having managed all these experiments, one can take up the mediumistic writing. The method is as follows:

Put a sheet of paper in front of you and take a pencil between thumb and forefinger like you do for writing. Now push a rubber-ring not too tight over your thumb, forefinger and middlefinger. You can manufacture this ring by cutting it off a bicycle tyre. The purpose of the ring is, not to have to concentrate entirely on the holding of the pencil. Now induce a trance in yourself, call your spiritual leader, prepare your right hand magically for him in the described manner and beseech him to write with the help of the right hand. In the beginning you will notice only some uneven lines, later on illegible words and, after some exercising, words and sentences will come about. If one sheet of paper has been filled with writing, change it for a new one. You can get a reply to every question. By constant exercising, you will acquire such a skill that the medial writing does not cause any difficulties at all. In this manner you will be enabled to call deceased friends, relatives and members of your family with whom you want to go in touch. The magician will be convinced that there is no such thing as "hence" and "beyond", that there are only the different degrees of density, in the fourth dimension, where the divers beings exist, and death will not mean the end of everything to him, but a passing over to the fourth dimension.

Finally I should like to remark that there are several kinds of medial writing, according to the aptitudes, which I shall mention briefly:

1. The automatic (mechanical) method: In this case, the hand moves absolutely automatically, without the magician knowing what he wants to write or what the spirit concerned is going to write. Messages in foreign languages will also be received, even in languages the magician himself does not know, and has never heard before. Paintings and drawings can be created as well.

2. The inspirational method—the most frequent—: here the messages will be given in a sort of thinking aloud inside or outside the own personality. In this case, one practically knows beforehand what the being is about to write. By frequent repetition this inspiration will become a loud thinking and listening in the passive communication. One will perceive messages from the depth of the soul or from outside of the own self.

3. The intuitive method where you have the feeling as if you did the writing yourself. Any questions will be answered instantly. Nobody but oneself appears to know the answer to the question. This is a kind of clair-knowledge. The hand writes words and sentences in full consciousness, without the person hearing anything or being inspired in any way.

The methods can also appear in a mixed kind, for example half automatic and half inspirational or intuitive and inspirational or all together. Which of the methods will be the dominant one, will only be known after a long spell of exercising. Each of the methods is good and reliable, provided you are using it honestly and candidly. Practice makes perfect!

Now I should like to give a comment with regard to the questions one is going to ask the beings and to the answers one can expect. First of all, the magician is supposed not to boast of his exercises and results. The more silent he is keeping about his communication with the invisible ones, the better for him. Furthermore, when choosing the questions to be asked, you always have to consider that the beings you are contacting are subject to laws different from those we have to deal with on this physical plane. Besides, beings which had been living before on this earth, will soon loose their orientation, because our physical plane is tridimensional, depending on time and space which does not occur in the sphere of the fourth dimension. Only highly developed beings are capable to give correct informations about time, events future, etc. Consequently, the magician will first inquire about the home of those beings and rather prefer messages about the fourth dimension for the sake of his own education. Later on, as soon as the scholar has developed his spiritual senses, he will no longer need the passive communication with the invisible ones, because he is himself able to achieve anything such a being could inform him about. The passive communication only serves the purpose to be convinced of the existence of another world which everybody will enter and live in, after passing away.

Summary of all exercises of Step V

I. *Magic Mental Training:*

Space-Magic.

II. *Magic Psychic Training:*

Projection of elements outwards:
a) through the own body, accumulated through the solar-plexus,
b) accumulated through the hands, especially dynamically through the fingers.

III. *Magic Physical Training:*

Preparation to the passive communication with the invisible ones:
a) release of the own hand,
b preparation of the fingers with the help of the pendulum, the pencil, the planchette, etc.

Passive communication:
a) with the own guardian genius,
b) with deceased people and other beings.

End of the fifth Step

STEP VI

Before I am going to describe the exercises of the sixth Step, I shall underline once more that all the previous exercises have to be under perfect control in order to keep the balance in the higher degree of development, too. It would be absolutely useless to skip one of the Steps or to omit and neglect one of the exercises. Any gap would become very perceptible and the scholar would have great difficulties to make up for one or the other problem in his development. Consequently, the main condition for success remains an excellent basic training.

Magic Mental Training (VI)

In this Step we are faced with the meditation on the spirit. I have already been talking in detail about the mental-sphere and the mental body, hence the spirit, in the theoretic part of this book. It is worth-while to have a look now at the functions of the own spirit with respect to the four elements, differentiating these functions, which can be achieved by special meditation. The properties of the spirit, in conformity with the four elements are as follows: the will is subject to the fire-principle, the intellect, with all its parallel aspects as there are intelligence and memory, underlies the principle of air, the feeling with all its aspects belongs to the water-principle and the consciousness with all its aspects establishing the connexion of all the three elements, is subordinate to the earth-principle.

Look inward as into your own spirit, observe yourself and the functions of the spirit and meditate on it. You must know how to imagine each of the functions corresponding to the element. If you manage to distinguish the functions of the spirit, i. e., if you have got a clear impression about it, you may continue. This preliminary exercise is very important, because it will enable the magician to influence these functions with the respective element on the mental plane in himself as well as in others, to master and strengthen or to eliminate them. Another exercise is to ascertain oneself of the whole mental body in the astral body, and, together with it, in the material body similar to a hand in a fine silk-glove which is put into a thick glove. Your hand ought to feel both gloves. The same thing is supposed to occur in the whole mental body. You should feel your spirit in the fine astral body and this one again in the material body. This feeling is the spirit. Meditate on this problem at any suitable opportunity. As soon as you are quite sure that your spirit is captivating the astral body as well as the material one, feeling and moving it, and that it is, as it were, your spirit which performs all the actions through the two wraps, you can again go one step farther.

Everybody whether consciously, half-consciously or nearly subconsciously is executing some actions suggested by an inner or an outer impulse, without himself paying any attention to it. The next exercise will teach you to accomplish actions fully consciously, little acts in the beginning, later on, great ones, and you ought to try to extend the duration of each conscious action. The wording "consciously" does not mean that one is all attention with the spirit but with the imagination and the feeling that the spirit with the help of the soul and the material body is accomplishing the action. For example, if I am walking along the road I do not think about the fact that I am walking, but that my spirit is walking and moving the astral and the material feet. The same thing happens to the arms and all the other parts of the body. If you are able to accomplish any action in this way, for at least ten minutes, you are mastering the exercise perfectly. The longer you can endure this without side-effects such as fits of dizziness, feeling of tiredness, disturbances of balance, all the better for you. For this particular reason, it is advisable to begin first with small actions over a short spell of time and to extend them until you get used to the attitude, and can extend them as long as you like to.

This experiment is very important, because it will give the scholar the possibility to accomplish any action in mental as well as astral connexion with the material body, according to his working with the mental or the astral sphere. Such an action is called the magic action. The scholar will certainly understand now why magic rituals never show any success with persons who have not been initiated or who have not been trained in magic, because people like these do not own the capacity of executing the ritual magically, i. e., they are not prepared to work in connexion with the material stuff in a mental and astral way.

Let us take the example of a magnetizer putting his hands on a patient's body or performing magnetic strokes, but without allowing his mental and astral hand to emanate at the same time, nor imagining that the mental force is pervading and influencing the spirit, the astral power doing the same to the astral body of the patient, and the material power influencing the material body, this magnetizer will never achieve anything else but a partial success, because the patient does, indeed, consist of all the three components, namely the body, the soul and the spirit. That goes without saying for the magician, that the mental body is only influencing the mental sphere or the spirit, in the same way as the astral body affects the astral sphere only i. e., the soul, and the material body concerns the material world only. This law has to be respected. Hence, it is necessary for the magician to adopt a mental as well as a psychic disposition in order to perform actions whether as spirit or in connexion with the soul. Once he has understood this problem very well, and mastering the practice perfectly, he can advance in his development.

The next task will deal with the magical training of the senses. First of all, a very important preliminary exercise: Similarly to the previous exercise, you are realising in this one as well that not your material eyes see everything but that it is the spirit which perceives all with the help of the astral and the physical eyes. Do meditate on this problem as often as possible. You will have to imagine, at least for five minutes, that the spirit is looking through the physical eyes and does actually see. The longer you are able to endure this, all the better for you. You will become a master here as well, by constant repetition of this experiment. Having achieved a success, in this exercise, with the eyes, turn to the ears by realising, that it is not your physical ear that is receiving the sound waves, but that the mental ears are perceiving everything with the help of the astral and the material eyes. If you can book the same result as you did in the case of the eyes, continue, in the same manner, with the senses and imagine that the spirit, with the help of the astral body, and this one again with the aid of the material body, is feeling objects, cold, warmth, etc. Practise this experiment diligently until you can master it, over the same period, with the eyes, the ears and the feeling. Should you wish to develop special faculties, try it also with the other two sense-organs, the olfactory sense and the taste. But the keenest attention should be paid to the three afore-mentioned sense-organs, that is seeing, hearing and feeling, which are most useful for practical magic. If you achieved good results in the mental ascertainment of the senses, try to adjust your spirit to two of the senses at the same time, as you did in the concentration of the senses. Begin with the eyes and the ears. If you manage to bring it about for, at least, five minutes, without any interruption, do adjust your spirit to three senses at once, that is to seeing, hearing and feeling. If you can manage this as well, you have, indeed, made progress in your magical development. This preliminary exercise is very important for the so-called clairvoyance, clair-hearing and clair-feeling and ought to be mastered perfectly.

The scholar will find the principal exercise in the seventh Step of this course.

Magic Psychic Training (VI)

In the fifth Step we learned how to project the elements outwards. Now we shall go farther and learn how to master the akasha-principle with respect to the elements. It has been mentioned in the theoretic part that the elements are originating in the akasha-principle by which they are dominated and kept in the correct balance, too. A magician who after a long time of exercising, has achieved good results with the elements, will also be capable to control the finest principle, that is the astral ether. The exercise is as follows:

Take up your usual posture (asana) and close your eyes. Imagine you happen to be in the centre of an unlimited space. Here is no above nor below nor any sideway. This unlimited space is filled with the finest energetic matter, the universal ether. Ether is colourless, but to our senses it appears to be of an ultra-violet, near black-violet colour and this is the colour in which we do imagine the etheric matter. You are inhaling this etheric matter and convey it deliberately, through the pulmonary breathing, to the blood. If you have achieved a certain skill in doing so, execute the same operation with consciously breathing, through lungs and pores, as you did in the accumulation of the vital power, but with the one difference, that you inhale the coloured ether and fill your whole body with it, instead of with the vital power. Performing this exercise you have to retain the feeling of being united to the entire infinite space. You have to be, as it were, completely secluded from the world. It is necessary to become familiar with this unusual state of mind. In any case you ought to avoid to loose your consciousness and to fall asleep. Supposing you do feel tired, better break up the exercise immediately and choose another time when you are more fit. After some successful exercises in the whole-body pore-breathing with akasha, you can go ahead. We have heard that akasha is the primary source, that means the sphere of all causes. Any deliberate cause, may be such as a wish, a thought, any imagination created in this sphere together with the dynamic concentration of willpower, unshaken faith and fullest conviction is bound to be realised with the help of the elements, regardless of the level or sphere on which the realisation has to be necessarily performed. This is one of the greatest magic mysteries and a universal key for the magician, who will under-stand its range only later on, in the course of his development. The scholar should always keep his mind on his own ethical develop-ment which will certainly help him to do good and noble deeds only. Our next exercise will be to win absolute control of the elements with the help of the akasha-principle, in all the three realms. The exercise is as follows:

You are sitting in your usual position inhaling, through the lungs and all pores, a stream of akasha and filling the whole body with it. At this point, I should like to mention that akasha cannot be accumulated in the same way as vital power. At the very inhaling, you must imagine that you are starting the control of the four elements. Consider that you have already got the faculty of mastering the elements and that they will fulfill everything you are ordering or wishing for, no matter on which plane the realiza-tion of your desires has to happen. You ought to feel with every breath your mastery of the elements. The faith and the confidence in your control of the elements has to be unshakeable and im-perturbable. You must not allow yourself the faintest doubt. Anyone who is working scrupulously through all these exercises will gain the absolute control of the elements after more or less exercising. A magician who has established the magical balance with respect to the elements, in himself, having ennobled his character, and having acquired the highest virtues and ideals, will very soon attain this power. He will feel his faith becoming as firm as a rock and will be absolutely sure of his conviction, which is excluding any doubt at all. On the other hand, a person who has not been working scrupulously enough, or scholars who did skip any Steps and neglected exercises, will feel doubtful about one problem or the other, and the influence of the one element which is keeping him in check most of all, will not tolerate to be mastered. Now and here the scholar will realise, why such a high value is set on scrupulousness and endurance in the execution of the exercises. There is no gap allowed to spring up, in the process of development, otherwise the scholar would fall behind, and some of the problems could only be set right under the greatest difficulties.

A scholar who is perfectly sure of his mastering the elements will soon notice that he is capable of projecting the elements on all planes, outwards as well as inwards, very easily, so that all seems to be a child's play to him. Having arrived at this point, the magician can turn to transferring the power of the elements into a suitable ritual. I have been talking already about this problem, in detail, in the chapter about the rituals. The magician forms any ritual, after his own liking, by means of finger-positions and gestures of the hands, into which he is transferring the power. According to his magical development, he will certainly dispose of a sufficient amount of intuition, so that he can compose the ritual suitable to the element in question. He provides it with a self-selected word (formula) and links it to a certain sound, corresponding to the element. It is quite impossible to make a mistake here, because these rituals are absolutely individual, purely personal. Therefore, rituals which the magician did compose for this purpose, are not to be imparted to anyone else! Another person could attain the same success in mastering the elements, by using these rituals, which of course would happen at the cost of the magician's power, who actually did compose the rituals. Supposing a person that does not dispose of the magical maturity, makes use of such rituals, he would certainly suffer great damages and bring ill fate to other people, too, for whom the rituals had been used. Be therefore very careful and select a kind of rituals only, which you can use in a large crowd as well, without anyone observing it, for example, a ritual with a finger-position in your pocket. The genuine magician will always regard this warning as fully justified.

First of all, the magician must try to compose one ritual for an element of the astral sphere with which he is putting the virtue of one element in operation, and at the same time a second ritual, with the help of which, he can dissolve this power again instantly, if he likes to. In the same way he ought to operate with the other three elements, thus creating by his power eight rites for the astral sphere and eight for the material production as well. As soon as the rites did become, in a way, automatic by a long spell of exercising and repeating, it will be sufficient to use the ritual only, which will make the element start working immediately, according to the purpose to be accomplished. If the magician wishes the effect to be cancelled, it will be enough to use the necessary revoking rite. This method should become a habit which renders performance easy and possible without any effort or imagination at all.

Before, I did mention, that the magician is capable to achieve everything, through the action of the elements, in the astral as well as in the material world. To obtain this state of maturity, a great amount of patience, endurance and tenacity will be required. Even then, when the scholar is developing more and more, on higher levels, he ought to work the mastering of the elements, until he really becomes a true master, and provided he be possessed by high ideals and wants to do good deeds only to help mankind, the Divine Providence will bless him, endowing him with unexpected faculties, to make the most of them.

Magic Physical Training (VI)

In this Step any special training of the body is no longer necessary, but we shall practically use all the occult powers which the scholar has obtained in the course of the exercises, provided he did follow all of the methods scrupulously and the practices did really become habits. The scholar can, of course, deepen the exercises to obtain a better success. It is impossible to describe the entire practice of magic which a scholar could master eventually, because it would comprehend another volume. I will only select some of the most interesting facts from the lot. In the meantime, the scholar has matured so much that he will succeed in the practice of lower magic without any exception, especially if he aims at high and noble ideals only.

Deliberate creation of Elementals

In contrast to thoughts living with their forms in the mental or spiritual sphere, the "elementals" are entities with a certain degree of intelligence deliberately created by a magician. Such "elementals" are capable of fulfilling certain tasks on the mental plane and obviously they may be looked at as obedient servants of the magician who can create for himself a whole flock of such servants, according to the purpose he aims at. Through the creation of "elementals" of the so-called elemental-magic type, the magician can accomplish everything in the mental sphere without any discrimination of his own or a foreign sphere. I will only quote a few examples just because of the great variety. With the help of the "elementals" the magician can influence the mind of any other person at will, he can strengthen or weaken man's mental and intellectual faculties, he can protect himself or others against foreign influences, transmute friendships in animosities or the other way round, he can produce a favourable atmosphere in associating with his fellow-men and he can bring under his control anybody's will, which is not yet developed or profiled. The business-man can enlarge the number of his costumers, and in many other ways, the "elementals" can be a great help for him. The genuine magician will always be inspired by good and noble intentions and keep the altruistic motive in mind, if he is aiming at the highest level of magical maturity. The practice of creating "elementals" is very simple and an affair of the magician's imagination, but the following rules must be considered:

1. The "elemental" has to be given a form corresponding to the desire one wishes to be fulfilled. The form is to be created by intensive imagination.

2. The form, the so-called vessel or housing has to be given a name of some sort. Everything existing, whether in a particular shape or shapeless does have a name, if it has no name, it does not exist.

3. The task is to be impressed on the "elemental" with the help of the willpower and the imaginative faculty, that means, an authoritative order has to be given with respect to the kind of effect to be produced. Here as well, the present or imperative form formula must be retained, in exactly the same way as I did, describe it in the chapter dealing with subconsciousness.

4. The effectiveness is to be impressed on the "elemental", regardless whether it be question of a permanent or a restricted effect.

These four fundamental rules are to be respected, at any rate, if one intends to work successfully with "elementals". I will render the practice even more understandable and an illustrative case may show how it can be done:

Supposing the magician intends to enforce somebody's memory or any other intellectual faculty with the help of an "elemental", the procedure is as follows: The magician imagines a large universal ocean of light, from the luminous matter of which he shapes an enormous ball of light, compressing and, hence, accumulating it more and more with the help of his imagination until this ball has the size of approx. 12—20 in. (30—50 cm). By this accumulation of light, the ball has become similar to a radiating sun. Now the magician impregnates this light-ball with the desire and the firm conviction that it will exhibit the same power and quality as is supposed to revive and reinforce the desired mental faculty such as memory, eloquence, etc. in the respective person. As soon as the magician has shaped this mental sun or ball, he must give it a suitable name, say LUCIS or the like. Besides, he is fixing the time when this ball is to affect the mental sphere of the person with terms like these: "You ought to work in the mental sphere until the person concerned has attained the desired faculty in such a way that this faculty has become a habit!" Having fixed the time, the magician orders the "elemental" to dissolve in, and return to, the ocean of light as soon as it has fulfilled its task. Expressing it magically, birth and death of the "elemental" are fixed in exactly the same manner as Man's or any other being's fate is.

Considering the fact that an "elemental" knows neither time nor space, it may be directed to the mental sphere of the respective person. Its sending off is happening quite suddenly as if the connecting link between the own person and the "elemental" were torn. At the same moment, one turns to another job, one ceases remembering the "elemental" which had just been created. One may also accompany the breaking up with a certain farewell gesture, just as one did while creating it. All this is entirely left to the scholar's discretion who, at his present state of development, should be quite capable to give such and similar instructions himself. The more detached from the magician such an "elemental" is, the more effective it will be in the mental sphere of the person for whom it was created. It can work independently in the mental sphere and will not be restricted, in any way, by the magician's mind. Now and again, it is advisable to re-load the "elemental", to give it a greater power of expansion. This is achieved by

131

calling the "elemental", by the name given to it, back from the mental sphere of the person concerned, rendering it more dynamic through a new accumulation of light, and sending it off again. As soon as the "elemental" has fulfilled the required task, it will dissolve itself in the ocean of light. This example should suffice to give the magician a rule of conduct how to create "elementals". The experiment described here is very often used by adepts to the purpose of inspiring and strengthening scholars of a lower standard.

Let us now turn to another, rather similar topic which makes us acquainted with the so-called Larvae:

The difference between an "elemental" and a larva is basically the fact, that an "elemental" is created deliberately by the magician, whereas the larvae form themselves involuntarily, in the corresponding mental sphere, as the result of a strong psychical excitement, no matter which kind of excitement this happens to be. The stronger the excitement is, the more mental material a person is subsiding, all the stronger, denser and more viable the larvae will become, especially in the case of a regular and frequent repetition of the same psychical excitement. This involuntary formation of larvae occurs in any human being, magically trained or not, young or old, intelligent or not, regardless whether the person knows or ignores it. If the psychical excitement is fading, due to the fact that no attention at all has been paid to the upsetting affair, the larva, too, will disappear, by and by, until finally dissolving itself. Consequently, there will be in the mental sphere a constant bringing forth and dying of larvae, naturally at the costs of the mental matter of each human being. We are causing these events by our own psychical excitements. The reasons therefore can be very different, usually fear, grief, sorrow, fright, hatred and envy and such like producing them. The shape which the larva shows depends on the cause of the psychical excitement and is always symbolic. Anyone who knows something about symbolism will be able to get a clear idea about this problem, for example, a thought of love will always be symbolised by a heart, a thought of hatred by an arrow or a flash, etc. In spite of the fact that the larvae, these undesirable mental inhabitants, cannot be seen by the normal human being, they do still exist, and the well-trained magician can perceive them on the mental plane. In sensitive or excitable persons, the mental matter is much more separable and the reproduction of larvae is obviously easier and more intense. Such people wreck themselves, their health, especially their nerves, but they also damage their intellectual faculties and involve other highly suggestible people, too. All kinds of mass-psychosis are originating here. There is no need of describing mass-psychosis in detail, because everybody will have made his observations and experiences regarding this problem.

Evidently the larva is becoming all the stronger, the more one is returning to the cause of the psychical excitement and the more attention one is paying to it. Any larva, being condensed very strongly, will always show a great deal of self-preservation instinct and will try to prolong its duration of life as far as possible. For this reason, it stimulates the mind of the given person, trying at every opportunity, to draw his attention to the cause of excitement and to revive it constantly. Such a well-fed larva can become fatal to a sensitive or emotional individual, and numerous mental disturbances such as persecution-mania and simi* lar are the result of it. How many people are living under the erroneous supposal to be haunted and destroyed by black magicians, whereas they are, in fact, victims of their own fancies, or putting it correctly: victims of the larva they have been creating themselves. People like these will usually find out all about this problem, not before they have left their mortal frame. Only very few persons are actually haunted magically. Think of the numerous innocent Inquisition victims of the past! No doubt that there is a certain advantage for the average man in that the old order has changed yielding place to a new one, for "if a man's belief is bad, it will not be improved by burning". But one has thrown out the child together with the bath-water, without touching on the roots of the matter, and without verifying the higher laws.

The magician will now realize, why there has been laid such a stress on the importance of introspection, control and mastering of the thoughts at the beginning of the practical part of this work. Supposing he did not get the thoughts under the control of his willpower, in the course of his development, he would unconsciously create larvae which might become fatal to him sooner or later.

Next, I am going to describe another group of entities existing in the mental sphere, namely the group of the phantoms or phantasms. The difference between a larva and a phantom is as follows: A larva is quite unconsciously adopting a shape in the mental sphere, appropriate to the motive of a single or a repeated psychical emotion, whereas a phantom accepts a certain form originating in the phantasy of Man. Exactly in the same way as it happens to be with the larvae, the phantom is likewise reinforced, revived and animated by the repeated evocation of the picture, regardless of whatever the matter might be, and it will be capable of influencing not only the mental or astral plane, but also the material level. Two examples may serve to illustrate this topic:

A very remarkable example is the so-called magic persecution mania which I shall describe from two points of view, with reference to the phantoms. There are certain human beings with an innate scowl or with demoniacal features, and whose outward appearance, consequently, gives the impression of black magicians, but who, probably, have not the faintest idea of any human science, to say nothing of magic at all. It is sufficient for any easily suggestible, emotionally excitable or rather conceited person to meet with such a type of man, whether in business or in personal concern, and our "test subject" as we shall call it, will instantly have the sensation of a strong dislike and antipathy towards the antagonist. It can happen now that our type is exhibiting a whimsical behaviour, without wanting to do so, nor even knowing about it. The first thought, entering the "test-subject's" mind will be, that he is facing a black magician. Maybe, for some reason or the other, this test person is not thinking too highly of this type of man, and the first step towards self-suggestion has already been done. Sooner or later, the test person will be met with small every-day incidents. The cause of these incidents will never be cleared up, but the blame for them will simply be set on our type of man. From now, the attention is stirred up, one is watching one's own self and the picture of the "type" becomes more distinct. One begins already feeling persecuted. The eyes grow more glittering, his appearance reveals itself in dreams, the picture becomes more vivid, emerges eventually even in broad daylight and finally one does constantly live under the impression of being persecuted at every turn. With the help of a very lively imagination, the picture can be condensed to such a degree, that it becomes visible even to other, similarly sensitive persons. Feeling persecuted in this manner, our test-person may be argued into anything, even the worst, the picture continually working on his mind. He is looking for help, begins to pray and does his best to scare away this terrible influence; he gets a nervous break-down, becomes gradually insane and ends up whether by committing suicide or else in a mental hospital for the rest of his life. The phantom has fulfilled its task.

How terrific is the shock, however, if such a spirit must convince itself in the mental sphere, that it has been committing a well-organised magic suicide! What a bitter disappointment! Our "type-man", of course, has not the faintest idea of what happened, indeed, and never will he realize that he was nothing else but a means to an end. His face, his conduct were only the form, the pattern, from which our "test subject" created the destructive being, the phantom whose victim he became in the end. Such and similar sad examples do happen more frequently than you would believe; sometimes faster, more drastically, in other cases more slowly, furtively, insidiously. But should you dare to tell such a persecuted person the truth, he would never believe it, because the phantom knows well how to hinder its victims from escaping. If the Divine Providence's guiding hand leads such an unhappy persecuted person to a genuine magician who is finding out the phantom's trickery, he will face a very difficult task to convince the victim, to lead him the right path and to teach him a different, normal mode of thinking. At certain times, especially if the victim is completely under the spell of a phantom, the helper will have to interfere very firmly, indeed, now and again, even drastically to restore the mental balance of the individual.

The second example shows the same occurrence but with a different motive underlying:

We have to deal here with a phantom of eroticism: The birth of such a phantom—if one may use the expression of birth at all—takes place in the face, the beautiful body of a living person, sometimes only a photo, a pornographic illustration or something similar with the purpose to provoke the lust, the sexual instinct, regardless of the person belonging to the female or the male sex. Provided any one being in love, have no opportunity at all of satisfying his personal longing, the stronger and the more vehement this yearning will grow, the stronger will, at the same time, the phantom's insinuations become, because it is thriving entirely on thoughts of yearning. The more the concerned person is trying to resist this unsatisfied love, the more obtrusive the phantom will become. At first it will turn up in dreams and allow his victim to revel in the most delightful transport of love. A little later it will provoke the sexual instinct and allow sexual intercourse in the victim's dreams. The pollutions produced in this way help the phantom to become denser and to influence the victim more and more, because the sperm is representing the concentrated vital power which the phantom is sucking up like a vampire. The point in question, here, is not the material sperm, but the animal vital power accumulated in the sperm. The victim is loosing the ground under his feet, his willpower is diminishing and the phantom gradually wins the upper hand. If fate is not so kind to such a one as to have him enlightened in good time and to find the right distraction for him, the phantom's mode of action will result in more dangerous effects. The person becomes confused, stops eating, the nerves are over-excited and such like. The love-phantom can be condensed to such a degree by unsatisfied passion that it can adopt bodily forms, seducing his victim to onanism and other artificial stimulation of the genital organs. Thousands of people have fallen victims of phantoms by committing suicide as the result of disappointment in love or unsatisfied passion. This problem recalls the remembrance of true occurrences of the mediae-val incubi and succubi and the trials for witchraft connected there-with. A very dangerous pleasure indeed!

In the light of the two foregoing instances, the magician may observe the activity of the phantasms, and he will be able to form such spectres himself. But do not forget: sooner or later, he always will run the risk of being influenced or mastered by them. He knows what is happening in the normal average-individual, and how to produce these phantasms consciously in a magic way, but never will he be induced to execute such practices himself, always remembering the magic sentence: "Love is the law, but love under a strong will."

There is one theme left to be described, that one of the phan-tasms or shadows.

Phantasms are animate presentations of people already deceased. I will pay particular attention to this theme to avoid many errors, and enable everybody to sift the chaff from the wheat. As soon as a human being is leaving behind the mortal frame, it is, at once, in the fourth state of aggregation, usually called the "world beyond". Without any mediating substance, it is impossible for a being to operate on our tri-dimensional sphere, just as a fish cannot swim without water. The same thing prevails to beings already passed away to the world beyond. Remembering, praising, mourning the deceased, any memory of, or tribute to, them will create and enliven imaginary pictures of the dead, which, as a result of frequent repetition, have rather a long duration of life. We call these pictures, created by the living ones, phantoms. It is this kind of phantoms which manifest themselves, in great numbers, to the so-called spiritualists, evokers, diviners, etc. The spooks and hobgoblins also are nothing else but phantoms preserving, con-densing, and thriving on the affection and attachment of the bereaved ones, as it happens in the case of the shadows. This can be stated, without difficulties, by citing, in different places, at the same minute, a being, which manifests itself, in all directions, at once, through the so-called mediums, which means nothing else but a manifestation of the dead person's phantom, because phantoms can be created by hundreds. It is very sad that these phantoms are always mistaken for the real dead persons by the spiritualistic mediums. A lot of mischief, self-deception and fraudulence is carried out just in this line. One can observe, for instance, that one of the mediums is communicating with a famous leader or general, a second one with an artist, another with a Saint, on a different place with a Pharaoh and immediately again with an angel. Therefore, it is not surprising, at all, that this particular field of knowledge will meet with an host of opponents and mockers, because of its amount of self-deception. No wonder that a phantom has such a strong instinct of self-preservation as to present itself as a vampire to the medium or the whole circle, and becomes, indeed, fatal to the nearest neighbourhood as well.

All this does not mean, of course, that a genuine magician who is mastering the fourth state of aggregation, that is the akasha-principle would not be capable of taking up a communication with a deceased person or with an intellect not yet embodied. I have quoted the practice already in the chapter about the mediumistic writing. Apart from that, any magician is able to form a housing, a shape, with the help of the imagination, transfering it in the fourth state of aggregation, and to persuade or even to force the true, desired being to enter this form and manifest itself to the external world. This practice belongs to the field of necromancy or conjuring magic and has nothing at all to do with the generally known spiritualism. The genuine magician will use this practice in extreme cases only, and he will not evoke a being, away from its sphere, because anything a being of the fourth state of aggregation has to say or to fulfill in the material or astral world, can be achieved by the magician himself through his maturity likewise.

Summary of all exercises of Step VI

I. *Magic Mental Training:*

    1. Meditation on the own spirit.
    2. Becoming conscious of the senses in the spirit.

II. *Magic Psychic Training:*

    1. Preparation to master the akasha-principle.
    2. Deliberate induction to trance with the help of akasha.
    3. Mastering of the elements with the help of an individual ritual from the akasha.

III. *Magic Physical Training:*

    1. Deliberate creation of beings:
        a) Elementals,
        b) Larvae,
        c) Phantasms (shadows),
        d) Phantoms.

End of Step VI

Magic Mental Training (VII)

In the sixth Step the scholar learned to become conscious of the own spirit, to act deliberately in the body as a spirit and also to use his senses consciously.

In this stage, he will consciously pursue the properties of the spirit or of the mental body, and use them as well. Here, of course, just like anywhere else, the analogy of the elements is to be considered. It has been mentioned before that the fire-element can be transformed into light and conversely. Without light, there would never be any reception of colour for the eyes, consequently we could not use our eyes without the existence of light. From this point of view, it is quite obvious that the sense of visual perception is analogous to the fire-element. This element, related to the spirit, shows as a specific property the Will. The mental property belonging to the air-element is the intellect with all its aspects, and it is imputed to the hearing. The water-element of the spirit is expressed in the feeling or in life. These three element-principles of the spirit, say fire, air and water together are producing the earth-principle of the spirit, which shows itself in the specific quality of consciousness. The akasha-principle, in its simplest form, manifests itself in the conscience.

The magician will at once understand the great importance of this analogy, if he has already developed so far as to achieve the magical equilibrium, in the astral body, by means of introspection. The next task he will be asked to fulfill is to analyse his spirit, and to find out which of the elements is predominant in his spirit.

In the case of people having a very strong will, which does not mean stubbornness, the fire element will, of course, be predominant. If the intellect or the intelligence with all its aspects is prevailing in the magician's spirit, the element of air is supposed to be the stronger one. In the case the magician should be, above all, an emotional character, the water-element will play the main part in him. If he has a weak memory, the consciousness will be affected very often, and one can take it for granted that the prevailing element is that of the earth.

This classification serves to establish the efficiency of the elements in the spirit and to arrange the development, so that the weaker elements are balanced by suitable concentration-exercises and deep meditation. The magician must neither allow the fire-principle, nor the ones of water, air or earth to prevail, and has to know how to classify his exercises in such a manner, that the intensity of his work will neutralize the elements. Let me explain this problem in detail in the light of an example.

Suppose the magician's intellect to be on a very high level, his will being weak and not quite up to the maturity of his intellect, then he must try to strengthen his volition by suitable concentration-exercises which bring out the fire-principle in the spirit. He should mainly select exercises which are training the eyes, that means exercises of optic imagination, considering that the eye corresponds to the fire-element.

But if the magician has a strong will and a weak intellect, we shall come to the conclusion that he has to give his keenest attention to the hearing by imagination-exercises, i. e., he has to choose concentration and meditation exercises which are fully engaging the ear.

Should, however, the magician own a strong will and a very good intellect, his emotional life or his feelings somehow lagging behind, then he will have to render his spirit more emotional, which he can accomplish through such imagination and meditation exercises which influence the feeling very strongly. If the magician should notice that his astral body as well as his mental body incline mainly towards the earth-element, say that his thoughts come very slowly in his spirit and that he gets the blues, that is to point out that the earth-element prevails and that first of all he must train his consciousness with the help of suitable exercises.

The magician has to develop his spirit to perfect harmony with regard to the elements, and to choose exercises corresponding to the elements and, at the same time, to the senses, so that the will or volition, hence the fire, the intellect, hence the air, the feeling, hence the water and the consciousness, hence the earth are enhanced and developed evenly.

The outcome of this description is the following schedule which I will quote for the sake of a synopsis:

Elements:	Fire:	Air:	Water:	Earth:	Akasha:
Senses	Eyes	Ears	Perception	Taste Smell	All in all
Fundamental qualities of the spirit	Will	Intellect	Feeling	Conscious-ness	Conscience
Exercises in concentration and meditation	Optic	Acoustic	Emotional	Expanding of the con-sciousness	Realising realities

The akasha-principle developing from concentration, there is no need of descending to particulars. It is also superfluous to quote single exercises of concentration and meditation, according to the specific qualities of the elements, prevailing in him, the scholar can easily compile them. He will select imaginations of objects, pictures, etc., for his concentration-exercises, if he has a weak will. After all, he went through these exercises, already, in the second Step of this course. The above harmony schedule is so-to-speak a sign-post, sort of a compass to find out which of the elements is pre-ponderant, and which of the exercises has to be taken up more intensively. As a result or success of this hermetic classification, the akasha-principle will reveal itself to him.

Magic Psychic Training (VII)

A very particular topic we shall deal with, on this Step, concerns the development of the astral senses with regard to the elements. The magician's astral senses have been trained and developed, in any case, in the course of all the preceding exercises, nevertheless, there is a need of an extraordinary drill in cases of only poor abilities for one or the other faculty, because every human being is differently talented. Therefore, it will be opportune to quote exer-cises here which enable the magician to develop the senses of the astral body fast and without difficulties.

In the magic mental training of the Step VI, the scholar did learn to become conscious of his spirit, and to act as a spirit through the astral body as well as through the material one. In pursuance of this, I will deal with one of the most fascinating problems, namely that of clairvoyance. Numerous books have been published about this theme, but the ones which came into my hands did not offer the slightest practical profit to any magician. It is therefore very useful, indeed, to labour the field of clairvoyance very thoroughly.

Generally speaking, clairvoyance means the second sight as it is popularly named, or the power of seeing, without the use of the eye, events taking place at a distance, actually or in the future or having taken place in the past, or seeing deceased people. Very few authors described this power from a psychological or from any other point of view, and that is why it shall be our next task to very thoroughly study the phenomenon of clairvoyance. First of all, the magician will realize that there are various kinds of clairvoyance. The principal kind is the inborn capacity of clair-voyance which its bearer has been granted whether in the invisible world already, or which he brought with him from a former embodiment into his present existence. This kind of clairvoyance is the best, but very few human beings do enjoy it, being hence born clairvoyants, who have developed this capacity to such a degree, without any effort at all, that they can practice it imme-diately. A second kind of clairvoyance is the one which, according to an involuntary shifting of elements in the spirit, occurs spon-taneously, and is therefore to be regarded as a pathological symp-tom. A shock in the case of severe illness can also cause the capacity of clairvoyance. This happens usually in the case of people who lost their equilibrium as the result of a stroke, a nervous break-down or otherwise through a physical, or psychical trauma, where, as a concomitance, a kind of clairvoyance will occur in a more or less distinct form. This sort of clairvoyance is naturally undesirable for the magician, because it will sooner or later lead to a complete breakdown, which not only implies a total loss of this power, but is also detrimental to the health and very often the cause of an untimely death. Clairvoyants of this kind are very pitiable, indeed, even then, if their success should be a convincing proof. To this category belong all the persons who, having a mediumistic pre-disposition, were induced to clairvoyance by some beings. Nor is this kind recommendable to the magic practitioner, because people like those, usually, end up in a lunatic asylum. A great number of persons who have been taken to Mental Hospitals and who were meddling with problems of spiritualism, without a reliable guid-ance, can blame their hopeless condition on spiritualism, and it does not matter in the least, whether the motives of this study were earnest intentions or mere curiosity or whatever may have induced them.

Another kind of bringing about clairvoyance which also belongs to this group, is the forced production of this power with the help of drugs like opium, hashish, mescal (peyotl), soma, etc. This will be without any interest to the magician, because most of these people will fall victims to the addiction to these dangerous drugs, which paralyse the ethical and intellectual faculties, the willpower and finally the nervous system, injuring, of course, the health as well as the development. By the millions, such cases are recorded in the Orient but they do occur, in great numbers, in the Occident as well as in all the other civilised countries, too.

The magician certainly has the opportunity—as long as he has not achieved the necessary maturity—of convincing himself of the existence of clairvoyance and other supernatural occurences in one way or the other, but usually—and that is the worst of it—he does not stop at this conviction: he, too, may become a prey to intoxication and fall into the same condition in which so many drug-stricken persons are. For this reason, I will not describe any method in this work which would tempt the magician to experiment on such things but I shall only point out quite harmless methods, which allow clairvoyance to occur automatically, in conformity with the **spiritual maturity and as a concomitance of the higher initiation.**

Another kind of clairvoyance is the one which is caused by impairment or temporary loss of a sense organ, in the case of clairvoyance the organ concerned will be the eye. Most of the books teaching clairvoyance by staring at an object, a magic mirror, a crystall ball or at gems are obviously good, but they are not adequate to everybody. These expedients for the development of clairvoyance are useful only in the hands of a trained magician, but they must not call forth clairvoyance by stimulating the "nervus opticus" but they are meant only to serve as a mere aid to an eye, that is already trained consciously. From the magical point of view, not a single recource, however highly praised or scrupulously executed, is capable to produce the gift of clairvoyance. This capacity depends 1. on the talents and 2. on the psychical and astral development and maturity of the magician.

Further chapters in which I shall teach how to make fluid condensers, will also include instructions for the production of magic mirrors and other appliances.

The magician ought not to forget that all the dodges and appliances mentioned, here, are nothing but poor expedients, by no means, however, are they the real factor which produces the desired result, the genuine clairvoyance.

I will finally mention the last kind of clairvoyance, which occurs as a concomitant of the correct magical development, and which is caused through the systematic display of the senses, in this case, the clairvoyant eyes. I resolved to quote, in this book, a secret magical method which has not yet been mentioned in any other work up to now, but which is exceedingly useful from the hermetic point of view as well as by analogy with the laws of the elements.

The practice of the development of the astral senses follows below.

The magic clairvoyance

Before I am going to describe the proper exercise, I must premise that we have got to deal here with the aspect of the light. As you know, light is an aspect of the fire, and therefore analogous to the will and the eyes. Consequently, what is the point, in this experiment is to intensify the imagination of the light i. e., to imagine the light optically to such a degree as to grant the success aimed at.

Take up your asana-posture and imagine you are imbibing the universal light—in form and brillance similar to our sunlight—from the universe into your body, whether through the pulmonary and porebreathing or imaginarily only. Regard your body as a hollow organ filled completely with this universal, bright white light. Now concentrate the quality of clairvoyance into this light in the body, i. e., imagine that the light is penetrating everything, seeing everything and looking through everything. Neither space nor time is any hindrance to this light. Your conviction of this quality of the light has to be rock-firm and not the faintest doubt is allowed to arise. If you are a religious man it should be easy for you to believe that this universal light is representing a part of God, who owns all the qualities described here. As soon as you have sucked in the light into your body, in this manner, together with the quoted qualities, and if you can inside feel its tension and penetrating power, do accumulate the light with the help of your imagination from the feet and hands towards the head, compressing the light to such a degree that it includes both your eyeballs. You can also fill first one and then the other eye with the accumulated light, as described here, if this way should be more suitable for you.

There are magicians who develop and enliven clairvoyance in one eye only, leaving the other eye free and undeveloped. It is left entirely to the scholar's judgement, whether this pattern is worth imitating but, as I see it, it is far better to prepare both eyes equally for clairvoyance.

As soon as you have performed the accumulation of light in your eyeballs, imagine that your eyes have got all the abilities concentrated in the light. Endure, in this exercise, for 10 minutes at least, and if you are quite sure that your eyes, which are imaginarily filled with the universal light, have also accepted the quality of this light, allow the light with the help of the imagination, to disperse again, whether directly from your eyes into the universal ocean of light, or to enter your body in its original form, and from there dissolve in the universal light. Both the methods described here are equally good, and the outcome will be the same. The important point is that the eyes, as soon as they are set free from the light, will become receptive again in the normal way. This is necessary for the simple reason that the astral eyes of the magician, developed in this manner, might not become over-sensitive so that they would be unable to discern what the normal eyes or the clairvoyant ones are seeing. Supposing the magician did fail to dissolve the concentrated light, his eyes would probably remain clairvoyant and he would hardly be able to distinguish between material and spiritual matters. Therefore he ought to have his power of clairvoyance well in hand, and allow it to become effective only, if he thinks it desirable. By frequent repetition of this exercise, the magician will achieve such a skill that he can allow his clairvoyant eye, the so-called "light-eye", to function in a few moments. Eyes prepared in this manner, whether closed or open, can see anything the magician wishes to, whether in a crystal globe or a glass-ball, on a polished wardrobe or in a magic mirror, his clairvoyant eye will see everything. The quality of the clairvoyant perception does then depend exclusively on the purity of his character.

An excellent remedy contributing to a quicker success and influencing very favourably on the physical eyes, so that people suffering from a bad eyesight or stricken with an eyecomplaint can gain a profit not only from the magical point of view but from the sanitary one as well, is the preparation of a magical ophthalmic fire-lotion.

The following ingredients are necessary:

1. A large bottle of distilled water available in any drug-store or dispensary.
2. Some camomile flowers (dried or fresh).
3. Some Herba Euphrasia also fresh or dried.
4. 7—9 thin osier or hazel-nut switches which you find in the open fields. They are to strip of leaves, to cut up even and to tie with a string at some spots. Then let the bunch of switches dry near the warm stove, in the sun or in dry air.
5. You will also need a piece of filter paper and a small funnel.

Now you can begin to prepare the eyelotion. Pour 0.44 pint ($\frac{1}{4}$ litre) of aqua destillata—distilled water—into a clean container, put it on the fire and when it begins boiling, add two teaspoonfuls of the camomile flowers and one teaspoonful of Herba Euphrasia. Let the whole boil up for a few seconds only, take it off the fire, and cover it with a lid. After 10 minutes, filter it into another clean container; when the tea has cooled down take the bunch of osier or hazel-nut switches, light the loose ends on an open flame and let them burn. Now dip the blazing ends into the tea. By doing so, the material fire-element has been transferred into the tea which one can already regard as a fluid condenser. I will write about this in detail in a further chapter. Now filter this fluid condenser through the filterpaper funnel into another clean container. This filtering is important to remove eventual chips, fragments of charcoal and ashes, produced by dipping the burning bunch into the liquid. Pour the tea into a bowl or a saucer and put it in front of you.

Now do inhale the fire-element through the lungs or pores or through both organs, at the same time, into your body and fill it entirely with this element. At this projection, there is no great attention to be given to the intensity of the warmth, as you will feel it in any case, but do not forget, that the fire-element has to be the bearer of your desire which you transferred to the fire-element through your imagination. After transferring your desire for having your material eyes strengthened and your astral eye developed, to the fire-element, in the same way as you performed the experiment of the light accumulation, project the fire-element, whether by way of the *solar plexus* or one of your hands or your breathing, into the liquid. If you get the feeling that the projection is not sufficient, repeat the experiment several times, but no more than 7—9 times. Thereby the so prepared condenser will factually turn into a strong essence which has not only a very fine effect on the eyesight, but also strengthens, enlivens and develops the astral senses. Now lock up the fluid condenser in a clean bottle and keep it in a cool spot. This ophthalmic fire-lotion may be used for strengthening the eyesight or for magical purposes. In the case of a weak eyesight, one could drop this liquid condenser simply into the eyes, without any hesitation, because the two-herb-combination is anti-inflammatory and an eye-tonic, but for the magical practice, i. e., the development of the astral senses, it will suffice to moisten a piece of cotton wool wrapped in gauze or a strip of clean linen, and to use it as a poultice, during the experiment of animating the eyes with light.

Later on, as soon as the astral eyes are better developed, the fluid condenser poultices can be omitted and it will be sufficient to perform the accumulation of light in the eyeballs. After frequent repetition, when the physical eyes are already developed by these light-exercises, one has only to direct the attention to the astral eye with the desire for being able to see with it. Apart from the duration of the experiment, one might also use these poultices, before going to bed, to achieve an automatic effect during the night, but there is a slight disadvantage: the eyes and the eyelids would become supersensitive as result of the intrusion of the fire-element, from the frequent use of the poultice. It is therefore more serviceable to use the poultices for the duration of the exercises only. The poultice is to be fastened with a scarf during the exercise to prevent it from falling off. This magic operation is to be performed without the presence of other persons. One ought to try to keep the poultice as well as the essence for a certain time, so it needs not to be renewed from one experiment to the other and does not fall into the hands of incompetent people, not even members of the family.

If the scholar has worked through all the foregoing exercises, he will develop his eye for clairvoyance, in an absolutely harmless way in a few months' time, when well talented even after a few weeks, following the method described and recommended here, and he will be capable to fulfil all the other tasks and operations still ahead of him in the knowledge of Magic. It is quite impossible to quote all the successes obtained with the different methods of clairvoyance mentioned here, they are so manifold and so reasonably obvious that it must be left to the magician himself how far reaching he will be able to train his astral eyes. At all events, he may be warned not to make boast of the abilities he did win, or even worse, to misuse them to harm his fellow-men. He ought to utilize them solely for the benefit of Mankind. Time and space won't be a handicap to him and there will remain nothing at all concealed before him, as far as his clairvoyant eyes are concerned.

The magical development of the astral clairhearing

This development is very much in line with the one of clairvoyance. The faculty of the astral clairhearing is based on the fact that one is able to hear voices even at the remotest distance and, at the same time, to understand the language of all beings. At the beginning, this faculty manifests itself in thinking aloud, coming from the inside, whether from the heart region or from the plexus-solaris. After a long spell of exercising, the astral clairhearing will develop to such a perfection that one can distinctly perceive everything with the supernormal hearing, similarly as if one were normally talking to somebody. This faculty is also a privilege of all magicians, and without it, there would scarcely be any progress in magic. For this particular reason, this type of astral clairhearing has to be handled with the same carefulness as astral seeing, and the exercises destined therefore, must not be neglected at any rate. All that has been said about astral seeing, about predisposition for it, about pathological symptoms will turn out to be true as well for clairhearing and clairfeeling. In connexion with this topic, I am going to treat the afore mentioned faculty.

Let us turn, without much ado, to the practice of clearhearing: For this exercise is required nothing else but a fluid condenser and a small piece of cotton wool. Make two small tampons from it in the size of the cavity of the ear. Moisten these cotton plugs a little with the fluid condenser and put both of them in front of you. According to the instructions you were given for training the astral eyes, you will work now with the air-element, filling your body with it by breathing through the lungs and pores. The whole body like a balloon, is assumed to be filled with air. Do imagine in this air-principle the desire for the faculty of clearhearing in your astral body as well as in the material one. Provided

you have the inward certainty that the air-element has been sufficiently impregnated with your desire and with your imagination,
do project the prepared air-element into the two small cotton-plugs
whether through the solar-plexus, one of your hands or your
breath by compressing and accumulating the air-element, which
fills your whole body, to such a degree that it will adopt exactly
the size of the two cotton wool plugs in front of you. You may
magically impregnate both of the plugs at the same time, or one
after the other with the entire amount of the element. The main
point of this experiment is the firm conviction and the unshakeable faith that this faculty is developing swiftly in your case.
You can use, as fluid condensers, a strong decoction of camomile
flowers in distilled water. Take two tablespoonfuls of camomile
flowers for 0.2 pint (⅛ litre) of water, filter them after scalding,
and keep the liquid cool to prevent the fluid condenser from
getting mouldy. By the way: a mouldy condenser is by no means
ineffective but insanitary.

Did you load these two cotton plugs several times with the
air-element, whether both of them, at the same time, or each one
separately, put both into your ears so that they are completely
crammed. Now, introduce the akasha-principle into your entire
head imaginarily, transfer yourself with your consciousness to the
ear region, and do imagine the faculty of the absolute clairhearing.
Imagine the akasha-principle introduced into your ears is instantly
producing the absolute clairhearing power in yourself. After a long
time of meditating and concentrating to this effect, dissolve the
akasha-principle again in the universal akasha, free your ears from
the cotton wool plugs, and keep them very well, because they
must not be touched by somebody else. In case the plugs should
fall into the hands of incompetent persons, you will have to prepare
new ones for yourself. Otherwise, it will be sufficient to remove
the plugs from the ears to allow the accumulated air-element to
dissolve again with the help of the imagination. It is obviously
of greater advantage to use new cotton wool plugs for every experiment, and to re-load them always anew, if one can afford the
necessary amount of time. Should you like to resort to your astral
sense of hearing, in one of the experiments, all you need to do is
lead the akasha, in the size of your auricles, into the inner acoustic
ducts of both your ears. After a long time of exercising, you will
be capable to use clairhearing for your purposes. As soon as you
do not need this faculty any more, try to lead the akasha-element
back into the original form, that is the universal akasha. By intro-

ducing the akasha-principle into the acoustic ducts, the mental as well as the astral hearing is influenced and developed and you will attain to the physical clairhearing with the help of the concentrated air-element. Anyone meditating intensely on this problem, will instantly find the coherence and may compare the operation with the wireless, where it is likewise the ether as the akasha-principle of matter—and the air which are playing their part as transmitters of the sound waves.

Development of the astral clairfeeling

Before passing on to the development of the astral clairfeeling, let us take up our magical diary and transfer ourselves to the time when we were engaged thoroughly with the introspection of the various good and bad qualities. According to the magic mirror we could establish, then, which of the qualities corresponding to the element in question were predominant in our mind. How important introspection, then, was indeed, is clearly shown by the fact that just this preponderance of the element concerned, points to our astral sensory centre. If the fire-element had been dominant, the sensory centre was the head, to put it correctly, the forehead; if it has been the air-element, it is the heart; in the case of prevalence of the water-element, it is the solar-plexus, and if it has been the earth-element, the sensory centre is in the hands or the thighs. Having, thus, established our astral sensory area, let us pass to the practice:

You have to act, in exactly the same manner, as you did, when training the two previous senses. The necessary requisites are: a piece of flannel, linen or a cotton wool plug which you slightly moisten with a fluid condenser. This condenser may again be a strong decoction of camomile flowers. At this performance, you are loading your body at once with the water-element through pulmonary and pore-breathing and with the desire, that this element may produce clairfeeling in you. The term of "clairfeeling" means the faculty of perceiving and feeling all the phenomena and powers occurring in the elements and in akasha. To this field also belongs the faculty of psychometry, that is the clear perception of present, past and future of any object, letter and so forth. Even the power of materialisation of any thought, any being, no matter whether the point in question is a self-created being, or an entity already existing in the akasha, belongs to this domain. Other faculties connected with sense perception and touch sensation can also be registered in the category of clairfeeling. Intuition, too, is originating in clairfeeling. These few examples may be sufficient to explain the clairfeeling power.

As soon as you have accumulated the water-element in the whole body through the pores and through breathing, load it with the intense imagination of the faculty of clairfeeling. You must be absolutely sure that it is strong enough to arouse this faculty really in your astral body. With the help of imagination draw the water-element from your body whether through the solar plexus, the forehead, hand or by breathing out, accumulating it in the cotton wool plug or the piece of flannel, soaked in the fluid condenser. You may repeat the loading but no more than 7—9 times. When doing this exercise, do not take up your routine posture, but lie down comfortably on a couch, or on the floor, whatever opportunity you have got. The main condition is to lie rather flat, only the head remains a little higher. To develop the astral clairfeeling, you need not directly utilize the water-element, but only the magnetic attractive power of the water. Before starting the exercise, put the fluid condenser on the pre-established sensory area. This exercise has to be performed with your eyes closed right from the beginning. Now do imagine your entire body is, as it were, actually swimming in the universal water-element, similarly as if you happened to be in the centre of the surface of an endless ocean. You feel nothing but water and again water only. Be very attentive, for it is quite possible that, during this exercise, you will fall into a state of doze and, in spite of all your carefulness, fall really asleep; in that case, make up your mind never to give in to sleep the next time, for, if this should become a habit, you would have great difficulties to fight against sleep, while doing your exercises.

In the previously mentioned imagination, you have transferred yourself, with your consciousness, to the sensory area, and now: imagine that the magnetical power of the water you have accumulated within yourself will enliven the finest particles of your sensation-field and produce the astral clairfeeling. You must be able to imagine the magnetic attractive power of the water so intensively that it becomes an incontestable reality. If, by long meditation, you have got the firm conviction that you have duly enough enlivened this sensory field, drop the imagination of universal water gradually, dissolve the water-element within your body into the universal element again, take off the fluid condenser, and reduce the concentrated element to the universal element, here also. The exercise is now at an end. In case, you should like to use the sensation-field practically, at one time or the other, the transfer of the consciousness into this field will be sufficient to put this faculty into action immediately.

To further the display of the astral senses of seeing, hearing and feeling, I deem it opportune to warmly recommend to you to continue these exercises even if you can spend very little time on them only. The real success will not be far off. We shall omit the development of the other senses, for the time being, because they are not important enough for the practical use of any magician. It is up to the scholar now to think out a scheme for himself to develop the other senses with the help of these three training methods. The faculties acquired by this astral development of the senses are so far reaching, that there is no need at all to talk much about. The enjoyment in the success can be compared, in a way, to a blind person who, deprived of the eyesight for years, is suddenly able to see again.

Magic Physical Training (VII)

If the magician is capable to manage the projection of elements to the outside, so that he knows how to project any element he likes to, out of himself or directly from the universe, he will be able as well to create "elementaries" for his own and other people's profit, too. He will succeed in creating beings which will be his faithful servants not only on the mental level but on the astral and material one likewise, according to his producing or rather condensing these beings in a mental, astral or material way. I have been talking already about the deliberate or conscious creation of thought-forms or "elementals". The difference between an *elemental* and an *elementary* is in that an *elemental* is produced, on the base of a deliberate form of thoughts, with the help of the magician's imagination and willpower, and works mainly on the mental plane for the magician's or other people's benefit. An *elementary*, on the other hand, is far more penetrating and more subtile, in its effect, because it is being created from one or several elements. In the light of practical examples, I will explain the real procreation act of an *elementary* as thoroughly as possible, demonstrating the manner in which the magician has to create an elementary. The intuition acquired by the previous training will certainly help the magician to contrive his own practice, responsive to the purpose he aims at. According to his ethical development, he will never dare to create elementaries for evil purposes; the invisible world would certainly vow ferocious revenge on him, because through the knowledge of how to create elementaries, the magician has got a plenitude of power, which allows him to achieve anything on the mental, astral and material level he likes to. He must always consider, that it's he himself who is responsible for his deeds, and not the elementary he has created. The elementaries are compliant tools in the hands of the magician, following his orders blindly and granting every desire to him, regardless whether a bad thing has to be turned to good account or the other way round.

In the same manner, as you cannot expect a baker's job done by a joiner, you cannot demand of an elementary created for a certain purpose the accomplishment of a second task it was not meant for. For this particular reason, you must never give two or more orders to any of the elementaries, for, in this case, the elementary will do neither one nor the other job well and reliably. Apart from that, there is also the analogy to the elements to be considered. It would be quite wrong and against the law, if a magician created an elementary which would not be in harmony with the analogous elements. As to the shape of the elementary, there are no limits to the magician's fantasy, and it is entirely left to him to choose the form according to his liking and his intuition. Avoid, however, to pick out the shape of living or deceased people you have known or who you have been, or are still, in connexion with. By doing so you might easily slip into the reach of the mental or astral body of the respective human being, and consequently, do him great damage. Apart from that, there is a danger that an elementary might turn against the magician, in consequence of its inbred intelligence, at any unguarded moment. It would understand perfectly to vampirise him or to influence on him indirectly when asleep, and to do any possible amount of mischief. Every magician is advised, therefore, to take this warning very seriously!

Each elementary has to be given a name, at the very moment of its creation. It is opportune to choose less common names, because the mere utterance of a name will be enough to bring the elementary near the magician at once. Supposing one has created several elementaries, it is advisable to take notes of the names in order not to forget them. But these names must not be mentioned to anyone else, because another magician, being clever enough, could easily seize the elementaries, and work with them without any effort.

The power and effectiveness of an elementary entirely depend on its loading. The stronger the magician's willpower is, all the greater will be the projection of the elements to the outside, and an elementary loaded, to such an extent, becomes, of course, all the more pervasive and far more effective. Sometimes an elementary can be so much condensed that it is visible even to an untrained physical eye. It is, therefore, up to the magician himself, whether he wants the elementary to work visibly or invisibly, just as the case may be. The duration of life of an elementary depends on the purpose to which it has been created, and this purpose has to be fixed right at the beginning of the creation-act. As soon as the purpose is fulfilled, the magician must dissolve his elementary in its original element, with the help of the imagination. Never omit this process of dissolution, because an elementary having performed its task becomes easily independent as the outcome of its instinct of self-preservation, and if you forget to do so, it likes to escape from your sphere of influence, and becomes a vampire. In this case, the magician would have to face all the *Karma-results,* caused by such an elementary transmuted into a vampire. Therefore carefulness and conscientiousness are seriously recommended, when you are handling elementaries. Many magicians determine, right at the creation-act, the kind of disintegration of the elementary by destroying the name of the elementary in question, burning it, performing a certain rite, a sign or a gesture, or using a formula which they fixed in advance. All this is individual and left to the magician's choice. A special attention has to be paid to the act of disintegration. Provided the magician be equal to this task, he will be able to force his elementaries to absolute obedience, at any time, by threatening them with disintegration. At all events, he should imprint on his mind that he is capable to bring the elementaries under his will and to have complete command of them. This is very important, if the magician does not wish himself to be the plaything of his self-created beings. He will make the experience, the better, the more faithfully, and the more reliably an elementary is serving him, the more engaging it will become and he will hate to dissolve it at all. But never must the magician give way to this sentimentalism, because he would get into the thraldom of elementaries. For this reason, it is more opportune to destine elementaries for a short life only, creating new ones for the same purpose in case of need. This does not mean, of course, that a new elementary should be created, every week, for the same purpose, but it is a disadvantage to keep the same elementary, for years, for one affair only.

Should the magician intend to create elementaries for his own use, he had better form them by the projection of elements through his body. Elementaries, however, destined for other people, should be created by the projection of elements directly from the universe. The magician knows very well that there is an invisible connexion between him and every elementary, which could be misused very easily, if he started to create elementaries by physical projection for other human beings as well. The way of how to manage it, will be quite understandable to every magician without any doubt.

It is necessary to talk about the places where elementaries should be deposited. In the Orient, elementaries—called there YIDAMS— are banished into a "KYLICHOR" where they are preserved. A kylichor is a diagram built from stone and corresponding to the yidam to which no stranger will ever be admitted. The well-trained magician, however, needs no separate place for it, but he will hide the elementary in a spot in the wall, realising that an elementary is neither limited to time nor does it claim a special space. Hence it will be quite allright in the wall as well as, if it would have been accomodated in an open space. It is even more suitable to keep it in a wall or any solid big object, because it is better to avoid banning it to places where other people are about all the time. Should a human being happen to come to the same place where an elementary is kept, the person would suddenly feel restless, and other bad consequences might occur.

Furthermore, it has to be fixed, right at the beginning of the creation-act, how the elementary ought to be called up. This can be done by whispering the name or thinking it only or simply, by a movement of the hand, a gesture or a ritual. The magician is at liberty to do as he pleases.

Before I am going to particularize the practical part, the proper act of creation, I should like to remark that it is not necessary for the magician to restrict himself to this practice, this being only a small part of practical magic and a hint, how the magician is to use his power. He should not specialise thereon, on the contrary: if he is capable to manage these practices perfectly, further possibilities are still at his disposal. This part of magic is to be followed up in the beginning only, and it is up to the magician to utilize it to help himself or other people, too. And, last not least, this is the purpose of this theme.

The act of creation

There are four fundamental methods devised for the creation act of an elementary.

1. The projection of one element into a ready form, no matter whether the point in question be a mental, an astral or a material form.
2. The projection of several elements into a ready form, which may be a mental, an astral or a material form.
3. The projection of one element without any direct form, which will be produced by the element in question.
4. The projection of several elements, which will be producing their form, successively.

I am going to explain all the four methods thoroughly in the light of practical examples.

Method 1:

Take any object of which you want to give the form to the elementary and put it in front of you. Choose for example a ball, it is of no importance at all, whether it be a big ball of wood or glass, solid or hollow inside. A rather large rubber ball will do as well. Draw the desired element, with the help of your imaginative faculty, from the universe, and imagine it in the form you did choose, in such a way, that the shape of the object—rubber ball— is completely filled. Treat each element you want to work with, in the same manner, except akasha, and always engage that element which best responds to your desire or your idea. Repeat this projection several times, each time imagining the sensation that more and more elemental matter is forming, accumulating and compressing. As soon as you are quite sure that this accumulation of the element is strong enough for the realisation of your desire, do impregnate this already completed elementary with the concentrated desire, that is, the purpose you aim at. Apart from that, give a name to the elementary, because it cannot exist without a name. At the same time, limit the period of its life-time, during which it has to fulfill its task. Supposing you did operate with the element of fire, the outcome will have been a fire-elementary and you have got a fiery ball. If it has been created from the water-element, the ball will be similar to a glass ball; created from the air-element, the ball will have a bluish colour and when produced from the earth-element, the elementary will appear clay-coloured.

Provided you did follow all these instructions, draw the elementary out of the object, and send it on to the job you did select to be done. But beforehand, order the elementary to go back into its shape immediately after having fulfilled its task. In this manner, you have the possibility of checking the elementary, whether it has or not done the job, by approaching the form with a sidereal pendulum. If the elementary has returned into the original form, say the rubber ball, after finishing its work, the pendulum will present vibrations, because such an elementary has a remarkable magnetical as well as an electrical radiation. The pendulum test is very important for you, as it demonstrated, whether your order has or not been executed. Later on, after having acquired the maturity, you will be enabled to watch the work of your elementary by clairvoyance. If the pendulum does not show any vibrations at all, it will prove the elementary to be still working, i. e., the job is not yet finished. When sending off the elementary to do its piece of work, you ought never to forget that there are no bounds for an elementary. Neither time nor space, can put obstacles in an elementary's way, and it really would be able to round the whole globe in a single moment, if necessary. You have to be firmly convinced that it will execute your order and obey your will within the time you have fixed, without any exception. Not the slightest doubt about the success must ever enter your mind. As soon as you have forwarded the elementary, cut off the connecting link between yourself and the elementary as suddenly, as if you had used a knife and stop to think of it, instantly, after having, sent it off. You may transfer yourself into a state of vacancy of mind, or give your attention to quite another story, in short, you have to forget the elementary altogether. The more skilfully you manage this, the more pervasively and undisturbedly will the elementary work. If the time you had fixed beforehand has expired, make sure, with the help of the sidereal pendulum, that the elementary has returned into its form. In this case, you have the opportunity of dissolving the elementary in the way you had previously determined, namely, by burning its name, with the help of a special ritual or, finally, by spelling its name from backwards to forwards in an undertone. This disintegration or, properly speaking, this dissolution can also be performed through the normal imagination, similar to the method we recommended for the projection of elements. You may use the elementary for the same purpose somewhere else, too, if you like to.

Should your elementary not have returned to the form it is preserved in, after the time you fixed, and should you suppose your order has not been fulfilled satisfactorily, just call back the elementary. Produce a more intense accumulation of the element, by reinforced imagination and projection of the respective element, and then, send the elementary off once more to do the required job. You may repeat this loading as many times as you like, until the desired effect has been accomplished. Such a repetition of the loading will be necessary when you bring your elementary up against a problem the solution of which would exceed its tension and power. Moreover, you have to consider that the effectiveness of an elementary depends on your own mental maturity, consequently on your ability to condense an element, besides, on your will, your conviction and your emanative faith which is capable to remove mountains.

This is the most artless and easiest method of creating elementaries, which the magician is using for simple effects only, narrowly limited ideas and influences which do not require any special intelligence, for example, to give an order to another person, to offer protection in simple affairs, etc. As mentioned before, mental, astral and material effects can be achieved with the help of elementaries.

In the manner quoted here, an elementary entity can be produced without any material shape as well. In such a case, one has to project the desired element into a form of thoughts, operating in exactly the same way you did in the material production. This kind of creation of elementaries is more difficult, it is true, but it has the advantage that the form can also be transferred somewhere else, where a material body would not have space enough, for example, into the corner of a wall, and into such spots where a meddling of other people is quite out of question.

This practice offers so many possibilities to the magician that it is left entirely to his intuition, to which purposes he likes to use the elementaries he did create. He can, for example, shield his house or his flat from injuries, with the help of an elementary, produce a more favourable atmosphere for himself, and similar things. All of us know that every science can be used for noble purposes as well as for evil ones, and so I am sorry to say, this practice likewise can be misused for egoistic and malevolent purposes. A merchant for example can create an elementary which will aid him to increase the number of his customers. All the haunted houses, discredited as such by spiteful magicians, may be, thus, interpreted as a production of elementaries deliberately created to such malicious purposes. A respectable magician will never degrade himself to such kind of machinations.

Method 2:

Although, according to this method, you may choose any object whatever, say a little statue, a doll or suchlike as a suitable form for your elementary, I shall, in addition, make you acquainted with a very ideal secret practice.

Take ²/₃ (two thirds) of loam and ¹/₃ (one third) part of wax —the parts to be understood in volumetric and not in weight sense— which means, for instance, that for one (1) liter of the mass you have to take ²/₃ l of loam and ¹/₃ l of wax, to get the correct proportion. Stir the loam with some warm water to a thick pulp and add the bees-wax, whether completely melted or very softly warmed up. Knead both ingredients to one mass until the loam is very well mixed with the wax. Do not take too much water to prepare the loam, otherwise the mass will turn out too soft and it would be difficult to operate with it. If genuine bees-wax be not available, any other suety ingredient will do, such as tallow, stearin, spermaceti and the like which are generally used for making candles. This would be a last resource, of course, because genuine bees-wax will be much better.

Now from the thoroughly kneaded mass, form a figure giving it the shape you want the elementary to have. If you want to give the shape of a human being to the elementary, the mass also ought to be moulded on this shape. With a rather big nail or any pointed object sink a wide opening while the doll is still warm and soft. Begin with the head, move down, as it were, along the spinal marrow to the feet, thus producing a large hollow inside the wax figure. Now fill this hollow space up to the opening, with a fluid condenser, and stop the opening while the figure is still soft to prevent the condenser from leaking out. Another way is, to pour the condenser into the figure, after it has cooled down and hardened, stopping the opening with liquid wax or with a candle. As to the treatment of magic condensers, I shall enlarge on this subject in a special chapter. If the magician intends to create the elementary for his own purposes only, he has to stop the opening of the figure with a cotton wool plug containing a few drops of his own, i. e., organic "prima material". This is the Alpha and Omega, therefore take a few drops of the own blood or sperm. In our case, one thing or the other would obviously be sufficient, but if both "Mumiae" of the first class were connected, it would be still more effective. Supposing a female magician is concerned, a drop of her own blood does, of course, serve the same purpose. The cotton wool plug prepared, in this manner, has to be put first into the hollow of the figure, pouring the fluid condenser over it, only then, not before; finally stop the opening. A figure like this, according to the magic rules, is the most ideal form to create an elementary. The size of the figure does not matter at all, although it is evident, that the bigger the doll's shape is, the more fertile will be your creative imagination. But a figure of approx. 4 in. (10 cm) will do for a skilled magician.

In case an elementary has to be created and a doll to be shaped for another person, the own prima materia is not to be mixed with the fluid condenser, otherwise serious damage will be done to the magician. The respective person, in consequence of the mental, astral and material connexion, would obtain the opportunity to influence the magician directly or indirectly to good as well as to bad effects. A figure for example prepared with the mumia and put into cold water, will cause shivering fits in the magician's body who created it, and, the other way round, if the doll were exposed to great heat, a high fever would be the result. Yet a great number of other possibilities are granted by the magic-sympathetic linkages, but I will refrain from quoting them so as not to seduce the scholar into any bad doings.

The afore mentioned doll can, of course, be loaded with one single element only, and an elementary can be created in the way described in the previous method, but I am going to particularize practice of the second method as well.

Take your wax-figure in the left hand and rub it gently with your right hand, as if you wanted to animate it with your vital power. Blow your own breath on it as if you wanted to resusciate the lifeless figure. Give your developing elementary the name you have destined to it and speak this name several times into the figure. Religiously inclined magicians do even baptize the figure in a way similar to the christening of a newborn child, and give the name to the figure while performing this ceremony. This, of course, is a matter of opinion of any magician and not absolutely necessary. At all events, ascertain yourself at this experiment that in this figure you possess a perfect body appropriate to your elementary. After your doll has got its name, fill your whole body, with the help of element-breathing, with the earth-element, do project it, whether through one of your hands or through the solar plexus outwards, and fill the figure with this element, beginning from the feet up to the neighbourhood of the genitals. The earth-element has to be accumulated dynamically in these parts, when filling the figure. Now concentrate all the specific properties of the earth such as gravity and the like into it, and while you are doing so, you must have the firm will and the conviction that the earth-element, with all its qualities, will remain in the figure, and work there constantly. Proceed, in the same manner, with the water-element, which you are projecting into the doll's abdominal region. After that, transfer the air-element to the chest region, and the fire-element into the head.

As soon as you have projected all the four elements into the figure, with the help of imagination, you may be sure to have created the astral body of your elementary, which has adopted the doll's shape but, in conformity with your desire, could also emanate from the doll, whenever you like to, accepting the size you prefer. The astral body of your elementary will always remain connected by an invisible bond to the material frame, in our case, the doll, and the life as well as the existence of the elementary depend on the physical doll, and are bound to re-assume the size of the doll, after the task is accomplished, re-entering and re-uniting into the doll's shape immediately. Up to this stage, you may repeat the experiment several times and reinforce its efficiency by deep meditation on the act of proceeding.

Provided you have produced the astral body of your elementary in the manner described here, you may turn to form the mental body of the elementary as follows:

With the help of your imagination, produce, in the doll, the mental body, which you think is made from the finest etherical matter, and see how it is surrounding and wrapping in the entire form of the doll. Concentrate into the head of the doll all the properties of the soul and the mind which you want your elementary to own, and deepen these qualities by meditation. Provided you are not interested in any special desires, you may concentrate on the four specific properties of the mind: will, intellect, feeling and consciousness, and deepen them by meditating on them. If you are sure that the figure has been sufficiently loaded and enabled to produce the intended effect, let us deal with the awakening of life of your elementary.

Accumulate, in your right hand, such an amount of light from the universe that the hand is shining like a sun, that means fiery, white or red. Take the figure in your left hand, and hold your radiant right hand some inches above it: Exhale your warm breath to the doll's navel region, and speak the name of the elementary aloud into it. When doing so, imagine that the light of your right hand is growing less and fading away from your right hand with each breath, entering into the puppet. Right at the first blowing your breath to it, imagine that the doll's heart is beginning to beat and the blood to circulate. Your imagination must be so intense that you can feel the life in the puppet quite distinctly, as it were, physically. At the seventh exhaling the light in your right hand will have completely disappeared, having passed into the doll: The astral form of your doll is throbbing and alive. At the eighth breathing to it, think that the astral body of your figure is accepting your breath and beginning to breathe regularly. At the ninth blowing your breath into it, call your elementary by its name and, at the same time, shout aloud and ecstatically: "live, do live, be alive!" The last "be alive" must be exclaimed enthusiastically and convincingly in the unshakable faith that the desired elementary has been created. Be positively sure that, according to the analogous laws of nature, a perfect being has actually been brought into the world.

Arrived at this point, one can either go on or wrap the figure in a piece of genuine silk for further use. Silk is known to be the best magic insulating material. The figure is to be kept in a favourable spot, inaccessible to anybody else, no foreigner must ever come in touch with the figure. Any further work is already a matter of imagination.

Provided you wish the advance, put the figure again in front of you, imagine the astral body together with the mental body emanating from the puppet. You have to imagine your elementary very much alike a tiny, complete human being, in a way as if you were looking at a normal human being through a minimizing glass.

It is also entirely up to you to see, in your elementary, a male or a female being, this depending on the kind of the task it is expected to fulfil. The same is true for the clothing of it, your fantasy may decide by the whim or pleasure of the moment. According to the task ahead, you may link the elementary, by imagination, to a self-selected ritual, allow it swiftly to grow as big as you want it to be. Impress on your elementary, right from the beginning, the command that it should adopt the size you decided for it. This will give you the chance to have your elementary shrunk to a dwarf or grown a giant. It depends absolutely on your will and your liking, whether you want to give your elementary an attractive or a less beautiful form. The purpose, too, on which you decide, also plays a part here. As every astral and mental body is independent on time and space,—matter being no obstacle for it,—it is necessary for you to communicate this property to your elementary right from the beginning, by imagination. It is, therefore, advisable for every magician to link important occurrences, when operating with an elementary, to a self-chosen ritual, because this occurrence wished for will become a routine matter, so that he is dispensed from using his volition or imagination, the ritual connected to the respective occurrence producing the necessary power and effect. When working with the elementary for a longer period, the elementary may be automatically or, in conformity with a desire, condensed to such an extent that it becomes visible even to an untrained physical eye. It is, however, better to make the elementary work in an invisible manner which, of course, has to be pre-set by an imaginary agreement with the elementary. At the beginning such a created elementary will fulfill first mental, later on astral, and after longer use, even material tasks. All depends on the purpose to which the magician has created it. The purpose, that is the task must be incorporated into the elementary in the very moment of its creation. Afterwards it would be more difficult to impress new qualities on it. Hence, before creating an elementary, one ought to form a written plan of action in which everything is carefully considered, before starting the proper creation.

Never permit an elementary to outmanoeuvre you, though it may have developed to such a degree as to set free grand mental, astral or even physical effects. Always confine the elementary, after having done its duty, to its own body, say the wax figure, with the aid of your pre-established ritual, never allowing it to pursue its own will. Be always aware of your own authority and magic power and make always sure, that life and death of the elementary are in your hands in the form of the wax-figure, representing the body of the elementary. The destruction of this figure or the flowing away of the fluid condenser will cause the elementary's death or its decomposition. As the wax-figure must always be wrapped in genuine silk, one may be certain that the astral body will neither enter the figure nor slip out of it, because the silk will stop it. To know and to remember this is most important. If you separate the elementary from its body, sending it off somewhere or ordering it to produce any effects, the figure must be free, that is unwrapped. If by any chance you have wrapped the figure in silk, when the astral body happens to be outside of it, you might be killing the elementary—eventually dissolving it instantly—in the same way as if you were touching a magician whose astral body is outside his physical body—killing him at the same moment, because the linking thread between the astral body and the mortal frame has been torn by the touch. As you see, you will have to treat a created elementary in exactly the same way as if you were dealing with any human being.

The dissolution of an elementary must not take place suddenly, because the power set free has its origin in the magician himself, and the sudden drawback could eventually cause severe damages to the magician, especially if his elementary is already capable to produce strong physical effects which even the magician himself would not be able to accomplish. In such a case, the disintegration has to be performed gradually. Therefore be on your guard beforehand against the elementary growing to such an extent as to outdo the magician's physical, astral and mental powers.

Hence I recommend the following two methods to disintegrate an elementary. As mentioned previously, the destruction must not happen all of a sudden, for example, by burning the figure, without unloading it, etc. One should always consider that, according to the method described here, it's a part of the own Self, of the own Ego that has been projected into the elementary, and that any abrupt destruction would result in a strong magical drawback. Should not the magician be sufficiently resistant or otherwise protected against such drawbacks, he would certainly suffer severe damages of his health, such as disfunctions of the heart, nervous break-down, paralysis of different kinds, mental defects and so forth. Therefore carefulness is always advised where magic is concerned, and one must strictly observe the directions and instructions given here. Then you will never incur any danger with respect to your health or otherwise. Only a fool ignoring or disobeying the rules will injure himself or other people. A sensible, righteous person will do good deeds only for the benefit of mankind, thus achieving high grades in magic, because he will never affront the laws of nature and spirit.

The process of decomposition is, in the case of an elementary, exactly the same as in the passing away of Man, unless the dissolving method was fixed at the very moment of creation, thereby deciding on another process. Take the figure in your hand and imagine the usual breathing process of the astral body in it. You feel the beating of the heart and the throbbing of the blood. Now load your right hand which you are imagining to be of a black-violet colour, with akasha. Do project akasha pointedly to the heart of the figure, all of a sudden, like a streak of lightning. By doing so, you have killed your elementary. The heart stands still, the breathing has ceased. Withdraw the mental body from the figure, because, through the streak of the akasha, the bond between the mental and the astral body has been torn. As soon as you did imagine the mental body being outside the puppet, dissolve it with the help of your imagination into the universal light, alike to steam evaporating. After that, pass to the decomposition of the astral body in the puppet by having one element after the other evaporated imaginarily into the universal element. Begin doing so with the fire-element in the head of the figure; then follows the air-element in the neighbourhood of the chest, the water-element in the abdomen and finally the earth-element in the feet. Now somehow open the hollow of the puppet, and to make short work of doing, break its head off. Catch the contents, that means the fluid condenser with a piece of blotting-paper, which you have to burn then. The puppet itself could be used again to make a new elementary, when kneaded and newly modelled, but it is more advisable to destroy it, by burning or burying it in a lonely spot. This would be the normal way of decomposition.

Apart from that, I am going to describe another method which is generally used, when an elementary had been condensed to such a degree that it did accomplish physical tasks or else had become so strong that it refused to obey the magician's power having got beyond his control. To protect yourself against any magic reaction or the cunning of the elementary, keep exactly within the following directions:

Prepare a very hot tub-bath, as hot as your body can endure it, go into the bath-tub and sit down. Hold in your left hand the figure, wrapped in silk. The right hand is loaded with akasha.

Now shake off the silk wrapping with your left hand, that is the one you are holding the figure in. The very moment you are holding the naked figure immediately above the water, direct the destructive beam of akasha to the heart of the figure. At the same time, dip the doll below the water and, while doing so, think that all the power, all abilities, the whole life is passing, with the help of the water, into your own body, your soul and your spirit. This process represents a very abrupt destruction of the created being, i. e., your elementary. Your body, soul and spirit are accepting the life in a tolerable manner. The rest of the power remains in the water and you are protected against any magic drawback or reaction. Now leave the bath, dry yourself, leaving however the puppet still in the water, until it has cooled down. The silk in which the puppet had been wrapped, might also have glided into the water. Let the cold water flow off into the drain or empty it, but make sure that nobody else comes in touch with this water. If your eyes are already clairvoyant and if you notice that the figure is still emanating an aura, throw it once more into the hot water and concentrate on the water taking away the last bit of life. The doll will dissolve and melt in the hot water and the fluid condenser i. e., the liquid will mix up with the hot water. You may perform this experiment in any case, even if you don't see the emanation. At least, you will thus be sure that all life in the elementary is extinct. Burn or bury the remains of the doll together with the silk. With this last operation the elementary is dead and gone for you.

Before I am going to terminate this chapter, I would like to give a few hints to the magician who has to work with elementaries. These hints are of a paramount importance for the practitioner. Exactly as the hours of birth and death of man are already predestined by fate, decide on the duration of life of your elementary in the same way at the very creation act, that means fix the exact dying-hour which you have got to keep to the very minute, even if you have determined your elementary to live for years. It is therefore recommended to write down everything beforehand, not to forget anything at all. If your elementaries have been created and condensed to such a degree as to be able to talk like human beings, they will try to beseech or even threaten you not to destroy them. On no account descend to promises of any kind, nor do yield to bluffs or threats. Sooner or later, you would lose the control of the elementaries and that would be disastrous for you indeed. Even though the elementaries had served you faithfully and you had become quite fond of them, it must be all the same to you to destroy them, indifferent and in cold blood, as soon as their hour of death has struck. Start the act of decomposition without any pity just as if you were performing any kind of magic operation.

How very important it is to fix the exact hour of death of an elementary, you may argue from the fact that, in case anything should happen to you, and you should die, before the elementary's hour is come, this latter would dissolve itself at the moment fixed by you. However, though departed, you might perform your destroying work in the akasha sphere, too, if you were as yet interested in it. I am not going to describe here, how anything like that could be managed, because it would be out of the scope of this book. Being however on the astral level, you would as a perfect magician understand that automatically. If in such a case the lifetime of an elementary were not limited to terms, that means had not the hour of death been exactly fixed, the elementary would go on existing for hundreds of years after the producer's death and constantly be viable. In the meantime it would probably grow into a spook, a hobgoblin or vampire, and, in akasha, its creator, i. e., the magician would be responsible for all the actions produced by the elementary.

Now the question will probably arise: how many of such or similar elementaries may be created by a magician? This problem is entirely left to him. He should decide how many he needs for his own purposes and how many he wants to create for other people. Some magicians have a throng of elementaries as their servants, fulfilling faithfully all the tasks they are ordered to do. Thus for example, the magician might have elementaries pointing out every danger to him in advance, others again will protect him, or forward messages to him, etc. There is no use to quote all the possibilities, because all of them are individual and depend on the desires which the magician wants to be realised with the help of the elementaries. The speaking pictures, columns and statues in the temples of the Ancients may certainly be interpreted as an outgrowth of elementaries' magic. The legend concerning the *Golem*, who is said to have been created by the wise Rabbi *Löw* in Prague goes likewise back to the creation of elementaries. But in the case of the Golem the creation has been produced with the rites of the Quabbalah. Anybody who knows of quabbalistic mysticism is informed about these facts. The synthesis remains the same as quoted in this method.

Method 3:

Before I am going to explain the practice of the third method, I would like to remark that very little is known about it, and it is used by a few oriental adepts only. If any magician should decide in favour of this third method, he has, of course, to consider everything I have written about the creation of elementaries up to now. First of all, he must think out a schedule and reflect very intensively about the purpose of the elementary, i. e., his own task and get a clear idea of it. Apart from that, he must have regard to the form which he intends to choose and whether he means to create a male, a female or perhaps a twofold nature being. Moreover, he has instantly to determine the appropriate name and make a note of it. Nor ought he to forget to fix the duration of life of the elementary, timing the exact day and hour. Supposing the elementary is meant for his personal use, he has to perform the loading through the projection of his own body. In case it is meant for somebody else he has to execute the projection directly from the universe. Furthermore, he has to make sure about the manner in which he intends to call his elementary, whether by a ritual, a formula, a gesture or the like. He must know if he wishes to bind it to a puppet, a figure or to any object else, a talisman or a pentacle. He has also to decide on the place in which the elementary has to be kept in order not to come in touch with strangers. Having considered all this carefully and having taken written notes of it, to be able to overlook the entire schedule, he may begin with the practical side. In this third method I am going to describe an elementary created with the fire-element, and which the magician may use for his own purposes.

Draw a circle on a piece of paper, in the middle of it two squares, one upon another, so that you get a regular octagon. This octagon indicates that we have to do with a symbol of the four elements in their positive and negative results. The circle itself represents the all-comprehensive akasha-principle from which the four elements are come. Mark the centre of the octagon by any sign you like, which indicates the symbol of the elementary. The paper you are using for the drawing has to be big enough to allow the created elementary to stand in the centre of the octagon, that means on the sign. Now engrave the same sign on a very tiny round object, best on a copper, silver or gold disk—any other kind of metal will also do—in a diameter of ½ in. (1 cm). If nothing else is available, a small piece of wood will do for our purpose too.

It is however more profitable to do the engraving with a pointed object on a small metal-disk, all the more, if the elementary in question is destined to have a longer lifetime. Lamas in Tibet working with it, name the big drawing the great *kylichor* and the small engraving the little *kylichor*, which they sometimes have about hidden in their clothing. The difference is, the great kylichor in Tibet is not drawn on paper, as quoted here, but it is built from stones, gathered there and erected in a lonely spot, where no human being will ever be admitted. The construction of a big kylichor has a diameter of approx 3—4 yards. For our purposes it is sufficient to draw the big kylichor on paper with red ink, chinese ink or any other liquid which cannot be wiped out very easily.

All these preparations being finished, let us begin with the real creation of the elementary. Sit down comfortably in your asana, spread the paper already prepared and put the small kylichor exactly into the centre of the big kylichor. As soon as you take your hand off the small kylichor, call the name you chose for the elementary. The small kylichor is now serving as a starting point and as a means of consciousness support in the projection of elements. Inhale the fire-element into your body through lung and pore breathing. You can either impregnate the fire-element with your desire now, or animate the fire-element with the help of your imagination after it has been completely projected outside of your body. In order to achieve a quicker success, both possibilities may be used without any incidents. Now project the fire-element out of your body through one of the starting points of your astral body and accumulate it to such a degree, that the entire contents of your body are compressed to a very small spark of fire. Confine this spark with the help of your will or your imagination to the surface of your small kylichor. Do repeat this experiment, at least, seven times, concentrate and accumulate the element on the surface of your small kylichor, mix one concentrated spark with another so that the spark is growing bigger with each repetition. After repeating it seven times, the spark might already have the size of a small flamelet, similar to the light of a candle. If you are getting tired, you may transfer the little flame with the help of your sending-off and guarding method into the spot where you intend to keep the elementary. This may be inside a wall or any other place not easily accessible where you will hide it. Now remove the small kylichor from the big one, guard it well, or carry it with you, if you find it more profitable. Do fold up the big kylichor, keep it well, too, and the first task will be finished.

Next time, all you have to do is to spread out the great kylichor in front of you, put the small one in its centre and call the being with the name given to it, and the flame will appear on the surface of your small kylichor. Repeat the projection with the fire-element and let the small flamelet grow bigger and bigger by each accumulation. If in this manner you have accumulated a flame which has reached the size and height of the wanted elementary, transmute the flame into the desired shape by imagination and therewith your elementary will have been created. Moreover you can still load it with the fire-element for a longer time to obtain a greater intensity of the elementary. The more frequently you will repeat this exercise, all the greater will be the effectiveness of your elementary. The way of working with it is the same as described in the two previous methods, except the loading takes always place in the great kylichor, and when calling the elementary, it will suffice to use your ritual or take the small kylichor in your hand and give it the corresponding order. This method is very popular in Tibet and the elementaries there are called *yidams*. The destruction of a yidam is brought about by the decomposition process with the help of imagination according to the instructions mentioned in methods 1 and 2, provided that you have not decided on any other individual method of dissolution, which you excogitated for yourself. The use of such an elementary is so manifold that I am unable to quote all the possibilities here.

For example, there are yidams created for the treatment of sick people, others transferring objects, bringing messages to scholars and friends, protecting the magician and pointing out any dangers to him, influencing other people and doing many other things of the sort, according to the creator's desire. It will always be advisable not to give too many orders to a yidam, and what is most profitable is to develop a single ability and one field of it activity only in such an elementary. One has to exactly observe the appointed duration of life as we described it very distinctly in the previous methods. It is entirely up to yourself to create several yidams if you like to. It is also remarkable that a yidam can be produced with the other elements and even with all the four elements in the same manner, the process undergoing a slight change in so far as one does not begin with the fire-element, but with that of the earth, then follows the water-element, the air-element and finally it is the turn of the fire-element. Hereby all has been said about the handling of the third method.

Method 4:

Following this method, you may operate in the same way as described in method 3, with a big and a small kylichor, but with the exception, that you imagine the complete shape of the elementary right at the beginning. The elementary created in this manner is instantly ready made and complete, its efficacy and power being increased by frequently repeating the projection of the elements. Although this method is somehow more difficult, an experienced magician possessed by a good imagination will manage it very easily as well. In the Orient, elementaries, consequently yidams are created in this way, while pictures of demons and images of gods serve as patterns for their representation. All the other conditions such as duration, loading, giving of a name, calling, preservation, sphere of activity, purpose, decomposition-process are exactly the same as in the previous three methods.

Magical animation of pictures

To the four methods concerning the creation of elementaries also belongs the magical animation of pictures. Pictures, images of saints, statues and the like especially in cultic places are very often told to emanate an exceedingly strong magic power producing miraculous effects on the bodies, spirits and souls of their worshippers and adorers. The blessed silence, calmness and the religious ambient the visitors in churches and places of pilgrimage are meeting with is certainly known to everybody, so there is no need to talk about it in detail. All the healings in places of pilgrimage, which have been in part substantiated even scientifically, but still unable to be completely explained, can be imputed to the animation of pictures and statues. The strange atmosphere, surrounding these objects causes their emanation which however has been first created by the attention or adoration of thousands of admirers and believers. This kind of animation of images and statues of saints is positively unconscious. But from the the magical standpoint, there exists a conscious animation of pictures and the like too, for the behalf of which I am going to quote a very useful and practical instruction.

The conscious magical animation of pictures belongs—as mentioned at the beginning of this chapter—to that kind of methods of creating elementaries where it does not matter at all, whether an ordinary picture or the image of a Saint has been selected to the purpose of animation. The synthesis is and remains always the same, emanation and its purpose undergoing change only. The main thing to know is not to animate portraits of persons who are still alive. As the result of the sympathetic connexion through their bodies, souls and minds, one could eventually do severe damages to the persons in question by creating images linked by an invisible, secret bond of sympathy with the original. Nor should portraits be animated which could produce sexual appetites or improper motives for example women in the nude and so on. In these cases the magician would incur the danger of thereby producing an elementary which might become a vampire, an incubus or succubus, for himself. Never create elementaries interested in evoking sexual sensations and feelings. These precautionary measures should be observed by anybody who is engaged in the animation of portraits of which I am going to describe the practice as follows:

Should you select an oilpainting in order to animate it, you don't directly have to use a fluid condenser, although it would contribute to intensifying the quick creation of an elementary. Do cut a piece of blotting paper or cardboard to the size of the painting in the frame, moisten it with a fluid condenser and let the paper dry. As soon as this little expedient has been prepared, open the rear part of the painting and put the paper with the dried condenser directly upon the back-side of the painting. It does not matter whether the painting has been done on canvas, silk, paper or any other material. Now put a piece of standard paper over it and fix it with nails or adhesive tapes. You can also secure the rear part of the frame with cardboard, to avoid any dust entering it. Thus the painting has been prepared for animation. You can hang it now on the wall or leave it standing on the table in front of you.

Now form the mental body with the help of your imagination, so that it has to correspond exactly to the form and size of the selected painting. In case you have a painting in front of you which is representing part of the figure in question only, you have got to make up the missing part in your mind. But supposing the picture in question happens to be smaller than the normal size, for example a small snap-shot, you will have to consider this matter during your working as well. The rest of the process is the same as quoted in the second method concerning the creation of elementaries where a wax-figure has been used. Provided you did transfer the imagination of the mental body into the painting, now transfer the respective properties of the spirit such as will, intellect, feeling and consciousness into it with the help of your imagination. After that imagine the covering of the mental body. In this covering you have to concentrate the faculties, the sphere of activity and so forth, in short all that seems desirable to you. If the elementary in question happened to be selected for the use of other people you must not project the elements through your own body, but you have to take the necessary element directly from the universe. But if the portrait has been destined to serve your own purposes, you had better perform the projection of the elements through your own body. This has to be done with one single element, but you may as well transfer all the four elements and even the akasha-principle into your portrait. Supposing you might work with all the four elements you have to operate with the projection in exactly the same manner as if you were creating a complete human being. As soon as you have projected the elements into your astral body and given a certain density to the portrait, call it into being. The kind of calling into being is the same as described in method 2 with respect to the wax-loam-figure. The kind of decomposition, too, can be the same, provided you have not prepared an individual method more suitable for you. The magician will do well not to leave the elementary in the pictures after frequent repetitions, but to keep it possibly in the wall behind the portrait. When the magician has animated his painting, he may allow it to emanate from the portrait and utilize it for his purpose in the manner previously mentioned. But if he left the elementary in the portrait, it could be condensed to such a degree that it might be spotted even by persons who are not initiated. Beware therefore of boasting of things like that, better keep the practice strictly secret in order, not to get ill reputed as a black magician or a sorcerer.

Statues, busts, etc., might be animated in the same manner, only, in this case, it would be necessary to manage the condenser somehow into the interior of the bust, or—if that is not possible, spread the bust externally with the fluid condenser and let dry.

In the light of some examples I have now discussed a very important chapter of practical magic on account of which every magician can work out many other methods. I found it opportune to quote these four methods only, the application of which will certainly be clear to everybody. It has to be said in advance, that any scholar who has not been working scrupulously through all the previous Steps, will never succeed in creating a correct elementary, perfect in every direction. With this hint I am terminating the seventh Step of this manual.

Summary of all exercises of Step VII

I. *Magic Mental Training:*

Analysis of the spirit with respect to the practice.

II. *Magic Psychic Training:*

Development of the astral senses with the help of elements and fluid condensers.
a) clairvoyance,
b) clairhearing,
c) clairfeeling.

III. *Magic Physical Training:*

1. Creation of elementaries with the help of four different methods,
2. Magic animation of pictures.

End of the seventh Step

STEP VIII

Magic Mental Training (VIII)

I am going to deal, in this Step, with a chapter which is of great importance in magic. I mean the problem of leaving the body, or the separation of the mental- and later on of the astralbody from the material one. Every magician who was working conscientiously in the magic art must own this faculty, because it is offering him the opportunity of leaving his physical body any time he likes to, in order to bridge the greatest distances, to visit strange continents, in short, to transfer himself to any place where he wishes to be. This apparently complicated faculty is very simple for a skilled magician. In the same way as a pigeon is leaving the dove-cote, as easily can the magician leave his physical body to betake himself anywhere else, where he will see, hear and feel everything. This faculty does not serve the magician to satisfy his own curiosity or to perceive more distinctly what is happening on the spot in question, but it is mainly destined to contribute to the well-being of other people. There is no material hindrance for him, neither time nor space exists for his spirit, and he can rush around the whole world in a single moment if he likes to.

Severing the mental body from the material one also enables him to move about freely not only on our planet, but he can also transfer himself, with his mental body, into other spheres as well, which depends on his maturity. Thus he will learn to know the whole universe, and in case of need, to be also active in some other spheres up to a certain degree. It ought to be the pride of every magician to get acquainted with the whole universe, that is the macrocosm, this being the proper purpose of the mental or the spiritual wandering. A good deal could be said theoretically about this faculty and everything else connected with it, but as this work is to be a textbook for practitioners, let us not waste any time with the description of experiences and occurrences, such as every magician will collect himself for the benefit of his own conviction. For this reason we shall give our attention immediately to the practical part, the development of the mental wandering, which is in fact a transference of the consciousness, consequently of the spirit.

It would be well for the scholar to pass at first through some preliminary exercises, to get sort of preparatory training. A very important preliminary exercise for the mental wandering is as follows: Sit down in your conventional asana in front of a mirror in which you can see yourself entirely. If you have a big mirror, you need not have a great distance between your body and the mirror, but with a small mirror the distance must be so great, that the mirror reflects your whole figure. Regard your reflected image for a few moments, then close your eyes and imagine mentally your reflection in the mirror. Provided you have been able to imprint your features very distinctly on your imaginative faculty, you may continue. If you did not accomplish any result, you have got to repeat the experiment until you have managed mentally to retain each detail of your reflected image. A particular attention has to be given to the head and the facial expression. As soon as you have been able imaginarily to grasp your reflected image in all the shades of the original, then transfer your consciousness into your reflected image in such a manner that you feel personified or embodied in it. This transference of the consciousness serves the purpose to teach you how to observe your body from the side of your reflected image. If you notice any success try to observe those objects which are visible in the mirror, but always from the side of your reflected image. This exercise will be very difficult for you at the beginning, therefore you had better resort to your imaginative faculty impressing all the objects which happen to be near you very scrupulously on your mind. In the course of time, you will certainly manage to notice everything, after transplanting yourself into your reflected image, as distinctly as if you did watch it with your physical eyes. When this faculty, too, has become a habit, you are fit for the actual mental wandering. The scholar may seriously be warned not to risk this experiment before having thoroughly practised every single previous exercise, because the detachment or severing of the consciousness from the physical body might cause severe mental disturbances in frail people. For this reason, the warning is absolutely understandable, and those scholars only, who can positively assert that they are mastering the exercises of all the previous Steps, may approach not only this exercise, but all the others still ahead without any fear of damaging their health or their spirit.

For the exercise of the actual mental wandering, the material mirror is no longer required, and you are working from now as follows: Take up your normal position—asana—and do concentrate on your spirit. Think, while you are doing so, that it is your spirit which is seeing, hearing and perceiving everything and—absolutely independent from time and space—able to move around freely as if still connected with the physical body. This operation has to be performed before every mental wandering. The deeper the penetration of your meditation will be, the stronger your sensory experience and the certainty that your spirit is unrestrained and able to step out of your body according to your will, all the better and quicker will be your progress and your success in mental wandering. Provided you have the sensation of inner liberty and self-determination, following this meditation, which will require a few minutes only, then imagine yourself stepping out of your body just as from a shell, and standing beside this body of yours. You must understand how to transplant your consciousness into your spirit in such a manner, that you can feel yourself like standing physically beside your body, just as if you were slipping out of a dressing gown or any other clothing. In exactly the same way this performance has to take place with the help of your imagination. After all, you have been exercising long enough the imagination of the own spirit, in the shape and size of your body, in front of your reflected image.

Now try to look at your body sitting in its customary position as if it did not belong to you at all. Try, then, often to practise this consciousness of self-determination and standing aside, the point being to focus your attention on the body. Seek to see with your eyes every single detail on your body, such as the expression of the face with your eyes closed, the calm, regular breathing, the clothing, the seat on which your body is resting and so on. At the beginning, everything is based, of course, on your imaginative faculty, as mentioned before. Later on, there will be no more need of any imagination at all. As soon as you are positively sure of consciously standing beside and watching your body, your next task will be to examine your nearest environs. Your imagination will be a good help for you here as well. After having finished your exercise always return into your body, just as if you were slipping on your garment, wake up and check at once if everything you did imagine is corresponding to the facts. You should attain to such a skill of imagination that your imaginary mind does perceive all the objects in the room as distinctly and truly as if you were looking at these objects with your physical eyes. Provided you can book a success after a long spell of exercising, you may go a Step ahead.

Now transfer yourself beside your body, and do not remain standing on one spot but try, similar to a child, to walk up and down in the room and do it in a manner, as if you were relying on your physical body. Your own weightlessness and the sensation of timelessness and spacelessness may tempt you eventually to move about with unusually long strides, unaccustomed to your normal body, an occurrence which you ought to avoid, in the beginning, in order to allow a manifest separation of the mental body. What matters is that you regard yourself as being earthbound. Much later, after a long time of practice, you can make use of the rules of the mental sphere. Providing the striding up and down in the exercise-room has been successful, go through the door, as if you were inside of your physical body, and try to leave the room, step by step. At first, it will be sufficient to go to the next room or to the hall, where you are repeating the imagination of the objects there, and, as soon as you have returned into the material body, identify these objects with the reality. Provided you are quite sure about being able to move about in your mental body and also to perceive everything in the same way as with your physical body, you are ready to continue. Practice makes perfect, and the whole secret of mental wandering lies in continuous exercising. It cannot be emphasized often enough, how very important all these exercises are, because they represent the preliminary step to the astral separation from the body, known as the so-called ecstasy, during which not only the spirit, but also the soul together with the spirit are separating from the body. I will treat this problem in detail in Step IX, under the heading "Magic Psychic Training".

Once you are able to move about with the spiritual mental body in the same way as with the physical body in the own house or flat, short walks outside of it may be undertaken, too. At first it will be quite sufficient to visit the house of a neighbour or to look up friends and aquaintances first, who live in the vicinity and whom you do know really very well. Provided you have obtained certain experiences after some of these exercises, other impressions, not only those of objects, are to be won, too. The consciousness is being skilled in the course of these exercises, to such an extent that it will be capable of receiving sense-impressions such as hearing, seeing and feeling in the mental body in exactly the same way as if one were actually present with one's physical body. Any result like this can, of course, only be achieved by persistent exercises during the training of mental wandering. Go on visiting friends, just to see what they are occupied with at this moment. For example you see people doing every-day work. At first, you can do this with the help of the imagination. In order to make sure whether the imagination coincides with the real facts, all you need to do is to imagine that the person, you did watch with your mental body, is doing something quite different, eventually the contrary. If you can manage this imagination just as easily, being, however, in contradiction to your perception, you may be sure, then, that neither one nor the other is true, that all is still a matter of imagination. In this case, you have indeed not advanced far enough and you have to repeat the experiments constantly until you are capable to discriminate the real facts from the imagination. At first, you will only sense that the imagination responds factually to the reality, because your senses have been already withdrawn, in a great measure, from your body and been transplanted into the mental body. Later on there is no more reason for apprehensions, because you are winning complete certainty about this problem, and consequently you will be able to differentiate correctly, whether the things seen, heard and felt, while being in the mental body, are real facts or imagination. After a long time of exercises, this faculty will become quite familiar to the magician, and wherever he is transferring his mental body, he will only perceive what is really true and coincides absolutely with the circumstances.

Provided you have made good progress in so far as you can walk greater distances without feeling tired, exactly like in normally walking, only then you have matured to such a degree as to occupy yourself with the laws of timelessness and spacelessness, not before. Do separate, in the manner just described, from your material body, and think that you are not bound any more, neither to time nor to space. While being in the mental body, do meditate on your being with it everywhere you want to be at this moment. You will achieve this firm conviction by frequent deep meditation while being in the mental body. Do you wish to be anywhere with your mental body, it will be sufficient for you to suppose you have already arrived there, and your wish will be granted instantly. In the case of greater distances, you will obtain a satisfying skill only after a long period of patient exercises and frequent transferences. You ought, of course, to visit places for the second time which are known to you personally. Only when you are finally convinced of being capable to perceive everything with your senses, no matter where your mental body happens to be, at whatever distance, at whatever time of the day, then you are allowed to visit places, absolutely unknown to you. The sense-perceptions accepted on the very spots will leave no room for a shadow of a doubt that all you have seen, heard or felt there, was not fully up to the facts. You must exercise for a long time and with great patience before you get used to such unfamiliar impressions. For this particular reason, while being in your mental body, you will do well to visit tropical countries, sea-coasts, large cities, to put it in a nutshell: go everywhere and see all your heart is craving for. You will achieve a wonderfull success after numerous exercises.

The purpose of mental wandering is not only to perceive everything on earth which is actually happening at the moment, but to be really active there, too. For example, you are not only capable to see an illness with your mental eyes, but you have also the chance of treating sick people with your mental body, right on the spot, or of performing other favourable influences. All the success and the work you have learned to accomplish previously with the help of an elementary, can now be managed by your own mental body on the mental plane.

If, at last, you are at home in the entire physical world with the help of your mental wandering, and if this world has nothing new to offer you, try to visit other spheres, in your mental body, contacting the beings there and acquiring a knowledge of things the average human being has not the faintest idea of. The elevation to any other sphere is now very simple and you have nothing else to do but to concentrate on the sphere which you would like to visit with your mental body: You will feel, as it were, whirled round and lifted up vertically through a funnel. The transition from our material world to another sphere happens as fast as if you were flying around the whole world in a single moment. I had better say no more about this problem just now, because the magician must make his own experience as far as this part of mental wandering is concerned.

At the beginning, in mental wandering, the magician will probably feel an invincible drowsiness which he must fight with all his strength. This kind of drowsiness is explained as the result of the separation of the mental body, i. e., the vital bond between the mental and the astral body is loosened which is, consequently, causing a transference of the consciousness, from which follows drowsiness. As soon as the sending-off of the mental body has become a matter of routine, by constant exercises, the drowsiness will gradualy vanish.

The mastery of this kind of wandering, described here, is an indispensable preparation to send off the astral body. The detailed description of this practice will follow in the next Step, under the heading of "Magic Psychic Training".

Magic Psychic Training (VIII)

The great Moment of Now

He who has arrived in his development to this point, has to consider the kind of thinking, mainly the plastical thinking very carefully. The concentration-power, promoted by many years of experiments is producing very impressive pictures in the akasha by plastical thinking, pictures which are animated to a high extent and therefore seek to be realised. Hence, one should always foster noble and pure thoughts, and endeavour to transmute passions into good qualities. The magician's soul should be ennobled by now to such a degree, that he is no longer capable of evil thoughts or of wishing anything bad to other people. A magician has got to be kind, obliging and ready to help at any time, to assist by word and deed, to act generously, considerately and discreetly. He must be free from ambition, superciliousness and avoid any boasting. All such passions would be reflected in the akasha and —the akasha-principle being analogous to harmony— akasha itself would certainly put the greatest obstacles in the magician's way to stop his further development, if not to make it quite impossible. Any further rising, in a case like that, would be out of question. Just remember Bulwer's novel: Zanoni, in which the guardian of the threshold—nobody else but akasha—sees the high mysteries not come over night to half-baked or unworthy people. Akasha will understand to derange such a person mentally, arouse doubts of all kinds in him or hold him prisoner by vicissitudes and reverses of fortune in order to protect the mysteries in every possible way. These mysteries will always remain hidden from incompetent persons, though hundred of books should be published about them.

A true magician does not know any hatred against religions or sects, since he knows, that every religion does have a fixed system which is intended to lead to God and that is why he does respect them.

It is a wellknown fact to him that every religion has made mistakes, but he does not condemn it, because every dogma is serving the spiritual maturity of its followers. In due course of his development, the magician goes through that stage of maturity where he can see with his mental eyes through every idea, every action and deed, no matter whether present, past or future, and it is quite obvious that he might feel tempted to judge and condemn his fellowmen. But by doing so, he would act against the divine laws and create a disharmony. A magician like that will not be ripe enough and make the experience, that akasha will dim his faculty of clairvoyance, and Maya will deceive him. He must realise that the good and the bad are entitled to exist and each has to fulfill a task. No sooner is a magician allowed to reprove or to reproach a person with his faults and weak points than he be directly requested to do so, and should he obey to such an entreat he ought to do so with delicacy and discretion. The genuine magician takes life such as it is, he is enjoying the good things and learning something from the bad ones, but never will he hang his head. He is aware of his own weak sides and tries to overcome them. But he ignores any thoughts of repentance, since they are negative thoughts which are consequently to avoid; it is sufficient for him to recognise his own faults and never to relapse into them any more.

For this reason, it would be fundamentally wrong to muse on the past and to feel sorry, that fate did serve you with this or that disagreeable thing. Only weaklings do complain all the time expecting to be commiserated. A true magician knows very well, that impressions of the past may be animated by recalling them to the mind, thus producing new motives for putting new obstacles in the way. That is why the magician lives, if possible, exclusively in the present time looking back only if need arise. He will limit to the most urgent any plans concerning his future and keep away from phantasmagoria and day-dreaming. Nor will he waste the abilities acquired in hard travail or give any chance to the subconsciousness to handicap him. A magician works purposefully on his development, without neglecting his material duties, which he is fulfilling just as scrupulously as the task of his psychical progress. Consequently he will always look himself straight in the eye. He is supposed to be modest, and, as far as his development is concerned, discreet. Since the akasha-principle ignores time and space, acting permanently in the present time—for the concept of time depends on our senses—the magician is advised to adapt himself, as much as possible, to akasha. He must acknowledge as representative the great moment of NOW, thinking and acting according to it.

The faculty of concentration with respect to the elements, depends on the magic equilibrium and is, at the same time, the best standard to check which of the astral body's elements have to be brought under control yet. For example, if the fire-element can still get hold of the magician's astral faculties, he will not succeed very well in plastical visionary imagination exercises. In the case of the air-element, the acoustic concentration will probably become more difficult for him, as for the water-element, difficulties will arise from the concentration on the feeling, and in the case of the earth-element, the control of the consciousness will be impaired. Mental wandering, for example, or trance, where a transference of consciousness is required, will become rather difficult indeed and, in such a case, it would be necessary for him to follow intensively those concentration-exercises, which are affecting and influencing the respective element. Finally the magician has permanently to perform and to deepen the concentration-exercises. A sure sign of magic balance will always be equally managing all kinds of concentration: visionary, acoustic, tactual and conscious ones. Arrived at this stage, the magician is supposed to keep any imagination, at least, for 15 minutes in his mind, without the slightest disturbance, no matter, which of the elements is concerned. He ought to manage all sorts of concentrations equally well, without feeling one or the other of them more in his line. Should this be the case, it would be a sure sign that the equilibrium of the elements in body, spirit and soul has not yet been established perfectly. Then, the learner has to seek to redress the magic balance by assiduous training. If he does not do so, all the shortcomings will delay his further spiritual work.

Now follows the psychical magic training. In particular, we are concerned, here, with the OR and OB of the Quabbalists and the control of the electric and the magnetic fluid.

The electric and magnetic fluids

According to the informations given in the theoretical part, there are two main kinds of fluids, originating in the four elements, namely the electric and the magnetic fluid. The electric fluid comes from the fire-principle, the magnetic one from the water-principle. The airy-principle is the mediating element between the two. The earth-element is bipolar, hence, containing both the fluids, and it is electro-magnetic, electric in the centre and on the periphery magnetic. According to their afore-described laws, these two fluids are working in all of the spheres, in the mental as well as in the astral sphere, and in the material world, too. These fluids are the cause of every thing being. Next let us deal with the knowledge and control of these two fluids, because managing these fluids will enable the magician to achieve everything in all spheres, no matter whether the mental, the astral or the material world be concerned. The effect of any of these fluids, however, depends on the magician's maturity whether he is strong enough and able to form the *cause* in the respective sphere. There are two fundamental methods in order to work with both the fluids, the inductive and the deductive method. The magician will learn how to use both methods in this Step. Let us, then, discuss the electric fluid first.

Control of the electric fluid—Inductive method

This exercise can be performed sitting down or standing up, just as it is more convenient for the individual. Take up your usual poise, close your eyes and think of your body as being hollow, furthermore, imagine that you are the centre of a fiery ball, which is including the whole universe. You have got to imagine the fiery element red hot and bright, similar to the sun. You will feel the warmth on the periphery of your own body automatically at this imagination, because you did already learn all about this sensation in the chapter referring to the projection; therefore, there is no need to draw your attention to it. Doing this exercise, you should perceive the expansion of the fire-element within your own body. You have to imagine that the universal fire-element, when expanding, presses the light into your hollow body. The more intensive and the more fiery you imagine the universal fire ball, the more light is pressed into your body through the pores of the skin from all directions, your whole body being loaded with light. You must perceive the pressure of the light inside of your body, feeling it like a balloon, swelled with light. The pressure of the light is supposed to go from the outside to the inside. At this moment, you will experience the sensation of an unusual fullness, as if you were ready to burst. Go on breathing calmly, while performing this exercise, because in this dynamic accumulation of light, you will be tempted to hold back your breath which you must avoid at all events.

As soon as you have produced so strong an accumulation of light viz. a light-dynamide that your body is nearly bursting, you will feel, at the same moment, that your whole body, mainly your fingertips have been loaded with a strong electric current. Do impress this perception very firmly on your mind, because this is factually the electric fluid I am talking about. If you accomplished this accumulation, allow the universal fire to fade away slowly with the help of the imagination, until it has gone out completely. At the same time you have to imagine, that the accumulated light is diminishing, too, the power of expansion becoming weaker and weaker gradually, until everything, inside and outside yourself, has turned pale and finally extinct.

Hereby, the first exercise of the inductive method concerning the electric fluid is at an end. When, after several practices, you will have achieved a certain skill in producing the electric fluid, without difficulties, in your body, you may begin to perform the desire-impregnation on the electric fluid. All you have to do is to imagine that the light accumulated inside of yourself, or better to say, the electric fluid contained in the light, does reinforce and increase your active powers in the spirit, in the soul and in the body. In this manner, you can arouse all the active faculties, qualities, etc., which are imputed to the fire-element and the air-element in yourself. You have the possibility, for example, to increase your willpower, your faith and your control of the element to a supernatural degree. It is, indeed, quite impossible to describe the range of power and strength achieved in this way with mere words, and you will be convinced of it best by your own experiences.

In the previous steps I did always point out how very important it is, to ennoble the soul, to be free of passions and to try to reach the magic equilibrium. If an unrighteous and passionate person who has not yet reached the full magic balance, wished to perform these exercises, he would increase his passions only by activating them.

He would hardly be able to control his passions which could become fateful for him. Everybody will see that these warnings are not mere words or a simple moral lecture. A well-balanced personality, however, has nothing to fear. On the contrary: He will have every opportunity to ascend and be fortunate enough to realise his highest ideals.

Control of the magnetic fluid—Inductive method

The performance with this fluid is exactly the same. You are sitting in your asana imagining that you are as hollow as a rubber-ball, but capable to take in the magnetic fluid. Now close your eyes and imagine the whole universe being filled with water and yourself standing in the centre of it. You will automatically perceive the wetness and coolness on the periphery of your body, but do not give your full attention to this fact, imagine how your body similar to a dry sponge, thrown into the water, is sucking in the magnetic power from the universal water-element. This imagination-exercise must be permanently increased, until you feel a "dynamide" in yourself, similar to a fully inflated pneumatic tire, and until you are quite certain, that a higher accumulation is impossible. You are feeling the magnetic fluid like a contracting, and in the same time, attracting force. As soon as you have reached the peak of the magnetic power accumulation, allow the imagination to melt gradually away, and the magnetic power accumulated inside of you to dissolve into infinity. If you are able to discriminate the difference between the electric and the magnetic fluid by means of frequent exercises, you will have the opportunity, just as in the case of the electric fluid, to strengthen those faculties in yourself which are indwelling in the watery- and the earth-element, such as mediumistic faculties, clairfeeling, psychometry, thought-reading, medial writing and others more.

Control of the electric fluid—Deductive method

You cannot work with this method before being able to manage both the previous methods. The deductive method is similar to the inductive one, but just in the opposite sequence. Do accumulate the fire-element drawn from the universe into your body through the pulmonary and the pore-breathing or through both of them, eventually by sheer imagination, too, in the same manner, you have learned it, with respect to the inhaling of elements and their accumulation. While storing up the fire-element, give your attention less to the warmth, which will be perceived automatically. The accumulated element will produce an enormous expansion causing a strong irradiation of the electric fluid in the body to the outside which will be mainly perceived by the skin of the whole body, just as if you underwent a treatment with an electric machine or a high-frequency current. The irradiation of the electric fluid will become stronger and stronger, more pervasive and more subtle, by frequent repetitions, and by increasing the accumulation of the element, it can even be condensed to such a degree that it can be seen and felt by people not being trained at all. You can increase this force so far that you can make a neon-lamp light up. These exercises are naturally not meant for such and similar purposes, and experiments like these are destined to serve your own conviction only. Apart from that, this power is for higher and nobler purposes. As soon as, in this exercise, you reached the peak-accumulation of an element, viz. the highest degree of irradiation, let the fire-element together with the electric fluid dissolve into the universe, the body get rid of the elements and the exercise is now at an end.

Control of the magnetic fluid—Deductive method

Similar to the deductive method of handling the electric fluid, described in the fore-going exercise, is the process concerning the control of the magnetic fluid with the only difference that, instead of the fire, the water-element will play its part. Accumulate the water-element as dynamically as possible in your body, which you have imaginarily made hollow. To perform this accumulation, you may use the breathing through the lungs and the pores or both kinds together, or else let the mere imagination play its role. Although you will perceive the wetness and coolness, in any case, during this accumulation, focus your attention on the external layer and the skin of your body. You will feel an astringent coolness and an attracting power like that of a real magnet especially on the periphery and the skin of the body. In the beginning and as a result of an extremely strong dynamisation, the sensation of this fluid will produce sort of a paralysing effect until you get accustomed to it. If you managed to increase the accumulation to the peak, dissolve the water-element together with the magnetic fluid gradually into the universe by means of the imagination. And this is the end of this exercise.

You ought to master all these four methods so well as to be able to perform each method in a few moments with your imagination, and to produce the magnetic or the electric fluid inductively. You will accomplish this by frequent and indefatigable training. Be very attentive, because controlling these two fluids is very important, since everything will be within your reach with the help of these two universal-powers, no matter on which of the spheres the magician wishes to exercise his influence. In the beginning, these exercises have to be performed with the eyes closed, later on with open eyes, without any regard to the situation one happens to be. It is important, too, to know, that in all the four methods the magician will be inclined to strain the muscles or to hold the breath, which ought to be avoided. These exercises must be performed in a calm and so-to-speak unconcerned way and should not be noticed by anyone else.

The magician will find out now that the inductive method serves to direct a power from the universe to the inside viz. into his body, his soul and his spirit, whereas the deductive method is destined to send off a fluid from the inside to the outside. If the magician has gained a very good experience in the four methods, he can extend the exercise as follows: While following the inductive method, he has increased the electric fluid in him to the highest point, and allowing the external fire-element to dissolve in nothingness, he can hold the electric fluid with its tension power and the respective fire-element inside his body. When he has kept this fluid for a long time, as long as he could endure it, then he may allow it to flow gradually back again into the universe. The magician can operate in the same manner, with the magnetic fluid. Do not advance before both these methods quoted here have not been practised for so long, until you are capable to master them very well.

The methods of controlling the electric and magnetic fluids described here are a kind of preliminary exercises, and as soon as they have become familiar to the magician, he may pass on to the final, namely the capital method concerning the mastery of the electro-magnetic fluid, which I will describe in the following chapter.

Consider the following analogies: head and chest correspond to the electric fluid, abdomen, thighs and feet to the magnetic fluid.

Now the magician'n task will be, to load the feet, thighs and abdomen up to the pit of the stomach with the magnetic fluid, the head, neck and chest, on the other hand, with the electric fluid, in the manner described previously. He must be capable to load both these fluids dynamically, one after the other, in the two regions of his body, to such a degree that he gets the sensation as if he were about to burst. After a prolonged period of exercises, he will be able to retain both fluids. Having arrived at this point, he presses the electric fluid into the right breast with the help of his imagination, forming a hollow around the heart region. But he better leaves the left breast free from loading, when charging the upper region of his body, that means he does not load the left breast at all. This done, he is withdrawing the accumulated magnetic fluid from the lower region of his body, with the help of his imagination, via the left breast, storing up this fluid in the entire left hand, right down to the finger tips. So the hand is turning out magnetic, and now possesses an astringent cooling irradiation. In the same way, one proceeds with the right hand, by accumulating the electric fluid imaginatively drawn from the upper region, that is the head and the right breast, into the hand. The right hand is hereby becoming electric. One can feel the expansive, hot electric energy in the whole hand, but mostly in the finger tips. Provided that there is no personal use for both powers, one dissolves them, letting them fly free from the hands into the universe in the imaginative way.

By managing these exercises perfectly, one has become master of the electro-magnetic fluid, viz. master of two universal powers, with the help of which one can practically achieve anything. Blessed be the magician's electric and magnetic hands which will be of potential value and may become a real blessing for mankind!

Magic Physical Training (VIII)

Provided the magician be perfect in all the stages of the magic training of the body, he will not require any special education in this line. I will therefore limit myself to give some instructions and hints, which may become useful in the following chapters. Subsequently follows an influencing method through the elements, which the magician can use for his own self-influencing or to influence other people.

Especially worthy of mention are the following four systems which may successfully be practised in self-influencing as well as in influencing other people. According to the elements, these methods are as follow:

1. Fire — through combustion,
2. Air — through evaporation,
3. Water — through mixture,
4. Earth — through decomposition.

It would be possible to quote hundreds of varieties and opportunities of producing such an influence through the elements, and a big book could be written about this problem. I will restrict myself to one example only for each element. In the light of this example, every magician can enrich his own practical experiments and elaborate new practices by himself.

These four methods exert an influence on the most subtile astral matrix of the material world, inducing the elements to exert their influence wherever the magician does allow them to work indirectly. Supposing that the point is to influence a human being, the material elements will analogously act on the connecting link between the astral and the material body. A magician mastering the elements perfectly, on every plane, does not require any of these methods, he will reach his purpose by a direct influence just as fast and surely. But now and again, even the highest magician will make use of the lower powers, for the simple reason, that the highest powers as well as the lowest do serve and obey him. On the other hand, as the result of an insufficient spiritual maturity, some magicians like to utilize these mean practices in order to satisfy their desires, because these powers do blindly execute the will of the person who understands to master them. One will probably ask now, whatfor these lower powers, and consequently, such methods can be made helpful? Two examples may serve to answer this question.

Supposing a scholar who is not yet quite closely acquainted with magic is asking a higher brother for help, because in spite of all his efforts, he is not able to fight alone a passion, a harmful habit, a heredity or such like by himself, or he would, at least, loose to much time before overcoming and equalizing this passion, the higher brother has the possibility to influence the element corresponding to the passion, according to the respective method and can, in this manner, reduce the negative form of the influencing element with the result, that the scholar can fight against it without great effort, or do away with the influence of the element altogether.

The second example: Supposes the magician to be about to treat a long-lasting chronic disease with the help of the elements. A couple of direct treatments would not be sufficient to fight the sickness, and a frequent repetition takes too much time. The magician can, in cases like these, use the Powers as helping factors. Hundreds of similar cases do exist, where the elements of this category will be of a great benefit to the magician. He may use all the powers he does know about. A magician must be a person of absolute moral integrity, his mind and his motives must be noble if he will follow the motto: Unto the pure all things are pure. Working with the four elements, the magician has three fields of activity corresponding to:

1. The immediate effect;
2. the timed effect which is limited to a certain time;
3. the permanent effect, which is fading as time goes on and finally ceases altogether if the operation is not renewed.

Subsequently follows the description of the practice:

The influence through the fire-element

—Combustion—

Arrange for a piece of flannel or blotting-paper, in the size of 4 by 4 in. (10 x 10 cm)—in emergency, a piece of ordinary paper will do as well. Moisten it with any liquid condenser and allow it to dry gradually. Now put the paper in front of you, and with the help of the imagination through the material elements, concentrate the wish you would like to get realised, into it. Do not forget, at this point, to time the effect, i. e., whether you wish an instant, a limited or a permanent effect. As soon as the paper has been loaded with your desire, do burn it in an open fire or on the flame of a burning candle. During the combustion, do concentrate once more on the fact that the power is released by burning the paper or the flannel, inducing the grosser elements to bring about the result you desire. The ashes left behind are worthless, from the magic point of view, and you may deal with them as you would do with ordinary ashes. Performing this experiment, you can arrange the effect, in a different way, too, so that it will occur the very moment, the person for whom the operation is performed does eat or drink something warm, enters a warm room or comes anyhow in touch with a heat factor. This operation offers the opportunity, too, to project the fire-element into the paper, to load it with a desire and to hand it over to the universal fire-element or to the akasha-principle in order to release the effect. There are still many other ways which might be followed, but I suppose this example will be sufficient to give the magician a useful hint in this direction.

The influence through the air-element

—Evaporation—

Pour so much ordinary water into a small basin or a saucer, made from any kind of metal, until it only covers the bottom up to a few millimetres. Add a few drops of a fluid condenser which corresponds to the air-element. If such a condenser is not available, you may use the universal fluid condenser. Now, operate in exactly the same manner as mentioned in the instructions given for the previous element, by concentrating your wish on the liquid. Having done so, put the basin on the hot stove, on a gas or spirit flame,—an electric cooker must not be used,—and let the desire-loaded liquid evaporate. While doing so, you have to concentrate on the steam, wishing the desire to be sucked in by the air-element, whereby the most subtile air-principle is induced to realize your desire. Do concentrate until the last drop of water has evaporated, and the experiment will come to an end. Together with the desire-impregnation, you can also combine the order that the person who is to be influenced, should, with every single breath, inhale the air-principle whereby the desire is beginning to be realized. This happens to be only one example, and every magician may establish similar versions of the influence operated through the air-element.

The influence through the water-element

—Mixture—

Take a new beaker, glass-dish or a small vase, and go to a running water—a well, a spring or a river. Try not to be watched while you are performing this experiment. Do fill the container with water and pour a few drops of the fluid condenser, responsive to the water-element, into it. In an emergency, take a universal fluid condenser. Now, performing the wish-impregnation, proceed in exactly the same manner as you did with the previous element. As soon as the water prepared, in the described manner, has been satisfactorily loaded, throw the water which is now impregnated, as it were ecstatically into the river, and give the respective order, which will be fulfilled promptly by the most subtile particles of the water-element. If the person who is to be influenced, comes in touch with the water-element in one way or the other, for example by washing, drinking, by rain, etc., the water-element will become immediately active, and release the effect which has been required. This example ought to be sufficient, and based on it, the magician can compose several individual methods, which will be just as effective as this one.

The influence through the earth-element

—Decomposition—

When working with this element, it can be done in two different ways. 1. Exactly in the same way as in the previous experiment, by taking some water from a river or rainwater—tap-water should not be taken—to which one is adding some of the fluid condenser corresponding to the earth element. One can use a universal condenser, too. It is also possible to work with the fluid condenser alone without diluting it with water, by throwing the impregnated liquid, together with the solid concentration, into the earth, instead of throwing it into the water, for the simple reason, that earth is sucking in the liquid, and thus the earth-element produces the required effect. Do not choose, for this experiment, a road, where other people are walking to and fro, but the solitude of a tiny spot in the garden, in a meadow or in the fields. Supposing you have none of these possibilities in a big city, a flower-pot, with some soil in it, will do as well. 2. Take an apple, a pear, or even better a potato and make a hole into it, with a potato peeler or with a knife. Into this hole pour a bit of fluid condenser, suitable for the earth. Instead, you may here use a universal condenser as a substitute. Now go on as you did before, when loading the potato with the desire-impregnation. Afterwards do bury the potato in the ground. Each manipulation requires the concentrated meditation that the earth-element will produce the effect you wish to obtain.

To this series also belongs the sympathetic and the mummial magic, the so-called transplantation. In this case, one does not work with fluid condensers but with mummies; these are constituent parts of the body such as hair, nails, perspiration, urine. I am not going to describe this lower kind of magic in detail, because every magician can compose these practices by himself, if he wishes to follow them.

These two examples should be sufficient to illustrate the influence of the earth-element. Following these instructions, the magician can work out various methods, and his intuition will inspire him to do the right thing. As one can see in the light of these examples, the magician's trained willpower remains the decisive factor, which is moving the universal elements to produce the desired effect with the help of the imagination. He can repeat the operations optionally until the success has been achieved. The magician can undertake these experiments for himself, too, that means for the sake of self-influencing. There is another kind of self-influencing, where the beings of the elements, the so-called salamanders, fairies, mermaids and goblins do execute the required effect with the help of the elements. In my second work referring to the "practice of magical evocation" I will publish the way of summoning forth these beings, making them visible and useful to the magician.

The fluid condensers

Any object can be influenced by any fluid, regardless of being loaded electrically, magnetically, with elements or akasha, through the aid of the imagination and the will. But according to the laws of analogy, and by experience, it has been found out that not each object and not each kind of liquid is suitable to retain an accumulated power for a long time or to accumulate it at all. Similar to the fact, that electricity, magnetism and heat do have good and bad conductors, the higher powers offer the same bipolar aspect. Good conductors own an enormous accumulative capacity, because the powers concentrated in them are stored up and can be held back at will. In the hermetic science such accumulators are called *fluid condensers*. There are three principal groups of them: 1. solid fluid condensers; 2. liquid fluid condensers; 3. aeriform fluid condensers.

To the principal group of solid fluid condensers belong, first of all, resins and metals. As for the metals, gold occupies the highest rank. Tiniest jots, even atomic particles of gold grant an enormous amount of condensation power to any liquid. For this reason, gold is added in smallest portions to any fluid condenser. But more about this subject will follow later on.

The second group comprehends lacquers, oils, tinctures and extracts composed from resins, which have been produced by certain plants. Just as gold occupies the first rank among the solid substances, being analogous to the sun viz. corresponding to the power and the light of the sun, so among the liquid substances, the human blood and the seed—sperm—play the part of the gold. Sometimes they can replace the gold completely, because tiny particles of blood or sperm dropped into a liquid will grant an excellent accumulative power to it.

To the third group are attributed all kinds of fumigations, flavours, smelling waters, evaporations, about which I will not talk in detail, because they are less important for the magic practice. Apart from that, I can extensively treat the most valuable fluid condensers only, which are required for the practice. Should I have to quote all these various kinds here, their production and the possibilities of using them, should I have, moreover, to consider all the precious—and semi-precious stones too, which doubtless may be excellent condensers, this brief summary alone would grow out into a voluminous book.

There are two kinds of preparing fluid condensers, in the first line there is the simple type, which is made from one material or one plant being useful almost for any purpose. The second kind consists of compound fluid condensers, which are prepared from several materials or plants owning extremely strong accumulative properties. Since a small quantity of gold has to be added to any fluid condenser whatever, the magician's attention was directed, of course, to the gold first. He can get it in special photo-shops as soluble gold chloride, called *aurum chloratum,* which is used for toning photographic papers. One gram of gold chloride diluted in 20 grams of distilled water produces a wonderful gold tincture, 5—10 drops of this tincture are sufficient for 100 grams of a fluid condenser. Those people who are experienced in laboratory jobs can produce a gold tincture by electrolysis themselves. In homoeopathic or electro-homoeopathic medicines are being sold, a gold preparation could be bought without difficulties. The homoeopathic gold medicines are mostly dilutions of gold chlorides or have been manufactured by electrolysis. They are tinctures like aurum chloratum D1—D3, aurum muriaticum D1—D3 or aurum metallicum D1—D3. The expert of homoeopathy does know, of course, that the capital D stands for decimal power.

Supposing you have neither the one nor the other opportunity to obtain a gold tincture, there is nothing else for you to do but to produce it yourself after the recipe of the ancient alchemists, a very simple thing, indeed. Take a piece of gold of the best quality—no new-gold—the more carats the better. The conventional 14 carat gold will do. The shape of the gold does not matter at all, it may be a ring, a brooch, a chain or the lid of a gold watch as well. Now prepare some distilled water, if you can't get it, some rainwater will do as well. Pour so much water in any container, that the weight of it is equal to ten times the weight of the gold. For example, if you have 10 grams of gold, add 100 grams of distilled water. Do heat this piece of gold on an open flame until it is red-hot, and throw it into the water afterwards. Take care that the wire to which the piece of gold is tied, or the pliers you are holding it with, will not touch the water. The best thing is a wire-hook, from which you are throwing off the red-hot gold. The water will hiss and squirt as a result of the sudden chilling off. Therefore be careful not to get burnt by the hissing water. Beware of your eyes! The pure gold only is allowed to fall into the water. Now let the water and the gold cool down and repeat this procedure seven to ten times. Cooling seven to ten times is enough for the gold, because with each cooling a lot of water, too, is evaporating, mainly if you are working with a small quantity of water. By the quick cooling of the gold—oxydation—tiny atomic particles are set free and thus the water will be saturated with gold.

The ancient alchemists called this sort of saturated water or any other herb-essence, chilled with red-hot gold, the "Quintessence of gold in the hot way", and they used it as an admixture to other alchemistic preparations. But we want to use it for our fluid condensers. The liquid saturated with gold will now be filtered through a piece of fine linen, filter-paper or cotton wool into a funnel and preserved for our purposes. One does usually pour 5—10 drops only of this gold tincture into approx. 3 oz. of fluid condenser. The piece of gold used for the preparation of this gold tincture, has to be cleaned with polishing powder for further use.

Preparation of the SIMPLE fluid condenser

Take a handful of fresh or dry camomile flowers, put them into a pot and pour so much cold water over them until they are covered completely. Let the camomile flowers boil for about 20 minutes. Cool them, but leave the lid on the pot and strain the decoction. Put this on the fire again and allow it to decoct slowly to about 50 grams. A few drops more or less do not matter at all. Let the extract cool and, for better preservation, mix it with the same quantity—in our case with 50 grams—of spirit or alcohol. If necessary, you may take fuel-alcohol, too. To this mixture add about 10 drops of your gold tincture. If you wish to use the condenser for your own purposes, you may still strengthen it, by adding a drop of your blood or sperm, if possible both together, on a swab of cotton wool, throw this afterwards without any scruples into the condenser and shake the lot well. Then, pour all, in a funnel, through filter-paper or linen into a small bottle and keep it, well corked in a cool and dark place, ready to use. Any fluid condenser which has been prepared in this manner does not loose its efficiency even after many years. The condenser must be well shaken each time you are going to use it, the bottle is to cork again after withdrawing some out of it. In the same way you can prepare several universal condensers from Russian or genuine Chinese tea, from lily-blossoms—best are the white ones— poplar leaves, alraune roots or mandragora roots, arnica montana, acacia flowers. Any simple fluid condenser, prepared from one plant is sufficient for normal use such as influencing through the elements, or developing the astral senses by means of the fluid condensers.

To achieve extremely strong accumulations of power or perform tasks which are destined to produce not only a mental, or astral influence, but also a material one as well, for example creating elementaries (wax-loam-figure), animation of paintings and other materialisation phenomena we are using the compound fluid condenser, consisting of the following herb extracts:

Archangelica officinalis, Salvia officinalis, lime-tree-flowers,
cucumber skin, melon seeds,
acacia blossoms or leaves,
camomile flowers, lily flowers, leaves or roots,
cinamon flowers or cinamon bark, leaves of urtica dioica,
leaves of mentha piperita, poplar-leaves,
leaves or flowers of viola odorata,
osier leaves or bark,
tobacco green or dry.

Three kinds of preparation are important to be known. The first and most simple is to put equal parts of the mentioned plants into a bigger pot pouring water over them and boiling them slowly for about half an hour. Afterwards cool off, strain and boil all to the point that it turns out as thick as possible. Now add the same quantity of alcohol or spirit as you have got of the extract, pour a few drops of gold tincture into it—10 drops to 100 grams eventually blood or sperm or both,—shake it well and strain the liquid through a fine sieve into a dark-colour bottle—green or brown—cork this bottle and keep it in a dark place.

The second kind of preparation is as follows: put the herbs, at equal parts, into a glass bottle, (preserving glass or bottle), pour pure alcohol over them until all the herbs are covered with it, and allow it to extract for about 28 days in a warm spot. Now press it through linen or any other kind of a press, filter it and corresponding to the volumetric measure, add the gold tincture to it, eventually your own mumiae, too—blood and sperm. Then fill all into bottles and keep them for your personal use. Add no more alcohol to this extract because of its preservation.

One of the best methods of preparation is, of course, to treat each herb or plant separately, whether in the described manner of the simple fluid condenser—camomile—, or else, one makes herb-extracts from spirituous extracts. After the separate extracts have been well prepared, mix them together, add the gold tincture and guard it.

One operates in the same way with the other four special fluid condensers destined to influence by the elements. The plants necessary to it are:

For the fire-element:
Onion, garlic, pepper, mustard seed or grains of mustard.
Comment: This fluid condenser must not come in touch with the body, first of all, nor with the eyes, because of their sensitivity.

For the air-element:
Hazel-nuts, leaves or bark will do as well, juniper berries, rose blossoms or leaves of it, cherry-leaves or bark.

For the water-element:
Oats, finely chopped straw of oats can be used too, rape-seed of different kinds, eventually turnip, sugarbeet, etc., peony, blossoms or leaves of it, cherry-leaves or bark.

For the earth-element:
Parsley, roots, leaves or seed, caraway seed, plantago lanceolata, broad or long leaves, carnation flower or balm-mint.

From the point of view of a layman the recipes quoted here will certainly appear as a dreadful pell-mell, and from the pharmacological standpoint one might describe them as pure nonsense. But the matter in question, here, is not the pharmacologic, but the magic effect. The eyes of expert practicants who know the secret significance of plants, which are so very mysterious, will detect the correct connexion by intensive meditation. One could compose hundreds of recipes on the base of analogies, but this outline ought to meet the requirements of the magician. All the recipes given here do originate in practice, and have produced fine results up to now. Before I am going to bring the problem of the fluid condensers to an end, I will throw some light on another alchemistic theme which is linked to it, I mean the

The so-called genuine alchemistic "life-elixirs" are nothing else but marvellously composed fluid condensers, which have been produced in analogy to the elements and the three levels of human existence. In accordance to them, they have been magically loaded. For the mental-sphere there are used essences, for the astral-sphere tinctures and for the material-sphere salts, eventually extracts, all of them loaded in the corresponding ways. Elixirs produced in conformity with them, consequently, influence not only on the material body of man, but on his astral and mental bodies as well. Such an elixir is, therefore, not only a good remedy but an excellent and dynamic regenerative, too.

Therefore, the elixirs of sincere alchemists are nothing else but exquisite fluid condensers.

Preparation of a solid fluid condenser

Since in the next step I am going to describe the genuine mirror magic, that means, the practical handling with the magic mirror, I shall teach the magician how to construct a magic mirror by himself. To manage this, he needs a solid fluid condenser which consists of seven metals. These are:

lead	one part
tin	one part
iron	one part
gold	one part
copper	one part
brass	one part
silver	one part
aloe resin	one part
animal charcoal	three parts
mineral coal	seven parts

The different parts are not to be understood, here, according to their weights, but volumetrically. Supposing you take one cubic inch (or one cubic centimetre) of lead, you have got to take of all the other metals one cubic inch (or one cubic centimetre) too. The same applies to aloe and the two kinds of coal. All ingredients must be pulverised. Softer metals like lead and tin can be pulverised with a crude file into the so-called filings, and as for the harder metals, take a finer file. The resina aloe must be crushed to powder in a mortar, if one can't get it pulverised. You deal in the same manner with the two kinds of coal. As soon as all the ingredients have been put together, mix them well and the mixture which you are obtaining by this procedure is, as a matter of fact, the real solid fluid condenser.

The Electro-Magicum of the old alchemists is not any different at all, it is a superb fluid condenser composed from:

30 grams of gold
30 grams of silver
15 grams of copper
6 grams of tin
5 grams of lead
3 grams of iron, and
15 grams of quicksilver

As one can see, it contains all the planetary metals, and from this metal alloy magic mirrors, bells and similar objects have been made. The solid fluid condensers I have recommended are very good, reliable and have many times proved useful.

Preparation of magic mirrors

Two kinds of magic mirrors exist: the concave mirror and the flat mirror. Normal mirrors are suitable for both kinds, which must be spread with silver-amalgam or black lacquer, or covered with a liquid or a solid fluid condenser. For our magic purpose, the ones mentioned before are of a special value, and I will describe the production of these mirrors on the base of some examples.

1. For the magic mirrors produced, in the most simple way, with the help of a condenser, the surface of any mirror, or of a bowl made of glass will be suitable. It must only be spread with a liquid or a solid fluid condenser.

2. Cut a circular disk from a pasteboard 8—20 in. (20—50 cm) in diameter, the size depending on how big you want the mirror to be made. Now cut the same disk from a blotting or a filter paper, moisten or spread it several times evenly with a painting

brush or a swab of cotton wool until it is saturated with the fluid condenser and let it dry. Glue the blotting-paper on to the pasteboard disk, wait until dry and the mirror is ready to use. Everybody will certainly be able to construct a mirror like this. Supposing somebody does not like the circular form, he may choose an ovale or angular shape. You can put the mirror into a frame, too, if you like. The fluid condenser which is required here, can be the simple one, but the compound condenser is more recommended.

3. The procedure of the third method is exactly the same, but here you have to cover the surface of the impregnated blotting or filter paper with a very thin layer of a colourless lacquer and strew the entire surface with the pulverised solid fluid condenser. You can use a fine sieve. A mirror which is ready for using immediately after drying is the best magic mirror, you could think of, because it contains both of the fluid condensers and is therefore especially useful for the practice.

4. Nor is the preparation of a parabolic or concave mirror complicated. From a glass-factory or from a watch-maker procure a curved glass such as is generally used for bigger clocks on the wall. An evaporation bowl will serve the purpose, too. Now spread the side vaulted outwards several times with black spirit or nitro-lacquer, of the kind which is used for motor-cars and contains acetone; it is drying very fast. Do you wish the mirror for optic clairvoyance, it will be sufficient to put it in a black wooden frame and the mirror is ready. But if you want to cover it with a fluid condenser you have got to paint the inner side with a good colourless lacquer in a thin layer, strew the solid fluid condenser on top of it and let it dry.

5. Supposing you would like to produce a magic concave glass-mirror and you cannot obtain the concave glass, instead of the glass, take excavated wood or a piece of paste-board which is easy to work with after moistening it. You can make a cheap concave mirror from loam, plaster, too, etc. The yellow loam or the plaster must be mixed with a liquid fluid condenser to render the mass kneadable. Now form the mirror with your hands, allow it to dry slowly, so that no cracks appear. Supposing here or there some cracks should show up, do smear them over with loam and let the shape dry again. Polish the completed shape of the mirror with

emery paper to avoid rough spots and spread the concave surface of the mirror with colourless lacquer, strew the condenser through a sieve on top of the varnished surface and let it dry again. Provided you did make an edge, you can lacquer it afterwards with a black nitro-lacquer, as well as the backside of the shape. The mirror is now completed.

As a matter of fact, such a home-made mirror happens to be more effective magically than the one made from glass, because it does own two very efficacious fluid condensers: the solid and the liquid one. The liquid condenser is in the loam and the solid one on the surface of the mirror. The only disadvantage is, that such a mirror is much heavier and breaks easily.

If, after the preparation of the mirror, there is anything left over of the solid fluid condenser, keep it well, because it might come handy for other purposes, for example for producing a magic rod, which you make from an elder branch, 12—20 in. (30—50 cm) in length. Drill a thin hole in its entire length and fill it with the solid condenser. Now cork the rod, seal it up and load it magically for different operations such as acts of volition, transference to living or other beings, exorcising, etc. I will write about these problems in detail in my second volume "The practice of magical evocation."

Summary of all exercises of Step VIII

I. *Magic Mental Training:*

1. Preparation to mental wandering.
2. Practice of mental wandering.
   a) in the room,
   b) short distances,
   c) visits to friends, relatives, etc.

II. *Magic Psychic Training:*

1. The great NOW.
2. No clinging to the past.
3. Concentration disturbances as a compass of the magic equilibrium.
4. The astral body and the light.
5. Mastering of the electric and magnetic fluids.

III. *Magic Physical Training:*

1. Magic influence through the elements.
2. Fluid condensers:
   a) simple condensers,
   b) compound condensers,
   c) fluid condensers for magic mirrors,
   d) preparation of a magic mirror with the help of fluid condensers.

End of the eighth Step

STEP IX

Magic Mental Training (IX)

In the chapter referring to the magic psychic training (Step VII) I have already clearly dealt with the problem of clairvoyance. In this step I want to examine it closely once more. The various instructions which have been published, up to now, for the obtainment of this faculty, did not bring about the desired success in anyone. Even people who are especially gifted in the mediumistic line, have only attained a partial success which is getting lost sooner or later. But people like these are very often struck by different diseases such as weakness of the eyes, nervous disturbances, etc. The main reason for such ailments can be found in the fact that the clairvoyance has not been produced as a result of the mental or astral development, but has been conjured up by force and is therefore one-sided and morbid. Following any of these incompetent instructions leads, without any exception, to an unnatural, morbid neutralisation of an element, which will result in an over-sensitivity of one of the sense organs. Consequently, it is not impossible that, in this manner, perceptions from the astral and mental worlds may take place, but all these effects depend on the spiritual intelligence of the exercising person, on the maturity and last, on the Karma, too. The neutralization of an element can be divided in four main groups, which are:

Group 1. Neutralization of the fire-principle:

To this group belong all experiments of clairvoyance which have been performed by fixation, such as crystal gazing, staring at one point, a shining surface, black ink, black coffee, mirrors, etc.

Group 2. Neutralization of the air-principle:

In this group are subsumed all those experiments of clairvoyance which are performed with the help of fumigation and by inhaling of narcotic vapours, gases and so on.

Group 3. Neutralization of the water-principle:

Here the neutralisation is brought about by experiments made on narcotics and alcaloides such as opium, hashish, soma, peyotl, mescal which, in the course of the digestive process, are introduced into the blood-stream.

Group 4. Neutralization of the earth-principle:

Answering the same purpose are all the practices which are causing any kind of dissociation or split-off consciousness, for example dancing, swaying of the upper part of the body, rotating of the head, spelling in the feet and things like that. To this group, too, belong all the unwanted and morbid visions of the insane, and all the pathologic cases, which occur as a result of shock, fury and exhaustion.

A great deal could be said about the variety of such exercises and their dangers and disadvantages. But this short description will be sufficient for the sincere magician. It is quite obvious that the neutralization of any element-principle results not alone in severe damages of the health, but it delays the spiritual development, too, mainly in the cases where such and similar experiments have been practised for a prolonged time and have become a habit. Based on these four principal groups, the sceptic has the opportunity to convince himself of the existence of higher powers, but if he can neither master himself, nor the elements, he will quite easily succumb to the temptations of lower forces. And once giving in to them, one will find it very hard, indeed, to ascend again!

Only a well-trained practicant with a firm will, who is mastering the elements and has developed the astral senses in the exercises of the various steps, can afford himself a temporary neutralization or elimination of any element-principle without jeopardizing his body, spirit and soul. The true magician will restore his elemental balance with the help of his exercises. His results in the practice of clairvoyance are satisfying, because he does not try out experiments, but works deliberately with the faculties he has achieved, which are the concomitances of his spiritual and psychical development.

Practice of clairvoyance with the help of magic mirrors

There are two kinds of magic mirrors, namely:
1. the optic mirrors, made from flat-glass or concave glass and covered on one side with silver-amalgam or black lacquer. As for the concave mirror, the side which is outward vaulted is lacquered and the inside, that is the concave part will be pure and shining. The crystal balls also belong to the magic mirrors: further, the flat or concave metal-mirrors, the surface of which has been provided with a coloured or a black liquid. The surface of a pool can also serve as an optic mirror.

To the second kind of magic mirrors belong those mirrors, which have been fitted out with the fluid condensers I have described previously.

First of all, the magician has got to know that it is not the mere mirror granting the success, but the astral and mental faculties, developed by the preceeding exercises. Consequently, the magician will regard any magic mirror as an appliance, an expedient or as a sort of tool. This does not mean, of course, that he would not be able to work without a mirror, but because of the manifold opportunities which a magic mirror may offer, the magician likes to make use of this help.

However, he who has worked through this practical course, step by step, will never just sit in front of a magic mirror and tire his visual nerves. He will operate in quite a different way, a way which is magically correct. Before I am going to describe some of these practices in detail, I will quote some examples, where a magic mirror may be a very useful help.

1. When working with the imagination, where optic exercises are required.
2. When loading up with powers, fluids of every kind.
3. As a transit gate to all desired planes.

4. As a help to induce a communication with living and deceased persons.
5. As a help to get contact with powers, beings, etc.
6. As an equipment for radiotherapy and room impregnations.
7. To influence the own or other people's personality.
8. As magic transmitter and receiver.
9. As a help to prevent dangerous and undesirable influences.
10. As an implement for the projection of all the desired powers, pictures, paintings, etc.
11. As television set.
12. As a help to investigate present, past and future times.

All the possibilities cannot be quoted, considering that the magic mirror represents a sort of universal help. Based on these twelve examples, the intuitive magician is now enabled himself to invent other new practices.

You are sitting in the asana, before your magic mirror, at a distance of 1—2 yards (1—2 m). The lighting does not play any important part at all. Now you start on imagination-exercises by imagining objects on the surface of the mirror, one after the other, which you are supposed to see with your open eyes as distinctly as if they were really there. Considering the fact that you have become a master of imagination in the meantime, this preliminary exercise will not be difficult for you. Hold on to the imagination of the object for some minutes, and dissolve it afterwards with the help of the imagination. Supposing you still have difficulties with the imagination of objects, do at first try imagination-exercises with colours, before proceeding with objects. As I mentioned before, the optic imagination faculty is analogous to the fire-principle, and magicians who master this element perfectly, will have the best success with the mirror magic, too. After the imagination of objects, you may turn to exercises with different animals, hereafter with human beings; first try to imagine features of friends, later on, of strange people and races. Now extend your imagination work over the whole body. As soon as you are capable to imagine a human being, whether known or unknown, male or female on the surface of the mirror, continue with the imagination of houses, areas, places, etc., until you have achieved a wonderful skill here, too. Only now you are prepared magically, to execute the correct mirror magic.

This preliminary exercise is very important, because the mental, astral and material eyes must get accustomed, with the help of these imaginative exercises, to perceive the size and the clearness of the impressions. Otherwise one will perceive distorted pictures only. Performing this preliminary exercise, one must never tolerate any pictures to appear in the mirror spontaneously, which could easily occur in the case of persons with spiritistic talents. Therefore one must firmly refuse all pictures which appear unwanted on the surface of the mirror, however beautiful and fantastic they might be, because anything unwanted one does see, belongs to the realm of hallucinations, reflections of the mind from the subconsciousness which like to appear to deceive the magician and to prevent him from his work. Performing this preliminary exercise, one will notice, that the imaginative work becomes much easier, the bigger the mirror happens to be.

The loading of the magic mirror

The next task of the magician will be to become familiar with the loading of mirrors. He must be capable to bind the desired power to the surface of any mirror with the help of imagination, drawing it whether out of himself or directly from the universe, to accumulate this power and to dissolve it again by imagination into the primary source. The following loadings are to be made:

1. with all four elements, one after the other.
2. with akasha.
3. with the light.
4. with the electric fluid.
5. with the magnetic fluid.

As soon as the magician has gained a certain skill in loading the mirror, he is fit for further mirror-experiments, for which I will quote some examples concerning the various methods.

The magic mirror representing a transit-gate to all planes

Performing this experiment, take care, that you are not disturbed by your surroundings. Sit down comfortably in front of your mirror and load its surface with the akasha-element, which you are sucking into your body by breathing through lungs and pores.

The loading of the mirror with the personal akasha can take place whether by your hands or directly via the solar-plexus. Now forget all about your body and think of yourself as a spirit, capable to adopt any shape and size. Now imagine your body becoming so small, that it is able to go right through the mirror. Doing this with the help of the imagination, then you will be on the astral-plane. Stay there deliberately for some time, have a good look round without losing your consciousness, or falling asleep. Having done so, return via the mirror and connect yourself again with your body. In the beginning, you will find yourself in complete darkness on the astral plane. After frequent repetition, you will perceive light. A strange feeling of freedom, timelessness and spacelessness will overcome you. Now you happen to be on the astral plane, which is usually called the other world or the Beyond. After frequent exercises, you will meet with deceased people and other beings, and if you wish to see one of the departed, you will be connected with this person instantly. After a few visits on that astral level you will know all about the laws valid there, and you will see the place which shall be yours, once you have left your physical body. The fear of death will be abolished hereby once and for ever.

Supposing you concentrate yourself, from the astral plane, on to a higher plane, you will very soon perceive finer vibrations: a sensation of extreme lightness, sort of being etherised will overcome you, and you will be able to go in touch with beings of these higher spheres. You will partake of cognitions, perceptions and experiences which none of the mortals could ever give you. You will always return to your own body with spiritual vibrations of a higher kind, which cannot be described in mere words. Which of the spiritual spheres you will be able to visit, depends entirely on the mastering of the elements and on your spiritual and astral purity, the ennobling of your character. There are no restrictions as far as the acquirement of higher knowledge is concerned. Having collected your experiences there, you may come in touch with high Light-entities, too, in exactly the same manner, but in this case, the mirror is not to be loaded with akasha, but with concentrated light, similar to a sun. No doubt that with the aid of the mirror method you will also be able to visit lower spheres, too, for example that of the elements and the beings there. In this case, you have to load the mirror with the respective element of the plane you wish to visit. Passing through the mirror, the form of the respective plane has to be adopted equally. If you wish to visit the kingdom of the goblins, not only the mirror must be loaded with the earth-element, but your own spirit has to be imaginatively transformed in the shape of a gnome and to be filled entirely with the earth-element. The same thing comes to pass with the spirits of the air, the so-called fairies, the spirits of the water or mermaids and the spirits of the fire, the salamanders. Here as well, the experiences you will accomplish are so abundant and marvellous, that books could be written about these problems. How the spirits of the different elements can be summoned to come down to our earth, and the way they can be made useful to do various tasks, I will describe in detail in a second volume entitled: "Practice of magical evocation."

The magic mirror representing a link between living and deceased persons

Supposing you wish with the help of the mirror, to communicate with a friend or somebody else, or to give orders to a person to write to you or come to see you, proceed as follows:

Load the surface of the mirror with akasha meditating on the fact that everywhere between yourself, the mirror and your friend there is akasha that means, neither space nor time does exist anymore. Hold on to this sensation in deep meditation, and do wish, at the same time, to see your friend in the mirror. A few moments later you will see the person you wish to see like in a panoramic picture, and notice what the person is engaged with at the moment, and the nearest surroundings, too. At the same time, you will experience the feeling of standing next to the person. If the surroundings are familiar to you, you will be able to convince yourself of the truth of what you did see in the mirror with the help of the mental wandering. Provided the magician has been trained correctly, his astral senses duly schooled, his experiences with the magic mirror will correspond to the real facts as he may state with the help of the spirit-wandering. Otherwise you have to repeat the experiment frequently until you are quite sure, that the things you did see, are in accordance with the real facts, which can be corroborated without any doubt by other personal scrutiny.

If for instance you notice that the person you wish to see is asleep, with the help of the imagination draw the spirit, that is the mental body into your mirror, and condense it, through your will, to such a degree that the person seems really to stand in front of you. If you managed to accomplish this, give the order you have been thinking about to the person. Doing this, you have to observe the mood of present and command, just as you did, when performing the self-suggestion, because it is possible, that the subconsciousness of the person in question begins to oppose. But not one truly wise magician will degrade himself to give any orders for the sake of an evil purpose. The akasha-principle would take severe revenge on him.

Furthermore, it is possible to make an astral contact with another magician of the same degree of development, with the help of the mirror magic, and everything the practicant is talking about in the mirror, will be perceived by his colleague, even at the remotest distance, sometimes so loudly as to be heard by a sensitive person who happens to be in the neighbourhood quite distinctly, although all is spoken from the distance.

Deceased persons can be called up, in the same manner, to appear in the mirror. In this case, one has to concentrate on the akasha and to imagine the person, or one has to think intensively that he or she may appear. If one wants to call a person one did not know, one has to concentrate on a certain clue dating from the time when the person was alive; one calls the name into the akasha and one waits in deep meditation for the appearance of the deceased being. In a very short time the being will show up in the mirror and the magician can express his desires. At the beginning, the communication with the deceased person will take place in a sort of thinking aloud, but later on one can really make conversation if one wishes to. One has the opportunity as well to make the deceased person step out of the mirror and condense the appearance with the help of the earth-element, so that the person becomes visible even to the eye of any person who is absolutely untrained. It is entirely up to every individual, how much he wishes to specialise in this work. Various other beings can be called up and condensed, too, but the details about this problem will be found in my work "The practice of magical evocation", because certain rules of conduct have to be considered here.

The magic mirror representing a help to make contact with powers, entities and so on

I will describe this method, too, in my second work "The practice of magical evocation". At this point, let me remark only for the sake of curiosity, as follows: Supposing the magician does load his mirror with akasha, drawing his sign with the element analogous to the entity, his character and his symbol imaginatively on the surface, he is capable to come in close contact with this respective being, if he pronounces the name of the entity according to the universal laws. The contact will enable the magician to achieve anything according to the original proprieties of the being. The same thing can be said about all the other beings and powers.

The magic mirror representing a help to self-influence or to influencing other people

Any magic mirror can serve as an excellent help for self-influence, but the best result will be obtained with a mirror equipped with a fluid condenser. There are so many different opportunities of employing it, that it is quite impossible to register all of them. Here I can quote a few practical examples only.

Draw such an amount of light from the universal ocean of light into your body with the help of the imagination or by breathing through lungs and pores that you can feel yourself red-hot like a sun. Do impregnate this light with the concentration on a desire, wishing for instance, the light and its radiation resp. might bestow intuition, inspiration or any other desirable faculty on you or make you recognise a certain truth. Now let the light flow, through your hands, with the help of the imagination, on to the surface of the mirror and accumulate there, until the tiniest spark of light has passed from your body into the mirror. Form the light accumulated there into a brilliant white ball or sun, emitting extremely intensive rays. Repeat this loading several times, at short intervals, until you are quite sure that the mirror has been loaded so intensely that the rays are penetrating right through your body, spirit and soul releasing the influence you have been wishing for. Now with the help of your willpower and imagination combined with a firm conviction bind this light to the surface of the mirror for so long a time as you need it, and then dissolve it again. You have got to be convinced so firmly of the effect and the influence of the light, that not the shade of a doubt will arise in you. It is just this unshakable and firm conviction which gives this enormous dynamic power to the radiance of the light, coming very near to a physical effect. I myself did, some years ago, load a magic hollow-glass mirror in this manner so strongly, that it burst into hundreds of chips and I had to procure a mirror made from oak-wood for my task.

Sit down in front of the mirror and meditate about the truth you wish to recognise or about the problems which you want to solve. After finishing the meditation, interpose the akasha-principle or induce a trance in yourself and you will soon accomplish your task. In any case, you will get a pleasant surprise by working in this manner, and later on, you can hardly do without this practice when performing your meditations. Supposing you keep the mirror loaded, you have to protect it from other people looking at it. The best thing to do is to wrap it in silk, because silk is well known to be a splendid insulator. You can also direct the rays from your mirror on to your bed allowing them to work all night long influencing your subconsciousness while you are asleep, to achieve the desired purpose. Your self-suggestion will reinforce the effect and produce a quicker success. It is quite obvious that you will not only arouse cognitions and faculties, in this manner, bringing them to a higher level of development, but your soul and your spirit will likewise be influenced in the desired respect. If you do not need the influence of the mirror any longer or a different task requires a different loading, such as the irradiation of akasha or of one of the elements, or magnetic- and electric-fluids may be wanted, then you have to suppress the first loading in the reversed order with the help of imagination i. e., to dissolve the light, sending it back into the universe. You can, by rays, exert an influence on other people, too, but in this case, the desired loading has not to be directed to the surface of the mirror via the own body, but it has to be led to the mirror directly out of the universe with the help of imagination. So it is possible to accomplish all kinds of experiments such as hypnosis, magnetic sleep, mediumistic conditions, a fact which the intuitive magician will find quite natural. He will therefore arrange his practice accordingly.

The magic mirror representing a ray-emitter in cases of room-impregnation and treatment of sick people

A similar procedure is followed in the impregnation of rooms with the help of the magic mirror. You are loading your mirror with the fluid corresponding to your wish such as light, biomagnetism, akasha, feeding its accumulation directly from the universe with the help of the imagination so strongly, that the radiance is spreading over the entire room which you wish to impregnate. Fix the duration of the effect already while performing this accumulation. In this manner, you can, if necessary, irradiate the room in which you are living for days, even for months in order to obtain success, health, inspiration, peace. You will also be capable to reinforce the loading, if necessary, by condensing the "dynamides" by means of frequent repetition. It is a matter of course that all kinds of diseases and ailments can be healed, too, in this manner, provided the mirror has been loaded in the correct way. You can also seat a sick person in front of the mirror, and he or she will feel well again after a few minutes, according to the power accumulated in the mirror.

The magic mirror representing a transmitter and receiver

The mirror can be used fabulously for this purpose as well, I mean to say you can perform experiments of animating pictures and transferring sounds. Similarly to the transmitter and the receiver of a radio, our mirror also can be used in this line. I am going to quote two practices briefly which the magician can execute without any effort at all, provided he did follow me to this point step by step. The first practice refers to the reciprocal animation of thoughts or pictures between two equally skilled magicians. The distance does not play any part at all, 10 or 1000 miles (km) do not matter. The possibility of communication varies, that means, it can take place whether by means of thoughts, pictures, letters, words or senses. The practice always remains the same and all work is performed with the aid of the same principle, that is, the akasha-principle. Below follows the description of the mirror, acting as transmitter, without the person who is to be influenced knowing anything about transmitting.

At the beginning it will be advantageous if the magician gets accustomed to a certain routine with his partner, who is supposed to be on the same level of development, or at least does manage to work with the akasha-principle. Fix the exact transmitting and receiving times in accordance with your partner. Both can take place at the same time. First of all, the practice of transmitting: The sending person has to load the mirror with akasha and to induce a state of trance with the help of the akasha-principle. Then he will eliminate the concept of space and time, between himself and the receiver, with the help of imagination, and thus he will have the feeling of standing next to his partner. This sensation will occur, later on, quite automatically, which we know already from experience and from previous experiments. Try, at first, to transmit simple shapes, and patterns such as a triangle or a circle together with the desire that the partner on the other end might be able to see them in his mirror. The receiver has nothing else to do but to load his mirror, too, with akasha before the transmission, to trance himself with the help of the akasha-principle and to concentrate on the fact that he will distinctly see everything in the mirror his partner is transmitting. Provided both partners are on the same level of training, the picture projected to the mirror by the transmitting partner will turn out visible to the receiving partner. As soon as the time for transmission and reception has run out, change over to become the receiver yourself, and repeat the experiment of telepathy in a reversed order. It is always a good point, if the magician is versed with the transmitting as well as with the receiving practice. Nobody ought to be discouraged by failures at the beginning, but he should continue to exercise with tenacity; success will certainly show up after several attempts. As soon as one is capable to receive simple pictures, one may reinforce the exercise by selecting more complicated pictures, later on pictures of living persons, of places and landscapes, similarly to the manner in which you were handling the preliminary exercises concerning the mirror imagination. Providing you are quite familiar with this experiment, you may pass to transfer ideas without imagination, i. e., ideas which have been registered with the intellect only.

Supposing one has gained sufficient experiences as a transmitter and a receiver, one may try to write short words into the mirror with the help of the imagination to be read in the receiver's mirror. Words may be followed by sentences, and finally one will be able to transfer written messages from one mirror to the other. Having attained the faculty of optical transference, you may proceed to the acoustic transference. Speak one or two words into the mirror with the desire that the receiver might hear these words. Here, likewise, the receiver remains in a trance state waiting for the message to arrive. At first he will feel it very similar to a sort of thinking aloud, but from one exercise to the next he will hear it more distinctly, and finally as clearly as having a conversation over the telephone. Later again it will be as if the words were spoken directly into the receiver's ears. As soon as one has become familiar with the transmitting and receiving practices, short sentences can be transmitted and received, until one has become capable to transmit and receive full messages and news by constant training. Many adepts in the Orient are using this method to send messages to each other. This faculty is called in the Orient "messages through the air". This is to be understood in a symbolic way, since all that is, in fact, done with the help of the akasha-principle. Consequently, it is quite obvious that also various feelings can be mediated between the transmitter and the receiver. This problem needs no further description.

If the magician masters the faculty to transmit to, and receive from, an equally trained partner, he will be also capable to intercept dialogues or pictures transferred between other practicants, in the same way as it happens in the case of broadcasting, a fact which is called radio-piracy in the magic terminology, too.

Now I am going to describe the magic mirror as a transmitter destined to transfer ideas, words and pictures to people who are not trained magically at all, who have not the faintest notion that such a transmission takes place or that, in this manner, they might be influenced eventually. In such a case the magician only has to blow his intention into the akasha-loaded mirror, including the command, this or that might be transmitted to these or those persons. If the magician interposes the akasha-principle between the unprepared person, the latter will perceive the message according to his intellect. Should anyone not be sufficiently experienced in this practice, the message will at first have the effect that the influenced person becomes restless at the given minute and feels the urge to think very intensively of the sender—in our case the magician. Later on the receiving person will feel the message as a thought of his own, being unable to differentiate whether it was transmitted or originated in the own mind. But if the magician is interested in specialising in this kind of transmitting, he can suggest to the person in question that the messages or thoughts are coming directly from him. This practice will exert its influence on the receiving person whether instantly or in the course of the transmission. The magician can also bring about a transmission through the mirror, the effect of which is to be delayed or to be perceived by the receiver only, when he has become fit for it. This moment usually comes if the respective person is not disturbed, restrained or diverted by external influences, and receives the message shortly before falling asleep or in the morning before awakening. In such cases, the magician concentrates the idea, the desire or the message into the mirror, together with the command, that anything he is transmitting should be perceived by the individual only if the necessary preparedness is happening. As long as the message has not been received, it will remain effective and adhere to the surface of the mirror. As soon, however, as the message has been sent out, which means, the mirror has served its purpose and the thought or the message has been correctly received by the person to be influenced, the surface of the mirror becomes perfectly pure once more. The magician can attend to his various duties without taking any notice of his wireless work and the mirror will produce its effect automatically for so long, until the thought or the message has really been perceived.

The magic mirror representing a ray-emitter for the impregnation of rooms, treatment of sick people, etc.

The magic mirror may be employed within this scope likewise, and in the hands of a skilled magician, it will represent an excellent help for his development. The practice of room-impregnation is as follows:

When you are working in a room which you want to be influenced by the magic mirror for your own purposes only, you have to perform the loading via your own body. As far as loadings of the mirror for the benefit of other people are concerned, you have to draw the power directly from the universe without allowing it to pass through your body.

Therefore, you are drawing an enormous quantity of light out of the universe—whether directly or through your own self-concentrating it, with the help of the imagination, in an accumulated form, to the surface of the magic mirror. This accumulation of light must be repeated several times, until the stored up light is adopting the shape of a ball or a disk, which is spreading a brilliant, white shine over the entire room, similar to the shine of a strong lamp. Frequently repeating this exercise, you ought not only to see the radiant light imaginatively but feel it directly streaming like X-rays through your whole body. Transfer your imagination of the desire into the light with the help of your conviction and your faith, and at the same time think that the light is increasing automatically from one hour to the other, from day to day, and that the effect of its emissive power is growing more pervasive and more dynamic. Fix the duration of the effect in the same way as you did in the case of biomagnetism, whether by limiting the emissive power to a certain time or fixing it as a permanent effect. Now transfer the task or the desire to be fulfilled by the emissive power into the confined light, namely, into your imaginary sun, for example success, inspiration, furthering of the intuition, peace, health or whatever you are mostly in need of. This done, arrange the mirror in your room similar to a reflector, so that you are constantly exposed to this irradiation. Take no further notice of the mirror afterwards, because it will work on automatically, influencing you or other persons in the desired way, therefore you will find yourself continually subject to the influence of the irradiation. You will hardly be able to manage your work, your exercises, your research and your meditations without this method.

In case the mirror has not only been loaded magically for yourself but for other people as well, say, in order to treat sick persons (for the sake of a complete recovery), you will find out that you can accomplish a great deal more being under the emissive influence of the mirror; you won't feel tired or worn out, and any sick person entering your room or coming directly in touch with the emissive mirror will feel an instant relief from the complaint. The efficiency depends on the loading of the mirror. Not only a single person can be irradiated, but as many people as there is space for in the room. Professional magnetizers or those who are engaged in treatment of the sick or in influencing people will find a marvellous sphere of action in this method.

The emissive power is not only available for the impregnation of a room and for its irradiation, but it can be transferred with the help of imagination to one or several persons at the greatest distance. The imagination must naturally be accordingly changed in such cases. It is not necessary to underline how valuable the magic mirror is in the hands of a magician and how many possibilities it offers. A wise magician will certainly never misuse his magic mirror and dishonour it by trying to exert bad influences with the help of it.

The magic mirror representing a protective implement against dangerous and undesirable influences

A magic mirror can also be used as a defensive or a protective tool. But then, of course, the impregnation of the emissive power in the mirror is to be modified in a corresponding way, and the room-impregnation or the spot to be protected have to be loaded with the emissive force of the light in such a manner, that the rays of the light will detain the undesirable and unfavourable influences or throw them back to the starting point. Having to do with bad influences or working with the impregnation of light, wanting a room to be insulated against good as well as evil influences, in all these cases you have to load the impregnation of the mirror or of the room with akasha, transferring the quality of intangibility and impenetrability into it imaginatively. Any accumulation of the akasha-principle, while working with it, is impossible, as mentioned before, but the wish-impregnation for the sake of a dynamic effect can be repeated frequently with the help of the imagination. It is left to the magician to manufacture several mirrors for different purposes. But if he works with long-distance transference or long-distance reception, naturally he must not insulate his workroom with akasha, because this would prevent him from each long-distance operation. How to screen from any adverse influences and how to insulate certain spots with the help of a magic mirror in order to accomplish different magic tasks, will be the argument of my second work: "The practice of magical evocation."

Apart from the possibility of using the magic mirror as a protective implement, other more advantages are offered to the magician. With the help of the mirror-magic he can put in operation all the known fluids, the magnetic, the electric or the electromagnetic fluids and work with them in his practice. Which of the powers will come into question for the various cases, depends on the activity and the effect of his wish.

The magic mirror representing a projector of all powers, beings, impressions and suchlike

The magic mirror can also be used to condense all the forces of the mental and astral planes to such a degree, that they can be perceived even by persons who are not trained at all. This is not a matter of mere imagination or suggestion, because the thoughts, elementaries, elementals, beings of all levels, entities of the elements, and so on, condensed with the aid of the practices described here, can be condensed in the mirror in such a manner, that it is quite possible to take a picture of them. Here follow the instructions for the practice:

The surface-loading of the mirror takes place with the help of the condensed earth-element which is not projected, first via the body, and then to the mirror—which would cause paralyses—but directly from the universe with the help of imagination. The stronger the accumulation of the earth-element happens to be, all the more condensed and visible will be the appearance of anything we wish to project. Consequently it will be opportune to repeat this accumulation of the earth-element several times. If you now wish an impression, a picture or an elemental to be made visible to any other, probably not trained person, proceed as follows: Introduce the akasha-principle whether to the head of the person only or, if you like, to the whole body with the help of the imagination and, at the same time, order the akasha-principle to remain effective only for the duration of the experiment. If it comes to making visible any impression, do by your own imagination transfer the picture or the impression to the surface of the mirror with such a clearness and distinctness as if it were reality. Hold on to this conception. Now, when the person being influenced with the akasha-principle observes the mirror, he will see your conception reproduced similar to a film. You can produce the same effect, in the same manner, with any self-created Elemental, Elementary or Phantom. But if you decide to call a being out of the astral or any other plane, you have to fill, at least, the space around your mirror in which the being is supposed to appear, with the akasha-principle. It is more profitable to fill the entire room with akasha. This preparation would not be necessary if you had a second mirror destined to the impregnation with the akasha-principle of the room in question. All the preparations being completed, develop a trance by introducing the akasha-principle to yourself, and in this condition of trance, call the being you wish to see, no matter whether it is an inhabitant of the astral or any other plane. As long as one is not absolutely familiar with the practices of the conjuration-magic, which I shall describe in the practical part of my next work: "The practice of magical evocation", one has to be satisfied with calling deceased people from the astral-plane, a performance which is brought about with the help of the imagination.

By means of the accumulation of the earth-element on the mirror surface, pictures or beings will be materialized so that they can not only be perceived with the physical eyes of an untrained person, but also be heard, too. Everything that has been seen is, therefore, not a hallucination, for the magician is able—as mentioned before—to take a photograph of the picture condensed by the earth-element. But mind! Pictures condensed in such a manner have a much higher vibration than the normal light which we know. It is therefore quite obvious that such higher vibrations cannot be taken in the ordinary photographic way because they do not correspond to our light-vibrations. Photographs like these must be taken in the shortest time ever possible. First class cameras will enable you to select a $^1/_{1000}$ second, and there are special cameras which even make possible a $^1/_{2000}$ second exposure for one photograph. Special cameras like these are the best, of course, because they produce concrete pictures, and it is much easier to work with them. Taking pictures, in the manner described here, it does not matter at all, whether it is day-time or night, whether the mirror is lit up or dark. But if you like to take a picture of the mirror and its background as well, a lighting will certainly be necessary. Otherwise, there will only be visible the materialized picture in the mirror. Experience has proved that, in these cases, photographic plates should be preferred to films. Considering the fact that the vibration-number of the picture in question is by far higher than that of the light of the physical world, a special kind of coloured filter has to be used. When taking photographs of the mental plane with all its Elementaries, Elementals, Phantoms and other entities of this sphere, you always need blue filters. For all the other beings, deceased people and so forth, violet filters have to be used. And other beings consisting of one element only, such as the essences of the elements, will require ruby-red filters. Photos of phenomena occurring in nature, mainly concerning the magic of nature, are taken with yellow filters only. As far as the colours are concerned, the filters are, therefore, analogous to the respective planes.

Moreover, the magician has got the possibility not only to show pictures and beings to any untrained person, but he can also display this person's or someone else's past, present and future in the mirror.

The magic mirror representing a television set

In our magic mirror we are capable to observe occurrences, or events which are happening to persons known or unknown, even at the greatest distance. Load the mirror, as usual, with the akasha-principle. Now, remain calm and comfortable in your posture, induce a trance with the help of akasha, and in this condition, concentrate on the person whose deeds and actions you want to observe. Think of the magic mirror as being a big telescope through which you can see everything at the remotest distance. The magician will immediately see the person and the surroundings like in a motion-picture. At the outset, the pictures will perhaps be a little muddy, but after frequent repetition they will become very distinct, and there will happen a feeling of immediacy and nearness to the desired person which will become so convincing that one is almost quite sure to stand next to the person one wanted to see. Even a distance of thousands of miles (km) is of no importance at all.

In order to verify and to be absolutely sure that everything one wishes to see is corresponding to real facts, one can imagine any different action of the same person. If one can manage this in full clearness with our astral senses, the things we have been seeing, are a deception, and the exercise must be repeated until one has obtained the faculty of distinguishing real facts from hallucinations and deceptions.

Under a skilled magician's guidance even an untrained person can take part in such a kind of television. Magicians especially trained and experienced in this field, will even manage to take photographs of the pictures and events seen at the greatest distance, using a red filter and considering the practices described here.

When you are not so much interested in the material occurrences which you are observing at a distance, but only in the psychic life, the character and the feelings of a human being, then do not think of the material body of the person you want to see, but imagine the astral body only. After a little while you will see the aura and the characteristics of this person in the various shades of colour, from which you will be able to come to logical conclusions concerning his character and his faculties, according to the rules of analogy.

If you are neither interested in the ways and doings of a person, nor in his psychic qualities and his characterization, and if you wish to see the spirit only in the mirror, imagine the material body together with the person's astral body as not being there. Here, too, the images corresponding to the spirit will appear, and you can, in this manner, pursue the train of thoughts of a person even at the greatest distance.

As one can see from the example quoted here, the faculty of reading the thoughts of a person at the greatest distance can be managed without any difficulties, and it depends entirely on your own will, how far you wish to extend this mastery.

The magic mirror representing an aid for the investigation of the past, the present and the future

Working with the mirror, one of the most difficult tasks is the exact investigation of the past, the present and the future of other people. It is comprehensible that the magician can perceive his own past and present in the mirror similar to a motion-picture but he will most certainly avoid to do so. Should he be as keen as to satisfy his curiosity to learn all about his future, it would not be difficult for him to concentrate on this problem and to inquire into every detail. But there is the rub: in the same moment, when seeing his future in the mirror, he is depriving himself of his own free will. One could compare him to a pattern which has to be filled in without the possibility that anything could be done for or against it. Quite a diffent matter of course it would be, if the akasha-principle in its highest form, let us call it the Divine Providence, gave a warning to the magician, in one way or the other, perhaps against dangers, without him having any intention at all to see or to learn something. It is quite obvious that the strictest attention has to be paid to warnings of this kind without any exception, because ignoring them would cause severe damages to the magician. Having arrived at this point, the magician will be capable to distinguish, whether the warning comes from one of the beings irrespective of which plane or directly from the akasha-principle.

The magic mirror is an excellent aid in instances concerning untrained people or such ones of whom the magician takes a great interest to investigate the past, present and future. All thoughts, perceptions, feelings and physical actions are leaving behind them exact records in the akasha or the primary source, a fact which enables the magician to read, like in an open book, in the akasha with the help of his magic mirror or directly, while being in a trance. All he needs to do is to concentrate on it by imagination. In the beginning, when the magician is not yet mastering this problem wholly, the images will probably appear incoherent or sporadical. By frequent repetition of this exercise, one picture after the other, will appear on the surface of the mirror in the correct connexion with the past, as clearly and distinctly as if the magician himself were actually realizing the events. The magician can unroll one occurrence after the other, beginning from the present back to the childhood and the day of birth. It is advisable to follow the past back to the moment of birth only, although, without any doubt, it is possible to investigate the life of the person in question in the previous embodiments as well. But the magician may be warned against doing so, because any investigation of the future as well as of the former life, in his own case or the one of other people, would mean a sort of meddling in the affairs of the Divine Providence, and such a curiosity would cause dangerous consequences. To begin with, he would instantly become as old as he was in all the former lives he did live, a fact which certainly would cause a very unpleasant feeling in him and an uninterestedness in any further life. Secondly, the magician is entirely responsible for all the blunders committed in his former lives. The only advantage would be that he would become conscious of the experiences in his former life, a fact which would never compensate for the disadvantages.

Supposing the magician would like to know something about the future of another person, for some really important reason, all he needs to do is to induce a trance. Provided he is quite familiar with this practice, there is nothing at all that will remain hidden. This kind of clairvoyance, where the magician is capable to perceive his own and other people's mental, astral and material planes in the correct connexion is the highest point which may be attained through working with the magic mirror. As soon as the magician has arrived there, I have nothing more to tell him with reference to the magic mirror, and he will himself find out new practices based on the examples which I have quoted here.

Magic Psychic Training (IX)

Conscious separation of the astral body from the physical one

In this chapter the magician will learn how to separate his astral body from his physical body, by means of conscious training, and how to get—not only with his spirit, but also with his soul—to places he wants, for some reason, to visit in the shape of his astral body. The emission of the astral body is, as you shall see, different from mental-wandering or the state of trance caused by akasha. The state during which the mental and astral bodies are separated from the physical body is, in the terminology of the occultists, called ecstasy. The perfect magician is able to go anywhere he likes in his astral shape, though, in most cases, he will content himself with mental-wandering or the state of trance. As a rule, the astral body, when united with the mental one, but separated from the physical body, will only carry out jobs that need be done by physical magic action. When emitting the astral body, certain precautions have to be taken, since in this case, in opposition to mental-wandering, both links between the mental and the astral body and the physical body, i. e., the so-called mental and astral matrix, are loosened from the body, the mental and astral bodies being connected to the physical body only by a very subtle elastic ribbon that shines like silver. If, during the period in which the mental and the astral bodies are loosened from the physical body, the latter were touched by another person, no matter whether skilled or unskilled in magic practice, the said ribbon, being extremely subtle, would break in two at once. The connection with the physical body being thus interrupted, physical death would be the consequence. Therefore utmost care has to be taken right from the beginning of these exercises that nobody should be able to touch the body of the magician when he puts himself in the described state. The thin ribbon would be torn to pieces, the electro-magnetic fluid in man being much stronger. Even the tender life-ribbon of an advanced magician would not be able to resist that fluid. A medical expert examining the body of a person killed in such a manner would come to the conclusion that death was caused by heart failure, embolism or paralysis of the heart. In its state of ecstasy, the physical body is, as in the case of apparent death, without life and feeling; its breath has stopped, its heart has come to a standstill. The following lines are intended to give you a clear picture of the practical side of the procedure. Apparent death, too, is a state of ecstasy, though caused by pathological conditions in the person concerned, which can be easily explained by any magician.

However, it should be added that the mental matrix, i. e., the binding agent between the mental and the astral body, is kept working by normal breathing, which supplies the blood vessels with the four elements, including akasha, via the lungs. We all know from experience that there can be no life without breathing. The astral matrix, the connecting link between the astral and the physical body, is kept alive, if supplied with enough food. The magician will now become aware of the connection between food-supply and breath and will have found its true cause in the preceding chapters dealing with conscious breathing and well balanced nutrition. If one point or the other is neglected during this stage of development, disharmonies, diseases and other inconveniences will be the result. Many mental and psychic disturbances are caused by irregularities in, or neglect of, these two factors. Therefore it has been pointed out right from the beginning that body, soul and spirit must be equally developed and kept in order. If the physical body is not well balanced, not strong and tough enough, and if it does not have a sufficient reserve of electro-magnetic fluids stocked by substantial food, rich in vitamins, thereby procuring itself an adequate elasticity, ecstasy-training could have an ill effect on it. Therefore any magician will agree in that ascetical training necessitating diet reduction must be considered extreme and therefore unhealthy. Many oriental methods demanding asceticism and ascetical training are one-sided and, no doubt, dangerous to people that are not natives of India, and whose physical structure is not accustomed to the local climate. However, if the magician has been able to equally develop the three steps of existence, i. e., body, soul and spirit, he need not fear that there could happen any disorders in his mental, astral or physical bodies. But the person not going through this course step by step, but neglecting, here and there, the neces-sary precautions must account for possible disharmonies. The magician will therefore not start practising the emission of his astral body, unless he is quite certain to have a thorough command over all the steps recommended up to this point. In the case of mental-wandering the most subtle part, the astral matrix connect-ing body and soul, remains in the body, but when the astral body is being separated from the physical body, everything is pulled out of the latter, which makes double precautions necessary when one proceedes to ecstasy-training.

The procedure to be followed when emitting the astral body is actually quite simple, especially for magicians that have a good command over mental-wandering.

The separation of the astral from the physical body is carried out as follows:

Sit down in your asana posture (though these exercises can also be done when lying down) and let your mental body escape from your physical body. Your consciousness now being transferred into your mental body, watch your physical body. You will have the sensation of your body being asleep. By the means of imagination you must now think that your astral body—much the same as your mental body before—is being drawn out of your physical body by your willpower. The shape of the astral body must be equal to the shape of your mental and your physical body. Then unite yourself with your astral body by entering the astral shape. When doing so, you will have a queer sensation, as though the astral body were not quite yours, and therefore you must at once consciously connect your mental to your astral matrix. Otherwise you would not succeed in keeping your astral body in your imagination, the same being constantly pulled towards your body, as though an invisible magnet were working on it. If you watch your physical body during this exercise, you will realize that there are irregularities in your body's breathing. But the moment you concentrate your thoughts on uniting yourself with your astral body and on breathing regularly, you will find yourself actually united with your astral body.

Right from the moment you are thus uniting yourself with your astral body—like a spirit beside your physical body—do not watch anything else but the breathing. This exercise has to be repeated until you have become accustomed to breathing in your astral body which you have drawn out of your physical body with which you have united yourself spiritually.

As you see, it is only conscious breathing in the astral body that brings about this separation of the astral matrix. If, by repeated practice, breathing in the mental as well as the astral body has become quite familiar to you, you may do another step forward. If you begin breathing in your astral body, your physical body will stop breathing. Because of the separation of the physical body from the astral shape, the former will lapse into a state of lethargy, a sort of morbid drowsiness, the limbs are stiffening, the face turns pale just like a dead body. But as soon as you will stop breathing outside your physical body, wanting to put an end to your experiment, you will instantly notice your astral body being at once, as if possessed by a magnet, pulled into your physical body which now begins to breathe again quite normally. But not before you spiritually re-transfer your mental body, i. e., your consciousness to the physical body, so that the astral body and the mental body re-assume their physical shape, will you recover your senses and gradually come round again.

What we usually call dying is the same process with the only difference that the matrix between the physical and the astral body is destroyed. In the case of normal death, the astral matrix between the physical and the astral body has been broken in two, by a lethal disease, or for some other reason, and therefore, the astral body, together with the mental body having lost its footing in the physical body, has to emanate automatically from the latter, whether willingly or unwillingly. During this process, breathing is transferred into the astral body, without the astral body becoming conscious of it. That's why, at first, deceased beings do not feel any difference between the physical and the astral body. They will come to realize it gradually as soon as they notice, that the material or physical body is no longer of any use to them, and that the astral body is subject to very different rules (the laws of the akasha-principle). I have written about this already in the previous chapters concerning the astral plane. Consequently, the practice of sending out the astral body deliberately, is an imitation of the process of dying. This evidently proves, how near you will come to the border between the actual life and what we call death, when you are practising such exercises. Therefore, proceed with caution.

Provided that the magician has got a perfect control of sending out his astral body,

1. the fear of death has become absolutely superfluous,
2. the magician does exactly know the process of his dying as well as the place where he is going after stripping off the mortal frame.

After frequently practising the deliberate separation of the astral body from the physical one, breathing in your astral shape will become a matter of routine, so that you will not notice it any more and you will experience the same sensations in the astral body, as if you were still in your physical body. If you wish to return into your material body, you have to hold the breath deliberately back in the astral body, so that the astral body is able to disentangle from the mental body and to re-assume the shape of the physical body. In this moment when the astral body re-assumes the physical shape, the body will automatically begin to breathe again, which makes the return into the physical body possible. This should always be considered first. The mental body, being subject to very different laws, does not breathe in the same rhythm as the material body does in connexion with the astral body. Only if you have become accustomed to the astral and the mental body going out from, and returning to, the physical body, so that you can do so as often as you please, considering the precaution measures with respect to your breathing, only then you are truly capable to withdraw successively from the physical body. In the beginning of this preliminary exercise, do not stray far from the side of your own body. Thus you have the opportunity, whether to stand besides your own physical body, or to take up its actual posture, namely, the asana.

A somewhat further exercise is to observe not merely the body, but, similarly as in the sending out of the mental body, to take notice also of the immediate surroundings. After all, it is the same process as the mental wandering; you should feel, hear and perceive every single object, with the diffence, however, that the mind is, in a way, taking a robe with it, in our case, the astral body, which allows sort of a more physical effect. Supposing you will pay a visit somewhere, in your mental shape only, in order to observe an event which might cause either a good or a bad psychical sensation, you can neither perceive nor feel it in your mental body, nor can you be influenced anyway. On the other hand, if you make the same experiment with your astral body, you will perceive it as intensively as if you assisted at it with your physical body.

In the next exercise you will learn how to withdraw gradually from your body, step by step. At first, you will feel, as it were, pulled back to your physical body by an invisible, attractive power similar to the one which a magnet exerts on the iron. This is to be interpreted by the fact, that the bond between the astral and the physical body is fed, preserved and kept in balance by the most subtle fluid. By performing the exercises of sending out the astral body, you are committing a deliberate act against the lawfulness of the natural elements in your body which must be overcome. Consequently the movement of your astral body requires a greater effort than if you would move away with your mental body alone. This is the reason why you should draw away from your body a few steps only, at first, and return to it instantly. Because the magnetic, attractive power is constantly pulling and influencing you, it will provoke various feelings in your astral body, such as the fear of death and the like. These feelings must be overcome at all events. Having advanced to this point, you should master all these occurences. Extend the distance from your physical body with every new exercise. As time goes on, you will be able to cover greater and greater distances. And the farther you can remove your astral body from your physical body, all the weaker will its attractive power become. Later on, when travelling very far, you will find it really difficult to return to your body. This will become a tricky problem for the magician, mainly if he is wandering about in planes or regions which allure him so much that he is beginning to feel a little sad at the very idea of having to return to his own body. Here you see, that the magician must be absolutely master of his feelings, because as soon as he gets accustomed to the idea of feeling quite at home in his astral body, not only on the physical level but also on the astral plane, he becomes usually weary of life feeling inclined nevermore to return to his physical frame. A longing will overcome him for destroying, by sheer force, the bond of life which still ties him to his physical body. Doing so would mean to commit a suicide in the same way as on the physical body. Besides, it would be an offence against the Divine Providence and would naturally have karmic consequences. It is quite understandable that the temptation to commit such a suicide is very strong, especially if the magician is nearly pining away for grief in the physical world after all the blissfulness he experienced on the other planes.

Having made good progress in these exercises concerning the sending out of the astral body, so that he can cover any distance, the magician now has the opportunity to use this ability for manifold tasks. He can tranfer himself anywhere with his astral body, wherever he likes to be, he can treat sick people by accumulating and condensing the magnetic or electric fluids in the astral body conveying them to the respective patients. The treatment with the astral body is by far more pervasive and effective than by the mere thought-transference or the mental wandering, because the fluids the magician is working with will become effective on the sick person's corresponding plane only.

The magician can exert a lot of other influences, too. He can materialize himself with the help of the earth-element, which he is condensing in his astral body on the astral plane under the very nose of an experienced adept as well as of a layman to such a degree that he can be seen, heard and perceived with the physical eyes. The issue, in this respect, depends on the duration of the training and on the capacity of accumulation of the earth-element in the astral body. It is obvious that the magician can perform physical acts, too, with the help of his astral body. Producing phenomena—as adepts see them—such as knocking sounds, and influence on terrestrial affairs, etc., find a satisfactory explanation here. Really and truly: no limits at all exist for a magician, and it is entirely up to himself in which line he wishes to specialise. In any case, he knows exactly how to manage all these things, as much as how to condense one part of the body only, say, one hand, whereas the other hand remains astral. If, with the help of his imagination, he is capable to accelerate the electronic vibrations of an object, he will also manage to "spirit" away any objects corresponding to the measure of his forces and his development, before the eyes of other people, and to transfer them to the astral plane. In these instances, the material objects are no longer subject to the material laws but will become astral. Therefore it is a mere trifle for the magician to transfer such objects to the farthest distance with the aid of his astral body, and to bring them back again to their original form. From a layman's point of view, such phenomena seem to be chimerae, but any experienced magician will easily be able to produce such and even more astonishing phenomena which otherwise might be spoken of as sheer miracles. But as you have gathered from what I have explained up to now, these phenomena are no miracles, for miracles, in the true sense of the word, do not exist at all. The magician recognises the Higher Powers and their laws, and he knows how to utilize them for the benefit of mankind. An amount of examples could be quoted here, but some hints may suffice to him who seeks illumination.

Impregnation of the astral body with the four divine fundamental qualities

When the magician has arrived at this stage of development, he will begin to express his concept of God in concrete ideas. The mystic, being trained one-sidedly only, or a Yogi, etc., sees in his

Deity nothing else but at mere aspect to which he renders worship and adoration. The truly wise adept, who always considers the four elements in his development, will represent the concept of God in four aspects according to the laws of the universe, namely, the omnipotence, corresponding to the fire-principle, the omniscience and wisdom belonging to the air-principle, the immortality with the water-principle and the omnipresence with the earth-principle. On this level, it will be the magician's task to meditate about these four divine ideas—aspects—in turns. Deep meditations, in a way, enable the magician to ecstasize directly with one of these divine virtues, fusing with it in such a manner that he feels himself to be the virtue in question. He has to experience the same with all the four virtues of his God. The arrangement of the exercise is his own business, that means, he is allowed to meditate on one of the virtues for so long, until he becomes quite certain that the respective virtue has become personified in him. He may perform the meditations, according to his spare-time, in the manner, that, through meditation, he recalls all the virtues, in turns, in one exercise. The meditation has to be so profound, so pervasive and so convincing that the astral body becomes, as it were, identical with the virtue. The magician's concept of God is universal, including all the four divine virtues, according to the universal laws. The magician should, therefore, give his keenest attention to these meditations, because they are absolutely necessary to realize this union with his God. As soon as, after long and deep meditation, he is capable to form an exact idea of these four divine virtues, he has ripened so far as to establish that connexion the practice of which will be described in the last step of this lecture. These meditations are producing a kind of deification of the magician's spirit and soul and, finally, they will influence his body, in an analogous way, enabling him to establish the union with his God which is the sum and substance of this training course.

Magic Physical Training (IX)

By continued practice in this course, the scholar has been led a great distance on the way to a state in which there is no more need of a special training of the body. From now he will have to intensify the powers he did develop so far and to use them in various ways. Below I will give a number of instructions which the scholar can follow, without any effort, according to the measure of his development.

Treatment of sick people with the help of the electromagnetic fluid

It is a beautiful and sacred work to help the suffering mankind. The magician is capable to do miracles as far as the treatment of the sick is concerned, just as so many Saints did in the past and are still doing in the present time. Not one of the lay practitioners, magnetizers or healing mediums will ever understand to release the dynamic powers corresponding to the primary principles, in the same marvellous way, as the magician does. The presupposition, here, is of course that the magician does know the occult anatomy of the body with respect to the elements, and their positive and negative effects, otherwise, any influence on the seat of the disease would be quite impossible.

With the help of the akasha-principle and his clairvoyant eyes, the magician will immediately recognise the cause of the illness and be able to influence the roots of the illness. When the origin of the sickness happens to be in the mental sphere, the magician, first of all, has to influence the mind of the patient to restore the harmony. As I did mention before, the astral sphere can only influence the astral plane, exactly as the material sphere influences the material plane only. This fact must always be kept in mind. Any transmutation, from one plane to the other, can only be accomplished with the help of the corresponding matrix or the connecting link of a more subtle power. A thought can never produce any physical power nor cure any physical ailment. But a thought which has been concentrated on faith and conviction, can cause strong vibrations in the mental sphere of the patient which are conveyed to the astral body via the mental matrix. An influence like this does not reach farther than to the soul of the patient. This induces the patient to set his mind on the healing process, thus producing the vibrations which are necessary for recovery, but nothing else. Evidently a sort of mental-astral palliation can be accomplished; the patient himself will mentally cause the acceleration of the healing process, but this influence on the material ailment is not sufficient, especially, if the patient is already lacking such an amount of internal strength that the fluids necessary for the healing cannot be renewed. Therefore the success would only be a very trifling one, and the recovery subjective.

To this category of healing methods belong suggestion, hypnosis, self-suggestion, faith-healing and so on. The magician will not exactly underrate these methods, but on the other hand, he will not rely on them, using them merely by way of a makeshift. By no means will these methods represent to him so high a value as it is described in numerous books.

More spectacular will be the work of a true magician who has got a great surplus of vital magnetism, by occult training and a corresponding line of life. He does neither need the patient's faith nor any kind of suggestions, hypnosis nor an aureole. A magnetizer like this loads his vital power, with the help of his own surplus, into the astral body—if necessary even against the patient's will—and this way does accomplish a faster recovery, because his magnetism has a stronger stimulus, thus strengthening the astral matrix of the patient. Therefore, a magnetopathist can treat very successfully a child, too, who neither through his imagination nor with his subconsciousness can contribute, in any way, to further the healing process. It is quite another thing if a magician specialised in the healing line, treats hundreds of patients daily, without his vital force diminishing in the least. A magician makes use of the universal laws and touches the sick physical organ directly with his influence, without passing first through the astral body together with the matrix. This is the reason why a magician has a much stronger influence on the sick organ than all the healers known up to date. The healing process can, in certain circumstances, happen so fast that it can be regarded as a miracle from the standpoint of the medical science.

I do not intend to prescribe any general rules to the true magician for the treatment of the sick, because I am sure that he already has his personal method of working based on the laws he did learn. It will be sufficient to give a few useful hints to him. The magician works with the willpower and the imagination, when the patient suffers from a mental weakness or disturbance, and the harmony has to be restored. Here the magician has to be fully aware of the activity of his spirit, so that not his astral or physical body, but his spirit alone does activate the influence. Therefore the keenest attention is to be paid to the spirit; body and soul must be completely neglected in order to intensify the effect from spirit to spirit. For example, if the patient happens to be in agony or in a state of deep unconsciousness, the magician will be able to bring the patient round again. If the cause of the disease is to be found in the astral body, the magician will work with the accumulation of the vital power which he impregnates with the desire of a quick recovery. He will convey the accumulated power from the universe into the astral body of the patient without allowing the vital power to go first through his own body. By doing so, the magician avoids any weakening of the own vitality and, at the same time, a mingling of the patient's morbid Od with his own one. If the causes of the illness are of physical nature, and if any organ in the body has been affected, the magician resorts to the elements and to the electric and magnetic fluids. If the patient happens to be of a strong constitution, the magician will work with elements only which have a favourable influence on the sickness; thus, he will fight a high fever with the element of the water. The element concerned will produce the necessary fluids—electrical or magnetical—by itself, and a line of conduct, a regime, kind of breathing, herbs, baths corresponding to the elements will be prescribed for the patient. But if the body of the patient has already become so weak that it is unable to accept the necessary element and, consequently, to produce the corresponding fluid, there is no other way out for the magician but to load the sick organ directly with the fluid. Here, the occult anatomy according to the polarisation has to be observed carefully. Any organ performing the function of the magnetic fluid must never be loaded with the electric fluid in order not to harm the patient. In organs where both fluids are at work, the magician will do well to introduce the fluids successively. Supposing he wants to exert an influence on the head by fluids, he will load the front part, — the forehead — the left side and the inside — cerebrum — with the electrical fluid; the right side, however, of the head and the back of the head — cerebellum — with the magnetic fluid. If the magician works by passing his hands on the patient's bodies, which is quite a good expedient, but not at all necessary, he will perform this act in accordance with the fluid. With reference to our example—head—he will influence the forehead and the left side with his electric, that is, his right hand, the back of the head and the right side with his left, magnetic hand. A magician who is extraordinarily well trained in the healing practice, will neither have to resort to any kind of strokes nor to passing his hands on the patient, he can accomplish everything by means of his well developed imagination. He must understand how to lead the magnetic or the electric fluid, with the help of the imagination, into the smallest organs as well, that means, he must be able to direct the magnetic fluid, say, into the inner part of the eyes, or the electric fluid into the edge of the eyeballs. In this manner he will not only successfully treat many eye-complaints, strengthen the visual power, but he will also be capable to make the blind see again, provided that the blindness has not been caused by a structural defect. The neutral parts of the body are therefore to be loaded whether with the element belonging to the respective region of the body or with the accumulated vital power. It would not be too serious a drawback neglecting the neutral parts at all, because the irradiation of the fluids will influence the neutral points of the organs indirectly, too. On the chance that not only one single organ is concerned but that the whole body has been affected, as in nervous diseases, or diseases of the blood, the electric fluid has to be led to the entire right side of the patient's body and the magnetic fluid to the left side. If, after the successive conveyance of both the fluids to the patient's body, the latter is no more receptive enough, the elements can be accordingly led to the regions of the body. Any extreme dynamic accumulation of elements inside a sick body is to avoid, because the patient will not agree with such a stimulus.

The most efficient magic healing process consists in successively influencing the patient's spirit, soul and body accordingly. Based on the mentioned examples and the analogous universal laws, the magician ought to know how to proceed without a particular hint. Answering the question, whether an expert and duly trained magician would be capable to completely heal every kind of diseases, even the most incurable ones, it may be said that the magician has, in fact, the possibility to cure even the most malignant illness, providing that none of the organs in the body is missing. But the magician will read in the book of Fate—Akasha—how far he is allowed to intervene, because certain ailments depend on karmic conditions, that means, the patient has to atone for this or that omission in his present or his former life by suffering the illness. If, however, the magician feels a call to act as a means to an end, healing or alleviating the sickness, or to cure it completely—which the truly wise magician can read in akasha, too—he will work astounding miracles based on these instructions and considering the universal rules.

The highest adepts who ever walked on our globe and brought about the most fabulous healings, resuscitations of the dead, etc., could do so only by considering the universal laws, their powers and fluids, and here it did not matter at all, whether the realisability of their faith did play any part, consciously or unconsciously, or if the living word—Quabbalah—has been the important factor. It does, indeed, depend on the magician's degree of development, how far the miraculous healings can reach.

Magic loading of talismans, amulets and gems

The belief in talismans, amulets and jewels goes back to times immemorial and has its origin in fetishism which is still widespread amongst primitive races. The belief in a talisman and similar things has survived from these earlier stages to the present day, but modified its character according to the modern style of life. What else but talismans are all the mascots, pendants, rings and brooches which are supposed to bring good luck? It is the birth-stones that are held in particularly high esteem to-day. So, if there were not something true or perhaps even magic in the nature of talismans, the thought of, and the belief in them would be bound to have disappeared long ago. Let us, then, sort out the chaff from the wheat, and lift the veil a bit.

A talisman, an amulet or any birth stone is meant to strengthen the trustworthiness and the credit extended to the person who bears it. By paying closer attention to his talisman, the bearer's subconsciousness is, by way of autosuggestion, influenced in the desired direction and, according to his aptitudes, various effects may be carried out. No wonder, if a materially inclined man, an uninterested scientist condemns such a belief, expresses criticism and pokes funs, marking it with the brand of superstition. The wise magician is aware of the true nature of such things and he will not be content of bearing a talisman for the mere purpose of raising the faith and the confidence, but he will endeavour to investigate the laws underlying the secrets of the talismans. He knows that talismans based on the belief of their bearers, become inefficient as soon as they pass into the hand of an unbeliever or a sceptic. With his knowledge of the causal nexus, the magician goes deeper and deeper into the matter relating to it.

Before dealing with this synthesis, let us treat the various differences. A talisman in the hands of a magician is nothing else but an implement, a clue, something material into which he is binding or enclosing his power, his ultimate cause, his fluid. Its shape whether being a ring, a pendant or a brooch, and its material value are of no importance to him at all. He neither considers beauty nor fashion or prestige. It represents to him an object, with the help of which, by binding his powers to it, he produces certain causes destined to liberate the desired effect irrespective of the bearer believing it or not.

A "pentacle", on the other hand, is a specific object, a talisman being in accordance with the laws of analogy concerning the desired effect, strength, faculty and cause. The magician has to consider these rules of analogy when he is producing and loading such a pentacle which he will always prefer to the talisman, especially if he wants to communicate with beings of other higher worlds, no matter whether good or evil entities are concerned, genii or demons.

An amulet again is a divine name, or a holy verse from the Bible, a Mantram, that is, a sentence expressing the worship of a deity, written on parchment or on ordinary parchment-paper. Carrying around various magic herbs such as mandragora and the like which are believed to possess a kind of protective power belongs to this category of amulets, too. Furthermore, this category includes fluid condensers in solid or liquid form or blotting papers moistened with them, loadstones and natural magnets as well as tiny artificial horse-shoe magnets.

Last of all let me mention the precious and semi-precious stones which are particularly suitable fluid condensers, and have been used, at all times, for protection, luck, success and healings. Astrologers have ascribed a special effect to each stone, on the base of the colour and hardness theory, and advised people born under a certain sign or planet to bear the respective stone as a lucky stone. But the true magician knows, of course, that these astrologically selected stones have a very insignificant effect, and that such a stone is absolutely worthless for anyone that does not believe in such things, whereas stones which are in accordance with an astrological effect are suitable to, and susceptible of, the corresponding magic loading as far as hardness, chemical composition and colour are concerned. The magician can, as far as possible, consider these astrological arguments, but he is by no means dependent on them. He can, if he wishes to, load any stone, even the one which seems to be most unfavourable from the astrological point of view, magically to such a degree that certain results can be accomplished, no matter, whether the person does or not believe in the result; there will always be the outcome the magician orders and nothing else. Having interpreted the different kinds and variants of talismans, amulets, pentacles and precious stones, let me talk about several loadings of which I am going to quote 10 kinds:

1. Loading with the mere willpower in connexion with imagination.
2. Loading with the help of timed accumulation of the vital power and the wish-impregnation.
3. Loading by binding elementals, elementaries, beings due to accomplish the desired result.
4. Loading with the help of individual or traditional rituals.
5. Loading with the help of magic formulas, mantrams, tantras and suchlike.
6. Loadings by accumulation of elements.
7. Loading by electric and magnetic fluids.
8. Loading with the help of accumulation of the power of the light.
9. Loading by electro-magnetic balls—volts.
10. Loadings by mago-sexual operation.

Each of the loading possibilities quoted here has numerous variants again, but it would take me too long to describe all of them. The advanced magician will find his own loadings with the help of his intuition. The ten ones mentioned here are supposed to serve as a rule of conduct only, and therefore a brief description appears indicated.

To 1.: Loading with the mere will in connexion with the imagination

This is the simplest and easiest method, the effect of which depends on the willpower and the imaginative faculty of the magician. Every talisman, every amulet, every pentacle, with the exception of paper and parchment-amulets, has to be cleared from the fluid clinging to it, before the magic loading can be performed. The best way to do so is with the help of the magic of water. Take a glass of fresh cold water and dip the talisman into it. While doing so, concentrate on the water taking away all evil influences.

Hold on to this concentration for quite a while. After some minutes of deep concentration, you ought to be perfectly sure that all evil influences have been sucked up by the water, and that your talisman is absolutely free from them. Dry the talisman and now be quite sure that it is receptive of your own influence. You have to perform this clearage on every non liquid talisman irrespective of the method you are about to use in order to load it. Hold the talisman in your hand and by imagination, fix your desire on it with all your willpower, with faith and confidence. Time the efficiency of your desire whether it is to last for a certain period only or for ever, furthermore, if the effect is meant for a certain person only or for anybody that is supposed to carry the talisman. Use the form of the present tense, that means, imagine that the desired result is working already. You can intensify the virtue of the concentrated desire by frequent repetition of the loading which will make the emissive power of the talisman more pervasive. Transfer the feeling, while concentrating on the wish that the effectiveness of the talisman should remain and become stronger if you do not think about it, and that, in case it is meant for somebody else, it should do the same effect. Provided you did load the talisman, to the best of your knowledge and with the greatest possible force, it is ready for use.

To 2.: Loading with timed accumulation of vital power and wish-impregnation

The talisman is to be freed from the fluid in the same manner as described in 1. If the point in question is a talisman which you want to use yourself, you will have to perform the accumulation of the vital power in your own body (see the instruction of step III). If you loaded your body expansively with vital power, lead it, via your right hand, into your talisman and compress the accumulated vital power to such a degree that it does fill the entire shape of the talisman, the amulet or the stone. While doing so, you have to imagine that the talisman is sucking in the vital power, keeping it inside for so long as you want it to. You must work with the firm conviction that, during the time you are carrying or using the talisman, its effectiveness will not decrease but become stronger instead. The vital power taken over by the talisman and pressed together, there, to a snow-white brilliancy seems to be very much like a shining sun. You see how far your imagination must reach. Transfer the desire concerning the effectiveness of the talisman to your body right away while accumulating the vital power. The duration of the effect can be fixed imaginatively afterwards, too. Choose the present tense to express your inner conviction that the talisman has got its full effectiveness immediately after the loading. Do not command several wishes to one talisman and, least of all, contrary ones. The most effective loading is restricted to one single desire only. Furthermore, always express wishes within the reach of possibility, and avoid fancy loadings which cannot be fulfilled. This command goes for every kind of talismans and loadings. How expansive the force of such a loading is, can best be checked up with the help of a sidereal pendulum.

If you load a talisman for someone else, the accumulated vital force is to be led not through the own body but has to be taken from the universe directly, being imaginatively condensed and conveyed to the talisman. All the rest of the instructions remains the same.

To 3.: Loading by binding elementals, elementaries, and beings supposed to release the desired effect

I have already described the creation of elementals and elementaries in the previous steps. Naturally any being like these can be bound to a talisman, a pentacle, an amulet or a stone. The spell has to be performed with a self-selected word, a short, specially composed ritual or a gesture with the help of imagination. It will suffice then to execute the gesture or the ritual, or to pronounce the word or the formula and the spell-bound elemental will release the respective effect. The magician will certainly know the times when he will be able to bind a being to a talisman. It is obvious that he will use elementals to influence the mental sphere, but for the achievement of astral or material results, he will resort to elementaries. Equally, entities or beings can be bound to a talisman in this manner, too, in order to obtain certain effects, and there is no magician who, duly trained, could not perform such acts. He is able to establish the contact by the practice of the passive communication, with the help of the magic mirror, or by inducing a trance in the akasha. No further directions are necessary, here, and the magician ought to know himself what he has got to do.

To 4.: *Loading by individual or traditional rituals*

This practice is preferred mainly by oriental magicians, who are endowed with a stupendous amount of patience which is indispensable as far as this kind of loading is concerned. The oriental magician makes a certain self-selected sign above the talisman, or he makes this sign with it directly in the air, with his hand, his fingers or even with one finger—quite individually. While doing so, he concentrates on the effect which the talisman is desired to have. He will repeat this experiment several times every day, thus producing so strong a battery—"the volt"—in the akasha by these constant repetitions that the desired effect is as good as granted. If, by frequent repetition of the experiment, the magic "volt" in the akasha has grown strong enough, it suffices to perform the ritual or the sign with, or above, the talisman (which may even be done without imagination or without any mental effort) in order to produce the desired effect. A magician familiar with the Quabbalah, will naturally know that he did load his own battery in the akasha ritually 462 times corresponding to the quabbalistic number of 462, on 462 days, for the purpose that his ritual should produce an automatic effect. This loading is practicable without great effort, but it is very wearisome and lengthy, and a European magician will hardly display this surplus of patience in order to achieve a result which he can sooner obtain with the help of one of the methods described here.

The loading by a traditional ritual is easier and requires a few repetitions only to bring about the contact, the effect being so amazing as to verge on a miracle. The snag here is that such traditional loading rituals happen to be the secrets of lodges, societies, sects and monasteries which I myself cannot give away. It is quite obvious that a magician well trained in clairvoyance could easily get hold of these secrets, but there is always the danger of being found out. And the oriental magicians who guard their rituals under the oath of death would proceed ruthlessly against anyone that should dare to grab them without permission. Therefore I warn every magician not to do such pilferings. It is usually by gestures that the secret signs of various deities—*Ishta Devatas*—are performed upon the talisman, in a similar way as I detailed it in the description of the individual rites. No doubt that a loading like this has an extraordinarily strong effect because this particular ritual is celebrated by hundreds of magicians thus being handed down traditionally from one generation to the other.

A member who has been declared to be mature is usually offered such a ritual as a sort of distinction. The grant of such a ritual which at the same time establishes the contact with the corresponding battery is called in the Orient *Ankhur* or *Abhisheka*.

To 5.: *Loading by magic formulas, mantrams, tantras, etc.*

This kind represents one of the greatest and most powerful loadings but it requires high knowledge and a lot of preparations which I will describe in my following two works, concerning the magic evocation and the practical Quabbalah. Therefore here I shall restrict myself to a short remark only.

The first kind of loading is realized by repeating a magic formula, and the desired effect is accomplished with the help of an entity selected for this purpose.

The loading by mantrams is done by imagining or speaking a sacred sentence, in sign of worship of a deity many times into a suitable talisman—Japa-Yoga. The quality of the deity in question becomes materialized in this manner. It is absolutely certain that fabulous results can be compassed on all planes in this manner.

A loading by tantras is nothing else but the correct use of word-magic where certain cosmic powers are employed with the help of suitable letters, words, etc., regarding the cosmic rhythm, sound, colour, quality.

To 6.: *Loading by accumulation of elements*

This possibility of loading is offered to every magician who went through his practical training up to now. Supposing the magician wants a certain result to be achieved through an element-principle, he will load the talisman or the pentacle he chose with the corresponding element. The loading itself happens in the same way as described in point 2, by accumulation of the vital power only excepting that the desired element is used instead of the vital power. For a personal use, the accumulation of elements takes place in the own body, but for other persons it is done directly from the universe. If for example, one element happens to be difficult to be mastered, the opposite one is to be used for screening with the help of a loaded talisman. Many other results can be accomplished through the elements and a magician, who is absolutely perfect in mastering the elements will intuitively compose the desired variants himself.

To 7.: Loading with the help of the electric or the magnetic fluid

One of the most powerful loadings consists in using the electric or the magnetic fluid. When the talisman is supposed to protect something, to screen it, to irradiate or to develop any kind of activity, one will mainly use the electric fluid, but if it is to produce an attractive power, to bring about sympathy, luck, or success, the magnetic fluid will be employed. The manner of loading is exactly the same as previously described, but if the point is a talisman for personal purposes, the accumulation is performed in the corresponding half of the body only, that means, not in the whole body. The magnetic fluid is accumulated dynamically in the left half of the body and projected through the left hand into the talisman. In the matter of the electric fluid, it will be the right side and the projection to the talisman takes place via the right hand.

To 8.: Loading through accumulation of light-power

To achieve subtler spiritual effects such as the enhancement of different occult powers, intuition, inspiration, etc., a talisman is loaded with condensed light-power. The loading is executed in the same way as the accumulation of vital force with concomitant desire-impregnation, timing and so forth. The light pressed together in the talisman is like a sun which shines brighter than the ordinary sunlight. A talisman destined for personal use is accumulated with light-power through the own body, whereas the power is to be drawn from the universe, when intended for other persons. Otherwise the usual rules and instructions as given before have to be observed.

To mitigate karmic influences, to be protected against influences of other spheres and to turn fate according to one's desire, a talisman is loaded for one's own or for other people's purposes with a magic "volt". This kind of loading is called "volting" and represents the strictest imitation of the akasha-principle, and only a magician aiming at the highest target, the union with God, should use this kind of loading not to burden himself with an interference in the akasha. As I did repeatedly mention already, everything existing has been created by the two fluids by means of the four elements. According to the universal law, the electric fluid will always be in the centre. On the periphery of the electric fluid, where expansion ceases, the magnetic fluid begins to work and this is where it is most powerless. The distance from the focus or centre to the periphery of the electric fluid is exactly the same as the one from the beginning of the magnetic fluid to the end of the periphery where the magnetic attractive power is strongest. This law is valid in small things as well as in the big ones, consequently in the microcosm as well as in the macrocosm. When loading with a "volt", i. e., when "volting", attention has to be paid to this law. If you wish to load a talisman, a pentacle or a stone for your own purposes with a "volt", you have to proceed as follows:

In the right half of your body, accumulate the electric fluid dynamically, with all your strength, via the hand and finally through the forefinger. Project the accumulated electric fluid to a powerful electric spark and encase it, with your imagination, exactly in the centre of your talisman. You have got to see this electric spark as if it were absolutely red hot. Now do the same with the magnetic fluid directing it through your forefinger of the left hand, and from there in front of you, so that you wrap the ball-shaped electric spark with the magnetic fluid to such a degree that it becomes invisible in your imagination. Imagine the compressed magnetic fluid as being of a blue colour. Did you manage this, only a small blue ball ought to be left comprising the entire shape of the talisman. Herewith the "volt" has been produced, and as soon as the electric fluid is irradiating inside of this "volt" and the magnetic one outside of it, impregnate the ball, that means, the ready "volt" with your desire and fix the duration of the effect. Supposing you wish to increase the loading later, which probably will not be necessary, all you have to do is to condense the magnetic fluid, the electric fluid which happens to be inside of it being increased automatically. A "volt" like this has such a powerful magic effect that it could, at will, even change the karma. A magician who can accomplish this is no longer subject to the customary karma, but only to the Divine Providence. Loading a talisman for another person with a "volt", it has to be done in the same manner, but the electric and magnetic fluids are not drawn from the own body but directly from the universe. "Volting" for other people should be practised only exceptionally, in absolute case of necessity, because the magician has to be absolutely sure that the person in question is really inspired with high ideals, longing for ideals only, but being haunted by karma or, to express it in a popular way, being an ill starred fellow whose run of bad luck continues. The magician's clairvoyant eyes will realize these facts, and his intuition will always teach him what to do and what to avoid. At this point, the magician himself will be responsible for all and everything. The most skeptic Thomas, however, would be greatly amazed at the enormous effect of such a magical "volt" bound to a small horse-shoe magnet so that the ball is wrapping in the whole magnet.

To 10.: Loading by a mago-sexual operation

There is still another kind of loading, a subject I shall only deal briefly with, here. For ethic and moral reasons, I desist from describing the practice in detail. The meditating magician will find out all about this practice, but he, too, will desist from working with it, since in the meantime he got to know so many different possibilities of loading. Only a magician on a very high ethical level could dare to make use of this practice, because lastly all things are pure to the pure ones. In the hands of an immoral man these practices would do more harm than good. At least, a lot of mischief would be done with them, and powers as high as those of love must not be misused. Therefore I am restricted to comment briefly on the principle on which this loading possibility is based.

First of all, certain preparations are essential, without which the operation could not successfully be accomplished. Any mago-sexual operation, whatever purpose it may serve, is a sacred act, a prayer by which the generative act of love is imitated. Everything created in the universe has been produced by the act of love. This universal law is the fundament of sexual magic. Obviously one ought to work with a like-minded congenial partner, who has gone through the same magical training. The male, that is, the magician represents the active, the begetting principle, whereas the female magician is the passive, the parturient principle. The female partner, familiar with the mastery of the electric and magnetic fluids has got to change her polarity, so that her head becomes magnetic and her genitals electric. With respect to the male partner, the conditions are reversed. The polarity of his head must be magnetic and that of the genitals electric. The intercourse between the two partners produces an exceedingly strong bipolar effort which gives rise to an enormous effect. Performing this act of love, its outcome does not mean new life, but the desired cause together with its effect has been begotten. Here the lower as well as the upper double pole are coming into operation, the four-pole magnet, the Yod He Vau He is working the highest mystery of love, here, the Creation. How easy it would be to degrade this creative act, the highest thing existent on this earth, to mere carnal appetites which would lead to damnation. The expulsion of Adam and Eve from the paradise finds its highest symbolism here. The magician who dares to approach the highest of all practices has to master the upper as well as the lower streams in order to transfer the loading eventually into his talisman. To dishonour this sacred act by carnal desires would mean to repeat the fate of Adam and Eve who were no longer allowed to enjoy the fruits of the paradise. The intuitive magician will understand without difficulties how great this symbolism is, and will agree with me if I stick to my duty of secrecy about the greatest of all mysteries.

Realisation of a desire with the help of electromagnetic balls in the akasha, the so-called "volting"

I have described the production of a "volt" by means of the electromagnetic fluid in the chapter referring to loading a talisman. The process is the same, here, excepting that the electromagnetic ball has to be bigger for a "volt" in the akasha. The practice is as follows:

Accumulate the electric fluid in your right half of the body with all the strength you can afford, and project it through the palm of the right hand to the outside, forming the electric fluid, at the same time, with your imagination, into a ball suspended in the air. This projection is, therefore, not going through the finger, but directly through the inner part of the right hand. The fiery ball which has to be turned out red-hot, by the compressed electric fluid, is becoming increased dynamically by frequent accumulation of the electric fluid in itself and by a reiterated projection, and enlarged by the repeated loading. This kind of accumulation and dynamical loading has to be performed until the ball has reached a diameter of one yard (1 m).

Perform the same process with the magnetic fluid, beginning to project the accumulated magnetic fluid, through the palm of the left hand, to the outside by wrapping the electric ball in your magnetic fluid, one layer after the other. By frequent repetition of this accumulation of the magnetic fluid and its projection, the wrapping is growing, until the diameter of the whole ball has reached 2 yards (2 m). The electromagnetic "volt" is now completed.

When doing such a "volt" destined for another person, the magician has to take the electric as well as the magnetic fluid directly from the universe. If such an electromagnetic "volt" has been prepared with a firm faith and conviction, the magician will impregnate this "volt", the strongest magic accumulator existing, with the respective concentration of the desire. By means of his imagination, he will create the desired cause which his "volt" is to produce. At last, having determined the duration of his magic "volt", the magician will, as it were, ecstatically fling it into the macrocosm, the causal world, consequently into the akasha by the way of his imagination. Imaginatively he interrupts the connexion with his "volt", stopping thinking of it the very moment he flings it, forgetting it purposely and paying his attention to other different things.

The "volting" quoted here is one of the most powerful operations which the magician is capable to accomplish in his present stage of development, for now he has succeeded in mastering himself as well as other people. The cause he did transfer with his "volt" into the akasha, will do its effect, and it is of no importance at all whether it concerns the mental, the astral or the material plane. The magician will certainly appreciate this great and responsible opportunity, and accomplish noble deeds only for his own benefit and that of his fellow-creatures for whom he did dare to undertake this operation.

The magician who walked on the path of hardships up to this very point, has balanced his karma with his troublesome exercises which were more than asceticism so far that it will do him no more harm. The magician is no longer subject to the ordinary influences of destiny, he became master of his fate and nothing but Divine Providence in its highest aspect can influence his will.

Summary of all exercises of Step IX

I. *Magic Mental Training:*

Practice of clairvoyance with the help of magic mirrors,
a) seeing through time and space,
b) distant effect through the magic mirror,
c) different tasks of projection through the magic mirror.

II. *Magic Psychic Training:*

1. Deliberate separation of the astral body from the material body.
2. Impregnation of the astral body with the four divine fundamental qualities.

III. *Magic Physical Training:*

1. Treatment of the sick with the electromagnetic fluid.
2. Magical loading of talismans, amulets and gems.
3. Wish-realisation through electromagnetic balls in the akasha, the so-called "volting".

End of the ninth Step

STEP X

Magic Mental Training (X)

Before the magician begins to follow the practice of the tenth, that is, the last step of this course, he may look back attentively and make sure if he achieved the positive realisation of all he has been taught up to now. If that is not the case, he must try to make up for all he is still lacking and must go to any length for developing every faculty completely. Any kind of haste or hurry with respect to his development is useless and will work out awkwardly later in his magic task. To avoid disappointments, the magician is advised to take a sufficient amount of time and to work steadily but systematically. He must realise that this last step really represents the end of his magical development with respect to the first Tarot-card and that he ought to be prepared for the higher magical tasks which I am going to describe in the following two works: "Practice of magical evocation" and "Key to the True Quabbalah". If there were gaps in his schooling, he would never be capable to control the higher Powers. It is certainly not important whether he will finish his course a few months sooner or later, the main point will always be to keep his aim in mind, and to advance steadily to the goal, the lofty heights of the God-cognition. Looking back to his actual development, the magician will realise that he has already covered a good distance on the path of his perfection, even more than he had supposed to do, but he has to know that all this is only the thin end of a wedge. Meditating on the fact how much knowledge and experience he has still to store, he will bow in a spirit of great reverence in front of the Divine fountain of Wisdom. There will be no more pride or ambition nor superciliousness to say nothing of bad qualities in his heart, for the deeper he penetrates into God's workshop, all the more humble and receptive will he become.

The first task which the magician is facing in the tenth step is to win his way to the knowledge of the sphere of the elements. With his mental body he will visit the different spheres of the elements, transfer himself to the kingdom of the gnomes, or earth-sprites, afterwards to the realm of the water-nymphs. He gets to know the kingdom of the fairies and finally that of the salamanders, the so-called kingdom of the fire. To a non-magician all this will be rubbish and he will regard it as an utopian idea. But for the true adept neither fairy-tales nor sagas do exist, because they are to be understood as a sort of symbolism concealing many a deep truth. It is the same thing with all the gnomes, water-nymphs, fairies and salamanders. Based on his own observations, the magician can convince himself that beings like these do really exist. On the other hand, a magically absolutely untrained person whose senses are mentally thoroughly undeveloped, is of course subject to the vibrations of the material world only and will never be able to form a mental picture of the existence of any other kind of beings, to say nothing of becoming convinced of this fact. Most people are preoccupied by the material mode of life to such a degree that they will not understand anything higher and subtler outside our physical world and, least of all, they will perceive it. It is quite otherwise with a magician who is developing his senses purposely and therefore will see and perceive far more, convincing himself very soon of the existence of higher powers, planes and beings. Properly speaking, it is the goal of our training to qualify the learner to perceive and to master not only the physical world but the higher spheres equally. But let us not advance matters but let us stick to the practice and consider what there can be done to reach the world of the elements.

In the previous chapters we learned that there is a kingdom of elements populated not only by the element itself, but by the corresponding beings, too. Then, which is the difference between a human being and an elemental being? The human being consists of four and five elements respectively, and is ruled by them, whereas an elemental being is composed of the purest element to which it does belong. According to our estimation of time, the duration of life of such a being is, probably longer but, in return, it has no immortal spirit. As a rule such a being is ressolved into its element again. Let us disregard the description of details, for a while, because the magician will learn everything by practical experiences. He will be able to do so by transference of his spirit. The magician is bound to understand how to transfer himself to the kingdom of the elements to contact the beings there. Later he will even manage to rule over these beings. In my next work entitled "Practice of magical evocation" I shall, in a particular chapter, treat the problem of summoning such beings to come to our material world.

First of all, the magician has to realise that the kingdom of the elements has nothing to do with our material world and that, consequently, he cannot transfer himself there, without being previously qualified to do so. On the other hand, an elemental being can come to an understanding only with a congener, a fact which ought to be considered most carefully. A bird is well matched only with another bird. In the same way, an elemental being will have an understanding only with a congeneric being, i. e., a being of the same element. Provided it should like to come in contact with a human being, it would be bound to adopt a human shape and human qualities to approach man in form of man. At this point, the magician will realize why he did have to perform transmutation exercises in the previous steps. A gnome will never understand a human being, and so it will be the other way round. When operating this way, either the magician has to become a gnome, or else the gnome has to be transmuted in a human being. Consequently, wishing to enter the kingdom of the earth-sprites, the magician will have to take the shape of a gnome.

If he can't imagine what a gnome does look like, he must use his faculty of clairvoyance whether in a trance or try to see the shape of a gnome with the help of the magic mirror. He will notice that gnomes are very tiny sprites, similar to the brownies described in the fairy-tales. Generally they are portrayed as dwarfs with long beards and caps, with long hair, bright eyes and garbed in little cowls.

Such or similar will be the appearance of the gnome the magician will see in his magic mirror. He will also notice that every sprite is carrying a little lamp of different luminous force in order to find his way in the subterranean kingdom. If, by means of his magic mirror, the clairvoyant magician has convinced himself of the gnomes' shape, he only has to mentally take the shape of a gnome. Moreover, he must identify himself with the earth-element, i. e., load his whole shape with the earth-element, without high accumulation. Now, the magician has to imagine nothing else but to sink down into the subterranean realm viz. the earth. Suddenly he will feel deep darkness surrounding him everywhere. His imagination forms a lamp illuminating the darkness with its bright light. At first, he will not discern very much, but repeating this experiment several times, his eyes will become accustomed to this dimness so that he will discriminate beings in his own shape wishing to contact him. And after a lot of attempts, he will see the sprite folk more distinctly; he will even have the opportunity of seeing them diligent in their business. But be on your guard against speaking to them. Do not ask a question, before any of the sprites has addressed you. It may happen that, in the course of the mutual work, the magician has watched something he might be tempted to criticize. He may be cautioned against doing so, for the earth-sprites would overpower him instead of his bringing them under his control, which ought to be the purpose of this experiment. In such an occurrence, it might happen that by their various magical tricks the gnomes could captivate him by means of the element, so that he would become a gnome himself, unable to return into his own body. Then, after a certain time, the mental bond between the astral and the physical body would break asunder which would mean the physical death. A medical expert would, in such a case, find out death from heart-attack, nothing more. But the magician who, in the course of his magical training, has obtained the necessary self-control, and considers this law has nothing to fear. On the contrary, as soon as the gnomes begin to talk themselves, they see in him a being higher in rank and superior to them and will try to make friends with him. This law forbidding to address gnomes first, is only meant for the first visits, later on, if the sprites are convinced of the magician's superiority in willpower and intelligence, they will enjoy it and become his most obedient servants.

The earth-sprites are nearest to man and like to serve him, especially if they recognise his superiority. Visits to the kingdom of the gnomes should be repeated as often as there is to be seen something new. He can learn a great deal from the gnomes and not one book in the whole wide world can reveal so many secrets about the subterranean kingdom to him as he can hear in the world of the gnomes. For example, the magician can get a great deal of knowledge about the power and the effect of different herbs, he can learn how to achieve a magical spell on certain stones, he can be informed about hidden treasures and other strange things. He will be witness of everything that happens and exists below the surface of the earth such as springs, coal, minerals, etc. Besides, from the gnomes the magician may learn several magic tricks which can be exploited through the earth-element. In course of time, the magician will notice that there are different groups of intelligences among the earth-sprites in the world of the gnomes.

He will meet gnomes who are able to give him a lecture on alchemy. When at last the magician feels quite at home in the kingdom of gnomes, and when he made all the experiments which these beings were able to teach him, then he is allowed to visit the kingdom next to it, namely that of the water-sprites or water-nymphs. In the very same way he may look for a water-sprite in his magical mirror, and he will find that there exists a significant likeness to a human being. There is hardly any difference to be noticed neither in shape nor in size. Usually the water-sprites—called generally nixies, mermaids, or water-nymphs—are very attractive females although there are male water-sprites, mermen, too. As for visits to the kingdom of water, it is not absolutely neccessary to adopt the shape of a woman; it is entirely up to the magician to transmute himself imaginatively into a mermaid. There is an advantage here: he will not be molested so much by the mermaids, because they are not only fascinating and dashingly beautiful, but also very obtrusive and sexy.

Providing the magician is mentally prepared, so that he has impregnated his spirit with water, he may transfer himself to a big lake or to the ocean, wherever he likes to, and submerge down to the bottom of the water. Here, as well, he will not at once meet the water-sprites, but repeating the experiment many times and according to his vivid desire for communicating with these beings, he will finally attract them. At first, he will only see female beings moving about in the same free attitude as human beings do. He will hardly meet an unpleasant mermaid; in spite of the fact that all mermaids are very beautiful, he might, indeed, happen to meet the more intelligent ones, the so-called royal leaders, since here likewise a very peculiar class-consciousness does exist. The magician will notice that they do not dance all the time as they are generally supposed to do, but that they do a certain amount of work, too. It's no use to write more about this theme, the magician will convince himself of. Here as well goes the rule that nobody must ever address one of the mermaids first, but he has to wait until the being starts talking or asking him questions about something. From the intelligent leaders the magician can learn such a lot about the water-element that he could write books himself. He gets information about the life of fish, about the different water-plants, the stones below the water and about other magic tricks related with the water-elements. But beware of the beauty of these beings! The magician be seriously warned not to fall madly in love with a mermaid and not to lose his balance. A love like this could become fateful for him. That does not exactly mean that he is not allowed to have fun with the mermaids. But he must certainly keep the motto in mind, love being the law, but love under a strong will. A mermaid is quite capable to fascinate the magician with her incredible beauty, charm and intoxicating erotism so much that he is in serious danger of becoming one of the kind, a fact which would cause his physical death undoubtedly. How many magicians have been wrecked by an unhappy love! Therefore the magician should remain firm commanding his own passions, because it's this kingdom in the sphere of elements that is the most attractive one and if the magician gave way to his passions, he would fall into the hands of the mermaids for good and all.

As soon as the magician can manage to visit the kingdom of the water-sprites as often as he likes to and if he has learned whatever concerns the knowledge of magic, he can pay his attention to the kingdom next to it, the one of the aerial spirits.

In contrast to the water-kingdom whose inhabitants, the mermaids or the nixies, like very much to communicate with human beings, the air-sprites are very shy and unsociable. Similar to the water-sprites, they have beautiful, dashing figures and, though male beings may be seen, most of them are females. Here the magician does not have to adopt a shape suitable for the air-spirits, he can impregnate his own spirit with the air-element and transfer himself imaginatively into the region of air, wishing for the air-spirits to contact him. He ought not to lose patience, if he does not succeed for a while, but he has to keep his mind constantly on his desire to see the air-spirits at any price. He will notice at first that the beings avoid to meet him, a fact which is not to discourage him. Finally he will see the most beautiful beings with a gorgeous etheric body, soft and supple. The magician must mentally imitate the air-spirits by moving about, as it were floating, carried by the air. Not long from now, the air-spirits will address him. Here, likewise, the magician be cautioned against addressing any of the beings first, lest the same ill fate should befall him as described previously. If, after repeated experiments, the contact with the air-sprites has been established, the magician will be informed by them about whatever concerns the air-element. He will be taught many magic secrets and practices which no man living would have the least inkling of.

Being fully acquainted with the air-element and its beings, and mastering the magic technique, the magician may proceed to the spirits of the fire-element which he will have to contact now. These beings have a certain likeness to human beings, but they are rather odd in some ways, and it is therefore advisable, for the magician to get an impression of these beings with the help of a magic mirror. He will notice that the fire-spirits have a much smaller face than men and an extraordinarily long and thin neck. He will therefore transfer himself imaginatively into the shape of a fire-sprite, loading it with the pure fire-element, and off he goes to the spirits sphere into a crater or a volcano, the most remarkable homestead of the fire-spirits. From what we stated before, the magician will have noticed that the beings of the air are restless and move about constantly. All the same may be applied to the fire-sprites which everywhere are roaming as nervous and fidgety, as the element they belong to. The magician ought not to forget the rule of not talking first to any of the beings. Here, there are likewise different groups of intelligences and the "high-brows" among these fire-spirits are those whose outer appearance is more beautiful. The highest ranks of these organisms are the most similar to man, and it is obvious that the magician will try to come into contact with the most intelligent of them. As for the practice of magic, he will learn a great deal about what can be accomplished with the fire-element. If the magician is now sufficiently acquainted with the fire-spirits and their leaders in the craters, so that they taught him all he wanted to know, he may be allowed to visit those of the fire-organisms who, living in the deepest centre of the earth, have a profounder knowledge. Not before having exhausted all possible sources of information about the fire-element, he may, with a good conscience, regard himself sovereign of all the elements.

There is one conviction which the magician will win, while visiting all the element-organisms, namely, however great the intelligence and knowledge of these sprites may be, they are still composed of one single element, whereas Man represents all four elements and moreover the fifth viz. the principle of God. Now he will understand why the Bible says that Man is the most perfect of all beings, created by God in his own image. This is the reason of the discontent of all the elemental organisms at the sight of Man's immortality, toward which all of them feel envy. It is understandable that each elemental being seeks to obtain immortality, and a magician is in a position to bestow such an opportunity on them Unfortunately it is not possible, for the time being, to particularize how all this is brought about, but it can be taken for granted that the magician will, by now, intuitively find out all by himself.

It is obvious that the magician will transfer all the experiences made, through his contact with other creatures, into his memory, that is, into the physical body and he will also be able to use these experiences, changed into practice, on the material plane as well. A magician like this will be able, in the magic of nature, to execute the most astounding performances under the nose of a layman.

After the magician's further progress in profoundly knowing and practically controlling the four elemental kingdoms, he may try to come into contact with his spiritual teacher, his guru or genius. As mentioned previously with respect to the passive communication with the world Beyond, Man was given by the Divine Providence a guardian angel or genius directing his mental development and watching over it. Here for the first time, man came into passive contact with his genius. But thanks to his clairvoyance, he could see his genius either when in trance or in his magic mirror, if he wished to contact him. But now he has advanced as far as to establish a visible connexion with his genius on the mental plane. The practical performance is not difficult, provided the genius did not make himself known already formerly to a magician mastering the mental wandering perfectly. The practice of the visible connexion with the genius needs only one thing, that is, to stand upright and to feel imaginatively grasped and carried off with a whirling motion in the air. Instead of being whirled into the air, one can imagine oneself the other way round, too, that is, being as light as a feather, and being pushed off the earth. This is left to the concentration of every individual. After several attempts the magician will find out by himself, which method is best suitable for him. If, thus, the magician is ascending mentally, he is climbing higher and higher until the earth looks like a small star and, while being completely removed from the globe and floating in the universe, he concentrates on the wish that his guide might appear before him or he might be drawn towards the guide. If not instantly, certainly after some trials, the guide or guardian angel or whatever you may call him, will become visible to the magician. The first meeting with his spiritual leader will make a deep impression on the magician, since, henceforth, he has the opportunity of mutual intercourse from mouth to mouth, from ear to ear. First of all, he will ask his genius when, how and under which conditions he can contact him at any time.

Every scholar, then, has of course to obey the instructions of the leader. From now, the guru is taking over the magician's guidance. As soon as the connexion with the guru has been established, the magician will enter the last phase of his mental development, and as the physical world has nothing more to offer and to say to him, he will visit other spheres. He will manage this in the same manner by ascending straight as a dart from the earth, concentrating on the sphere he wishes to visit, and according to his will, being attracted by the sphere. As there does not exist any perception of time and space for his spirit, he can visit any sphere instantly, either alone or in company of his leader. According to the quabbalistic tree of life, he will reach, in turns, first the sphere of the Moon, next the one of Mercury, then that of Venus, of the Sun, Mars, Jupiter and finally the sphere of Saturn. On all spheres he will meet the organisms living there, and he will learn to know all about their laws and secrets. If the magician has gone so far as to he able to visit the universe, that is, the spheric planetary system of the organisms and to master it, his mental training is completed. He has grown to be a perfect magician, he is a Brother of the Light, a true adept who has achieved a great deal but not yet all.

Magic Psychic Training (X)

In the theoretic part of this course I alluded to the notion of God, and the magician who has made appreciable progress in his development can start on the meditation of this concept of God. Before he begins to work through this last chapter of his development, he has to examine whether or not he is already mastering the psychical training of all the previous steps, whether he has accomplished the magic balance and ennobled his psychic personality to such a degree that the Godhead can live in it. Many religions are talking about the practical connexion with God, giving expression to the personal point of view that this connexion can be established already by addressing God in the form of a prayer, of adoration, or of giving thanks to God. The magician, of course, who has trod the stony path of development up to here, is not at all satisfied with a statement like this. God is, for the magician, the highest, all the most true, the most lawful concept that exists. For this particular reason, right at the beginning of his initiation, the magician learnt to respect this lawfulness regarding the universal laws, and he did observe it, since the conception of God has to be interpreted as an outcome of this universal lawfulness. Whichever may be the spiritual group the would-be magician belongs to, he may be a Christian, a Jew, a Buddhist, a Mohammedan, a Hindoo, a Brahman, or whatever be his creed or his path to initiation, he has to respect this universal lawfulness in his conception of God without exception. The Christian will worship our Lord Jesus Christ as his highest ideal attributing to him the four fundamental qualities or basic aspects which are manifest in the omnipresence. These four fundamental qualities are: Omnipotence, wisdom or omniscience, all-love or charity and immortality. The magician will not regard his Christ as a manifestation endowed with one quality only, but, regarding the universal laws in analogy to the four elements, he will revere him as the highest Divinity. The same may be applied to the followers of Buddhism or any other religion. Provided the magician does work correctly after having matured in magic, he will establish his God-principle on these four fundaments with their basic qualities corresponding to the elements, and these four fundamental aspects of his Deity will represent his highest concept of God. The concept of his God has not to be linked to any person living or having lived, it can be also expressed in a symbolic way. Fundamentally it is absolutely the same thing, whether the magician does think of Christ, Buddha, a Devi, a sun, a light or a flame as being a symbol of his supreme Godhead. It is not the imagination that matters, here, but the quality he does impute to this imagination. In any case, to a magician of whatever religious faith or ideology, the imagination of God has to be the highest, the dearest, the most precious and the most venerable of all things above which there cannot be any kind of "Super-God". The communication with his God can be effected by the magician in four different ways:

1. in the mystical passive manner,
2. in the magic active manner,
3. in the concrete manner and,
4. in the abstract manner.

The true magician ought to be master of all these four methods and it is left to him which of them he will choose for his future permanent connexion.

The mystical passive manner of unity with God is a privilege granted to most of the Saints and all the believers to whom the Divine principle manifested itself somehow in ecstasy. As the magician does not know in which form God will manifest himself to him, the kind of manifestation will be expressed according to his religious faith. In the instance of a Christian, this may happen in the form of a symbol such as a white dove for the Holy Spirit, in the person of Christ himself or in the shape of a cross; all this is, however, of secundary importance. The main point is the quality of the Divinity which manifests itself to the respective person. How strong and pervasive this manifestation of God to the individual will be, depends entirely on the measure of his mental and psychical maturity. This kind of manifestation will be experienced by all persons in whom a state of bodily rapture or ecstasy has been produced by deep meditation or by prayers. All the mystics, theosophists, bhakti-yogis, etc., regard this kind of manifestation of God as the attainment of their aims. As history offers so numerous instances of this mystic unity with Christ-God, I deem it superfluous to dwell on minute details.

The second kind of revelation of God is the magic-active one, peculiar to most of the magicians. The well-trained magician will try to come near or in touch with his deity by invocation. This kind, too, may be spoken of as a form of ecstasy which, however, in contrast to the previously described concomitant manifestation, is being produced deliberately, step by step. In this kind of manifestation, the interior that is, the spiritual part of the magician rises up to God half-way and the latter comes to meet him half-way down. This invocation of the Deity, in the magic active manner, is a "theurgic", or a real magic form which a magician is allowed to use only, when he has gained the right measure of maturity. The manner of invocation is absolutely individual, because there does not exist any concrete method.

The mystical-passive as well as the magic-active invocation of God can again be carried out in a concrete or an abstract form. The concrete invocation imagines God in a certain shape, whereas the abstract invocation is based on the imagination of the abstract idea of the divine qualities. The practice of the possible Divine revelations is very simple. Supposing the magician is meditating in the akasha-principle, that is, in a state of trance, about his God and his qualities, and when the expected symbol of God makes its appearance during this meditation, then one can speak of a mystical-passive kind of revelation. But, when the magician, with the help of his plastic meditation, whether outside or inside of himself, does invoke the single qualities of his Deity, regardless of his imagining these qualities in a concrete or an abstract form, then it all turns out to be a magical-active invocation of God. He whose development has reached this point, can attain not only to the mystic passive, but also to the magic active union with God. I myself prefer the methods of the concrete and abstract forms which can be managed by every magician. An excellent exercise preliminary to the concrete manifestation of the Deity is to put a picture, a figure or any symbol of the respective Deity in front of oneself. The magician is sitting in his asana posture staring intensively at the picture, until an effigy of his God will appear before his closed eyes. While, staring at the picture of the Godhead, the magician is worshipping, he can again perceive it, afterwards, on any white surface near by. This visualization of the Godhead is an excellent prelude allowing the magician to make the image of God appear before him.

This preliminary step is to be repeated, until the magician is capable to imagine his Deity as being alive, at any time, in any position, at any place, without the slightest effort. Then he can combine the picture he did imagine with the corresponding Divine qualities. At first, he will not at once succeed in coordinating all the four Divine fundamental qualities he has been meditating about in the previous step, with the picture of his imagination. He will, therefore, concentrate on one quality after the other. The concretisation of the Divine quality in the imagined picture is very important and has to be repeated so many times, until the magician's deity can be actually perceived by him as endowed with the four fundamental qualities. If the magician did achieve this, he must imagine the object of his adoration not as a mere picture, but as a living being, acting, irradiating with such an intensity, as if his personal God were standing real and alive, in front of him. This is the so-called concrete union with the Godhead outside the own Self. The more frequently the magician is following this method, the stronger and the more effective will be the visual and sensuous Deity before him. When he feels to have put all he knows about God's conception and realization into the object (picture) of his invocation, then he may think of his living Deity which appears before his eyes, with all the brilliance of the four basic qualities, as filling and entering his body, thus occupying the place of his soul.

This has to be repeated by the magician, until he feels the Godhead so strong in himself that, losing his personal consciousness, he gets the sensation, as if he himself were the Deity he had imagined. By frequently repeating this union with the Godhead, the magician adopts the qualities condensed in his imagination, and now it is no more the personal Self that is acting through him, but his Godhead is doing so. Thus he is experiencing the concrete union with God, union with his personal God, and it is no more his consciousness, his soul or his spirit, but the manifestation of God's Spirit that is speaking through his mouth. Here the magician is uniting himself with his God, becoming God himself, for the time of the duration of this unity, sharing all the basic qualities of the Godhead he is united with.

The method of the realized union with God is of utmost importance for the magic practice, since a magician ought to be able to contact any Godhead whatever, irrespective of the creed, in this manner. In theurgy as well as in the conjuring magic, this practice is indispensable, as it is the only way for the magician to bring about this union with a Godhead at any time, forcing the lower beings to execute his will. It is evident that, in this manner, a magician can unite himself with the God-principle to such an extent that all the properties and powers dwelling in the realized Godhead he is psychically united with, will become his own too, and continue, as it were, being his qualities, even if he is not bound to the image of the deity any more. This goes without saying. Such Divine qualities are called by the adepts magic capacities or powers or Siddhis.

If the magician masters the performance of the concrete union with his Godhead, he is going to realize the abstract form of the unity with God. In the beginning, he may link the conception of God to an auxiliary conception such as light or fire, but later on, he must refrain from doing so, projecting nothing else but the quality first outside, then inside of the own Self. Now, the aspect of the Divine quality has to be connected to the organ corresponding to the elements in a manner that e. g. omnipotence is, in the abstract, experienced in the head, or love in the heart. By repeating this exercise frequently, one becomes identified with the abstract idea of God to such a degree that there is no need of any imagination of a region or of a part of the body. Next, the four basic qualities can be combined into one idea which permits the introspection of the highest form of our conception of God. By repetitions, God's manifestation is deepened so much that one feels oneself God. So deep must be this unity with God that, during the meditation, there is no God, neither within myself, nor without, subject and object being molten into one another, so that there is nothing but: "I am God" or as the Indian in his Vedas puts it: "Tat twam asi—That Thou art."

Arrived at this stage, the magician has completed his magical development in the astral form, and any further exercises will serve the purpose to deepen his meditations and to strengthen his godliness.

Communication with Godheads

When the magician has advanced so far in his incarnation of God that he can communicate with any deity, any intelligence, with every higher divine being, then he is able to work in every sphere he wishes to, not as a magician but as a God.

Herewith the magic psychical training of the last step has come to an end. I have nothing more to say to the magician in this direction, because he did become one with God, and anything he will express or order, during his unity with God, will be just the same as if God himself did say it. Henceforth, he partakes of all the four basic qualities of his Godhead he is united with.

Magic Physical Training (X)

Brahma and Shakti

He who knows other systems of initiation will find a certain parallel with my system since all paths leading to truth must be the same. Let me mention, here, the Indian Yoga-system concerning the snake power which is in accordance with the systems of the Egyptian mysteries I have quoted. In Kundalini-Yoga the scholar is exhorted to meditate on the Muladhara-centre, the seat of which is in the coccyx and to perform there Pranayama exercises. If we look closely at the symbolism of the Muladhara-centre, we shall find that this centre has the shape of a yellow-coloured square with a red triangle in it. The centre of it is a phallus, the male genital, three and a half times swathed with a snake. The muladhara-centre is the first, most primitive and grossest centre which is symbolised by an elephant placed in a corner together with the respective goddess.

This symbolic expression, called Laya-Yoga in India is unequivocal, and means the key for the first stage of yoga. There are several explanations of this sign, but the correct one is, that the square represents the earth, the triangle the three peaks or kingdoms namely the material, the astral and the mental world—, the phallus the generative power or the imagination, and the serpent the path and the knowledge. The fact is well known to the scholar that the earth-principle is composed of four elements, and it does not need any comment. The growing yogi has first to learn to know and to control the three worlds, namely, the material one, the astral-psychical and the mental-spiritual world.

The muladhara-chakra is, consequently, nothing else but an initiating diagram corresponding to the first tarot-card. Such an unsophisticated definition like this has never been given in India, and it is left to the scholar to find out by himself, if he can master the muladhara-centre, that means, if he has accomplished the development corresponding to the muladhara-diagram on his spiritual path. The muladhara-centre has not for nothing been called the Brahma-centre, because, in this phase of development, the yogi scholar recognises Brahma, consequently the Godhead in the most subtle manifestation. Brahma is the eternal, the inscrutable, the universal, the indefinable, the steady and the calm, therefore, the positive part. Brahma does not create out of himself, but all that has been created has been done so by his Shakti, the female principle. Shakti, therefore, in the muladhara-centre represents the serpent winding round the phallus and using the creative power of the latter, namely, the imagination. A lot more could be said about this centre, but the experienced magician will be satisfied with these hints to understand that a parallel does exist between religious and initiating systems. Consequently, the Shakti or the Kundalini power represents the imagination which the magician has to develop systematically. Casting a retrospective glance at our entire developmental system the magician will certainly find that it is just this creative power of the phallus, namely, the imagination and its development which are playing the main role in his training.

I have already finished the magic physical training in the ninth step, therefore I will restrict myself to discuss some occult powers in the following chapter. Although the magician will not necessarily have to master all of them, nothing must come as a surprise to him in his development, and he ought to have the correct explanation for every occult phenomenon.

Suggestion

In the chapter concerning the subconsciousness I have been talking about this theme in the way of describing the self-suggestion. These instructions go for the suggestion of other people, too. What is necessary, here, is to utter the suggestion formula strictly in the present tense and in the imperative form.

A magician will always transfer the desired suggestion into the subconsciousness in the case of somebody who has the mental maturity not yet. The suggestion has not always to be induced aloud, it can also be performed by telepathy. It is very easy, indeed, for a magician to practice suggestion at the greatest distance. He can do so in two ways, whether visiting the subject in question mentally in order to influence him, best while he is asleep, or also removing the distance between himself and the subject, with the help of akasha, in order to work with suggestion. It is obvious that any long distance suggestion can also be carried out with a magic mirror. The effect of a suggestion can also be timed, i. e., any suggestion may be given in such a way as to be carried out at a fixed moment in the future, too, the time of the suggested effect having been transferred to the subconsciousness of the subject.

Telepathy

Akin to suggestion is the field of telepathy. It is certainly a mere trifle for a magician to suggest his thoughts to any person. All he needs to consider is the fact that he has to transmit the thoughts not to the body nor to the soul but simply to the spirit of the subject. He imagines the subject's spirit, omitting the material and the astral body, dealing only with its spirit, to which he transfers the thought. Here it is entirely left to the magician, whether to suggest to the subject that it is his—the magician's—thought or that of any other person, or else to allow the subject to think it to have been his own idea. Not only ideas but feelings as well can be transferred at close quarters or at the greatest distance. The magician ought never to forget to transmit good and noble thoughts only, with the help of his magic powers. I am quite convinced that no scholar or magician will degrade himself to any kind of misuse. Naturally thoughts can also be suggested against the will of a person. Mastering the elements the magician can wipe out the thoughts of the subject who is to be influenced, by way of telepathy, suggesting him thoughts which might appear desirable to the magician.

Hypnosis

Another field very similar to telepathy and suggestion is that of hypnosis by which a person is sent to sleep forcibly and is deprived of the own free will. From the magical point of view hypnosis is reprehensible and it would be better not to specialise in this line. This does not mean that the magician is not capable to lull people to sleep. The practice is imaginably simple. The magician need only suspend the function of the spirit, by means of his will or with the help of the electro-magnetic fluid, and the person will instantly fall asleep. Here it is less important, whether the magician is using telepathy or suggestion. He can use both of them as a makeshift but he does not depend on them. Nearly all the books which have been written about hypnosis do recommend the use of telepathy and suggestion. A master of the powers does need neither one nor the other, because the very moment he does not take any notice of the body and soul of the test-person, paralysing his will by way of imagination, sleep or unconsciousness will occur instantly, which will set free the subconsciousness making it susceptive of any kind of suggestions. Just this act of violence, i. e., the intervention in the individuality of a human being is not recommended from a magic point of view, and the magician will not resort to it unless to give his subject good and noble suggestions with an extremely strong effect. Even though the test-person should insist on being hypnotized by the magician, he should avoid to do so, if possible. The true magician will always keep away from satisfying the curiosity of others by hypnotic experiments. At times of great danger, a well-trained magician may induce a sort of shock-hypnosis by paralyzing the spirit of the opponent by a flash of the electro-magnetic fluid, a method which is only to be followed in an emergency which, I hope sincerely will never happen in the life of any magician. It has been proved scientifically that animals can be hypnotized, too. If a magician wants to do so, he will hit the instinctive side of the animal, so that even the biggest and strongest animals are immediately knocked senseless.

The mass-hypnosis induced by Indian fakirs and jugglers which meets with so many admirers is no problem at all to the magician. The fakirs engaged in these performances generally do not know themselves how such phenomena are brought about, their secret being a matter of tradition, handed down from one generation to the other. Supposing a certain spot, room, and so on, is being loaded with the akasha-principle, all the bystanders are likewise pervaded by the akasha, too, and this principle will prevail in all of them. Whatever has been induced in the akasha-principle, has to be necessarily realised, since akasha is the ultimate cause. In the light of this law, the mass-hypnosis produced by the fakirs performing their shows in front of a crowd, can be understood without any difficulty. The magician can do exactly the same things. With a traditional word or a formula, the fakir calls akasha into the room transferring the pictures which the audience wish to see, into this principle. By repeating this experiment so many times, it has already become automatical, so that the fakir has to apply neither to the imagination and the akasha, nor to the act the spectators want to see. It is sufficient for him to utter the akasha-formula to hold people spell-bound, and afterwards he only needs to express the desired occurence packed into short sentences or tantras, and so on, in a low voice, in turns, and the audience will perceive one picture after the other in the same order. The fact that these formulas are genuine incantations sounds absolutely credible, since such a secret is traditionally handed down from family to family for hundreds of years. Not even the owner of such a formula does exactly know what sort of powers he is going to release. All he knows is, this or that will happen if he expresses the respective words, and he does not bother his head about the cause of it. Performances like these are very much admired, indeed, mainly by people who haven't got the faintest idea of the higher laws of magic. In India such a performance of an illusionist is nothing else but a mere money-matter. Making a snap-shot of an experiment like this would bring about a great disappointment, because nothing at all would be seen on the plate or film, nothing of the marvellous scenes but the fakir and his partner, sitting quiet there and smiling a polite smile. This seemingly miraculous experiment is easily explained in the light of the magic laws and, therefore, it must be left to the individual to work at such things or even to specialise in them. But for the magician's development and rise, such experiments are absolutely useless. I only did mention them to put the magician in the picture and let him find the explanation from the magical point of view.

Thought-reading

A lot of publicity has been made about the problem of thought-reading. This seems to be a matter of course for the magician and he is regarding it as a concomitant of inferior value for his mental development. Thought-reading can be performed by pictures, intuitions, inspirations, and so on, according to the mental attitude of the magician. It is not necessary to underline the fact that a subject's thoughts can be read not only if he is close by the magician, but also at a far distance, which is nothing else but the result of working in the akasha. Every idea, every word and every act does find its exact pattern in the akasha. Cf. the chapter dealing with this akasha problem! If the magician does concentrate on the spirit of the person in question, loading himself with akasha, he can read the actual thoughts, and if he looks back with his innermost desire, he can also read the thoughts of the remotest past without any effort. As soon as he has achieved a certain skill in thought-reading, after a rather long training, he will be capable to read any thought, even the most hidden one. The forming of thoughts is an intellectual or imaginative act. Imaginative thoughts are easier to be read. A perfect kind of thought-reading can be obtained only, if the magician has gained the absolute mastery over his spirit and, therefore, over his world of ideas, too. This is the fundamental condition. Otherwise, he will be able to read thoughts only partially or only, if they are effective ones. Thought-reading is no problem at all, it requires the contact from mind to mind, the magician has to feel himself a spirit, (the exercises of the previous steps should have given him sufficient help in this direction) and all he needs to do is to establish the connexion between himself and the person in question, by imagining the subject's body and soul as not being there, in order to seize all the thoughts he wants to know.

Psychometry means the faculty to read the present time as well
as the past and—if it should be essential—the future, too, of any
object whatever, a letter, a gem, an antiquity, and so on investi-
gating all the events related, at whatever period, with this object.
This ability is a concomitant of developed astral senses and easy
to be managed, if the magician has undergone all the practical
training taught during this course, and if he has learned how to
use his astral senses in seeing, hearing and feeling. All he has to do
is to take the object which is to be investigated into his hand or
to put it on that part of the body which is important for the
exploration. If he wishes to see the happenings in pictures, that
means, to investigate them visually, he ought to press the object
on his forehead, if he wants to perceive them acoustically, he must
put it in the region of the heart and if he wishes to search out the
object intuitively or emotionally, he must bring it close to the
solar-plexus, or he simply holds the object in his hand. After concentrating on what he really does want to know, he induces akasha
or a trance, and now he is capable to read the different events of
the past, present or future with his mental eyes, ears or the feeling.
The magician is also allowed to use his magic mirror. In this
manner, he can, say, from an antique object, unroll all the events
connected with it, like in a motion-picture, and he will learn all
related anyhow with the object. Naturally, he has got the opportunity, too, from every letter addressed to him or to other people
by persons known or unknown, to see not only the sender but also
the thoughts which happen to be in the person's mind at the given
time. He can, to put it in a nutshell, read between the lines of
any letter.

To the field of psychometry also belongs the faculty to communicate with any person that came in touch with any object,
because an object—no matter of which nature is happens to be—
does always represent the connecting link between the body, spirit
and soul of the magician and the person in question. No doubt
that the magician is able to read thoughts with the help of an
object even at the greatest distance. At the same time, he is capable
to learn all about the psychical side of the person concerned, and
to detect the qualities of the character and the mental development
in the world of akasha without any effort. The same can be said,
of course, about the material side, and he can fathom the past,
the present and the future, once he has established the communica-

tion between his spirit and the one of the person with respect to akasha.

A variant of psychometry is psychography, but it is of little importance to a magician, which results from what I just have said. Through the connecting link not only the sender of a letter can be detected in all phases of his existence, but the object itself can serve to establish the contact with the respective person, influencing him mentally or physically and psychically. From these arguments it has become patent that psychometry is nothing else but a subvariety of clairvoyance which has already been dealt with in a previous chapter.

Memory suggestion

As we know, memory is an intellectual property possessed by every human being whose normal five senses are intact. But at the same time the memory is the receiver of thoughts and ideas from the mental and, consequently, from the akasha-world as well. We know that all thoughts and ideas are transferred to the akasha, and that the memory, thanks to its receptive quality, does call back these ideas from the akasha and the mental sphere to the consciousness. Being quite at home in the akasha, the magician is capable to influence the memory in a direct or an indirect way. The direct way is to reinforce the memory by means of the corresponding element or the electro-magnetic fluid or by mere influence on the subconsciousness with the help of the imagination. But when working on the memory, he can, if he wishes so, wipe out, or weaken or diminish certain ideas and impressions in the consciousness and, consequently, in the memory by means of his imagination. The indirect way of influencing the memory is to do so indirectly, with the help of the akasha-principle. The magician seeing everybody's train of thoughts and pictures in the akasha, can evidently make them fade away, destroying the connexion between the pictures in akasha and the person concerned, with the help of the imagination. Because the magician has the possibility of depriving every person of the memory, in this manner, he may be warned seriously against misusing this strong power. Nobody who is aspiring to ethical development will be persuaded to do a deed like this.

The magician will certainly utilize this faculty only, when he wants to weaken or to wipe out anyone's bad experiences or occurences which did leave deep impressions on the person's memory. The magician can do all the good in the world by effacing a deep sorrow or a disappointment a person cannot get over. He can experiment with it in his own life as well, provided he did once suffer from mental shocks or bitter disappointments, perhaps before his magical development, which keep on coming back to his memory. Such pictures will never enter his memory again, once they have been wiped out in akasha. But if he does manage to master these remembrances by his will, by self-suggestion or other methods, there is no need of a drastic interference with akasha to have these pictures wiped out for good and all. The pathologic loss of memory can be explained by the fact that the connexion with the mental world and, therefore, with akasha, too, became paralysed from time to time. But this condition is already a disharmony, an illness, a mental disturbance if it did occur as the result of different causes such as a shock and the like.

Working in the akasha

In the same way as the memory can be influenced and certain remembrances be wiped out with the help of akasha (which I explained in the previous chapter), the magician is capable to obliterate not only certain ideas and recollections but also certain causes which are registered in the akasha and turn out as influences of the fate, on himself or on other people, provided he has got the correct motivation. Supposing he wipes out a cause which the subject did create himself, he has to establish another cause in place of the one he wiped out, which is destined to have a corresponding effect on the fate of the person in question. This interference in man's life must not happen for frivolous reasons whether the magician himself or other people be concerned. The magician can intervene in such a manner only, if he can take the full responsibility for his action before the Divine Providence. Wiping out a cause and creating a new one, whether a favourable or an unfavourable one, is best done with the help of an electro-magnetic "volt", a practice which has been described in detail under the head of physical training in the ninth step. There are some more methods yet, but all of them are based on the willpower and the respective imagination, and the magician can determine them after his own free will. The fact that a magician can change fate wiping out its cause and with it, the sins as well (sins so far as regarded in the religious way, for sins are nothing but moral views of religions) has been pointed out by our Lord Jesus Christ when he said: "To whom I forgave the sins, they will be forgiven for ever!"

Long-distance impregnation of rooms

I talked previously already about the impregnation of a room in which the magician himself happens to be, and I also recommended several implements, such as the magic mirror combined with a fluid condenser. One fact I did not mention, up to now, is that the magician can impregnate a room at a distance, too. There are two ways to do so, firstly the magician does visit the room in his spirit or in his astral body, performing the desired impregnation there with the help of his imagination. Here, of course, hold good the same instructions I did give in the chapter concerning the room-impregnation. The second possibility is linking this room to the room the magician is living in, with the help of akasha, so that the two rooms are becoming one room in the akasha. In consequence of thus connecting the two rooms, the greatest distance will, of course, be bridged. Whatever the magician is impregnating his own room with, is naturally passing over to the other room, too, irrespective of its distance.

Messages through the air

This kind of transmission is in general use in the Orient and mainly in Tibet between magicians and adepts. If the distance, however great it be, between a person or a room has been bridged through the akasha-principle, thus spanning time and space, a person communicated in this condition with somebody is able not only to read and transfer the thoughts but also to produce and to receive physical manifestations by conveying the electro-magnetic fluid to these two bridged poles which are already linked in akasha.

In this manner, sentences spoken in the magician's room can be heard physically quite distinctly also in the room connected to the one of the magician through the akasha. If now the distant person does answer in his room, he can be heard in the magician's room as clearly as if the sender were there personally. It is essential to produce the electro-magnetic fluid in the exact way I described in the chapter about the "volt" except that it does not adopt the shape of a ball but the one of a room. Such an electro-magnetic akasha combination allows words and sentences to be spoken and transferred to the greatest distance. These messages can be heard or perceived by persons who are neither initiated nor magically trained. This method can be materialized physically to such a degree that it can produce even a material effect. The point, here, therefore is not so much to transmit ideas but physical words, a fact which is known in science as wireless transmitting and receiving. The ether in which the vibration waves of the words are moving is the akasha-principle, and the electricity necessary for it in our case, is the electro-magnetic fluid. The magician does know, of course, from experience that whatever science has produced in the physical way—no matter whether by electricity, magnetism, warmth and so on—can be accomplished with the help of magic, too.

In this manner, it is possible to transfer not only words and sound waves but also pictures. Visible, consequently, materialised pictures produced by imagination in such a magically prepared room, can be seen by people anywhere, provided they are connected acoustically with the "broadcasting studio" that is, the room in which the magician does work. Regard the modern television technique. It is evident that other more transferences, say, of feelings, smells and the like are possible by means of akasha and the electromagnetic fluid which transmit them to the greatest distance. The effects of elements can be transferred in this manner, likewise. The material ether is, by no means, exhausted already, and the future will teach us that, one day, we shall not only transmit sound-waves similar to those of the wireless, and pictures like those in television, but also other quite different powers. Here is still a wide field of activity for science, and I am sure that there will be a time when thermic waves, i. e., heat will be transferred to the greatest distance through the ether. Here the magician can start a lot of events which could be accomplished through the ether, and he will also be able to put the magic knowledge in perfect harmony with the technical arts and with chemistry. Based on the universal laws, he would be capable to make more and greater inventions, but every anticipation, as far as evolution is concerned, would certainly be fateful to the magician.

Exteriorization

The magician has learned in this course how to sever his mental and his astral body from the physical body, and the problem, therefore, does not represent anything new to him. What he ignores is the fact that he does not have to separate the whole mental or astral body, while performing this experiment, but that he can exteriorise or disconnect single parts of the body. The mental and the astral body not being confined to time or space, the magician will be able to transfer different parts of his body even to the farthest distance, as soon as he separates these parts in the akasha, with the help of imagination. For example, he will be able to transfer one or both of his eyes anywhere else, in order to get impressions, there, in exactly the same way as if he were there physically, without wasting force in transferring his whole mental or astral body. He can do the same with his mental or psychical ears in order to hear things at unlimited distances. At first, he will perform it, through imagination, with his spiritual body only and later with his astral and his mental body. In this manner, he will be capable to see and to hear anywhere, at the same time, by means of his transferred eyes and ears, without being in a state of trance or in the primary world.

As soon as he possesses a certain skill in the eye-ear practice, he can try the same experiment with his hands and, gradually, with his feet as well. He will do so mentally, at first, too, after that, in connexion with his astral hands, and condensing the latter with the help of the earth element, he can materialize them physically. It is obvious that he will be able to make himself conspicuous by these materialized hands, at a distance, causing knocking sounds and other noises. After many exercises, he can move objects, too. Naturally a lot of spooks could be performed in this manner, but a true magician will not waste his precious time with such childish tricks.

The faculty of writing at distance between living persons may be interpreted in this manner, too. Supposing a skilled magician has exteriorized his mental and his astral hand, with the help of imagination, by thinking of the hand as being somewhere else, where a piece of paper and a pencil are prepared, his mental and his astral hand can seize the partner's hand at the greatest distance and give normal messages. It is even possible to transfer the magician's correct handwriting by this experiment at an unlimited distance. This particular feat is called by adepts "Writing at distance between living persons".

If the magician has gained a certain mastery in exteriorizing his hands and feet, objects can be transferred, in the same way, at the greatest distance, too. I am going to describe, in a further chapter, how to make an object invisible. The magician will notice that he can neither hear nor see with his physical eyes, nor will he perceive anything at all that happens, while exteriorizing his eyes or ears outside his body, even if he kept his eyes open. As to the exteriorization of other limbs, the respective limb, say, the hand will remain lifeless, cataleptic, until the mental or astral limb has been re-connected with the body.

Magic of becoming invisible

In many fairy-tales the story goes that a sorcerer has made himself invisible, and that there is a peculiar ring which makes people invisible if they twist it round their finger. Many books describe talismans and gems granting the bearer the gift of invisibility, and give instructions in this line, too. But nothing of the kind is reliable nor of any use for real practice. On the other hand, based on the universal laws and on what we have learned up to now, we shall try to prove that, from the magic point of view, making invisible is a matter of fact.

To start with, we have to distinguish between a mental or spiritual, an astral or psychical, and a physical invisibility. Making the mental body, that means, the spirit invisible has no particular value, but it is, nevertheless, possible that situations will occur in life, where this practice could be useful. Suppose the magician wants to transfer himself mentally or psychically somewhere, and he does not wish to be perceived by beings of some kind or by the skilled senses of anybody else, he can utilize the mental invisibility. Take example by a Guru who wants to visit his scholar, mentally, in order to check him. Thus made invisible, the master will be quite near to the scholar, without being noticed by the scholar, even if he had already fully developed his senses. Furthermore, a magician could attend to the evil works of the so-called black magicians in order to learn everything about their doings or, if necessary, to perform a certain influence, without being noticed by these black magicians and their beings. There may be other more conditions in life where it will be advisable to resort to making invisible oneself mentally or astrally.

Becoming mentally invisible is very simple and it is accomplished by filling the mental body with akasha from head to toe. The mental body will instantly vanish out of any being's sight, since akasha is without any colour and without any vibration. If the spirit of a magician should perform any act on one of the mental planes, this would be registered in the akasha-principle, and in spite of being invisible, he could be found out in consequence of his activity, by means of clairvoyance. To prevent this, the magician has to wrap his whole body with a black cover, as soon as he has filled his mental body with akasha. It does not matter, whether this cover has the shape of a ball or of an egg. He must not forget to seclude himself from all, underneath his feet as well as above his head, completely, with akasha. Before going somewhere else, in this condition of being invisible, he ought to concentrate on the fact that his activity should be neutralized by the akasha that means, is should not be written into the akasha, i. e., leave no traces at all. This concentration is necessary, for, otherwise, the magician must fear that, though rather illegibly, several new causes might be registered in the akasha. The magician is fully responsible for every action he is, though invisible, carrying out in the mental world. Fate is no longer able to do him any harm, because he has become the master of akasha, master of his fate. Henceforward, he is merely subject to the Divine Providence. Should he misuse his knowledge for evil deeds, it would be the Divine Providence that would punish him, instead of fate. The Divine Providence would give him, so to speak, the cold shoulder and he would have to live on as a lonely individual forsaken in the universe. The only possibility of relying on the Divine Providence would be lost forever, which, to be sure of it, would be worse than any curse. Such a magician would be doomed to destruction, and he can easily realize, what that would mean from the magical point of view.

Provided one is proficient enough in making and becoming invisible in mental wandering, the same procedure can be also used in sending out the astral body. Here, as well, the practice of loading the whole personality with akasha is very much in line with the loading of the mental and the astral body together. The other measures are the same as previously described. From the magic standpoint, it is also possible to make invisible on the material plane, but, here, invisibility is not produced by akasha but by means of the light. Filling the physical body with light, it must be in harmony with the intensity of the light prevailing at that moment. If the accumulation of light were stronger than necessary, one would not become invisible, but transparent and bright, similar to the sun, shining white without and within. Physical invisibility is very difficult to be produced, it requires years of training and practice, and hardly anybody but adepts of higher, if not the highest ranks, can execute such an operation correctly.

Supposing this great skill of making invisible his mental and his astral body, eventually his physical body, too, the magician is in a position to bring about the disappearance of any material object. Another way to do this, is the transmutation of an object from the solid into the astral form, by means of imagination, in connexion with akasha. The object vanishes instantly from the sight of any person whose magic senses have not sufficiently been developed. An object transformed in the astral form, can be transferred by the astral body of any entity or of the magician himself, to any distance. The magician or the entity, performing this transference, at last, has the task of re-transferring the object from the astral condition into its physical form. This kind of object-transferrence is often practised by creatures of spiritualistic mediums, provided the point is a phenomenon based on an unmistakable materialization, although such things are extremely rare. But whatever planetary and extra-planetary intelligences may be able to perform, all this can also be done by the magician who is acquainted with the universal laws and has made good progress in his development.

There is still one method of making invisible, I mean the deviation of the senses which is practised in all kinds of hypnosis and in that form of suggestion in which entities produce a number of vibrations corresponding to that of the light in the physical body, thus effecting invisibility. Some more instructions referring to this problem will be found in my book "Practice of magical Evocation".

A great number of possibilities are offered to a magician who wishes to specialize more particularly in the use of the elements, provided he has materialized, i. e., condensed the element with which he is working, in such a manner, that the elemental power has become a real physical power. Being perfect in doing so, he can, through condensation of the earth-element in his body, produce such an invulnerability of his body that it resembles to that shown by the Indian fakirs in their performances. He is capable to run pointed objects through his muscles without feeling the slightest pain or losing a tiny drop of blood, to say nothing of a scar left. Fakir's insensitivity to pain, when lying on a nail-board is, to a certain extent, brought about by auto-suggestion, but a magician produces the same effect much faster with the help of the earth-element. He is indeed able to cure big cuts on his own or any other person's body, directly with the help of the earth-element, without leaving a scar behind. A gaping wound which normally would require a surgeon's aid, can really be healed in a few minutes. The earth-element which he is condensing, outside of his own person, enables him to condense every thought, every impression, every being—whether deceased or not embodied—to such a degree that it becomes visible to the eyes of a completely untrained person, and can even be photographed.

The magician has the great advantage of being able instantly to paralyze anybody—man or animal—even his deadly enemy by the extremely quick projection of the earth-element. There are some more possibilities of employing this element but I hope that the above remarks may be sufficient meanwhile.

The water-element, projected and condensed very strongly in itself, helps the magician to stand the greatest heat, without his body being scorched or burnt. Projected into the hands, the element permits the magician to hold red-hot coals or irons, without any damage being done to his hands. He could even stand smiling in the middle of a blazing stake, and nothing at all would happen to him. Let me draw your attention to the biblical event, where the Young Man in the red-hot oven remained unharmed. John, the favourite disciple of our Lord is said to have been immersed in a boiler with burning oil, and no harm was done to him either. The magician will now see, that events like these are not only legendary traditions, but they did really and truly take place, and such apparent miracles can be performed by mastering the elements. Every kind of fire, regardless of its extension, can be extinguished with the help of the projected and condensed water-element.

The magician can, of course, perform such almost miraculous feats with the air-element, too, in the same or a similar manner.

With the help of the fire-element the magician is able to stand the greatest cold if he does accumulate this element in himself. The lamas in Tibet can, with the help of the concentrated fire-element, produce an enormous heat in their bodies, so that they can, in no time, dry wet towels spread on their bodies in the depth of winter. This experiment is known in Tibet under the name of *tumo*. Any kind of combustible material can be lit with the help of the outwards-projected fire-element. The Bible describe similar occurences, where stakes soaked with water were set on fire by means of the fire-element. There is no doubt that a plant, for example, a tree can be made to die down, through the projection of the fire-element. Did not our Lord Jesus Christ make dry up the leaves of a fig-tree in order to give tokens of his power? He did consider the same law, performing the projection with the help of a magic word—Quabbalah—which indirectly caused the fire-element to carry out his command. Backed by the universal laws respecting the mastery of the elements, the perfect magician will bring about an amount of other magic performances with the aid of the elements.

Levitation-Phenomena

Levitation means the abolition of the law of gravitation. Based on the universal laws the magician has found out that the power of gravity depends on the magnetic attraction of the earth. The gravity of the own body can be abolished in two ways. Firstly, through constant loadings or accumulations of the air-element (Waju Tattwa), the primary quality of this element is realized to such a degree that man feels light as a feather, and as rising and floating in the air like a balloon. The second method demands the mastery of the electro-magnetic fluid. By accumulating the magnetic fluid in the body to such a degree of density as corresponds to the weight of the body, that means, the attractive power of the earth, the effect of the gravity will be neutralized altogether. In this condition of loading, the magician will hardly touch the ground and he can even move on the surface of the water quite sure, regardless of its depth. Condensing the magnetic fluid more and more, he can, at will, raise his body in the air and, by means of the condensed air-element or the self-produced movement of the air, he can be carried on in any direction. The speed of transport in the air depends entirely on his own will. Many of the yogis possess a remarkable ability in mastering these levitation-phenomena and even in the Bible we read that our Lord Jesus Christ, was walking on the surface of the sea. Considering what has been told hitherto, it seems to be quite evident that, in this manner, objects or even people who are not magically trained can be carried away by a magician if he wishes to do so.

The accumulation of the necessary magnetic fluid can be performed by the magically trained imagination or with the help of some other practices such as Quabbalah, interference of beings or, ghosts and so on. The elimination of the electric fluid in the body and the increase of the magnetic fluid can take place not only deliberately but unconsciously as well, for example, in the cases of spiritualistic mediums and somnambulists, where the electric fluid is, by trance, abolished and, in return, the magnetic fluid, increased. In consequence of a sudden loss of the electrical fluid, moonstruck people, generally, when asleep, may be overwhelmed by the magnetic fluid. Many times such moonstruck people may be observed to be able to climb a wall like a fly, or to move about on the most dangerous spots of a house or even on a wire-rope. The magnetic overloading of moonstruck subjects while being asleep can be traced back to the influence of the moon. That's why somnambulism is also called moon-madness. In any case, this condition means a disharmony, a disturbance of the electromagnetic fluid and, consequently, a pathological state, or an illness. A person afflicted in this manner can be treated only by harmonising the electric fluid which has to be increased in the sick body.

This summarized interpretation of the levitation phenomenon should, for the present, suffice to the magician, although, from the afore-mentioned arguments, he might draw the conclusion that it will also be possible to produce the opposite effect, that is, an increased attractive or gravitational power. And as a matter of fact, here the result is brought about, in the same manner, with the electric fluid instead of the magnetic one. This explanation is unequivocal if the magician takes into consideration the basic law of physics which says that like poles of two magnets repel one another just as two unlike forces attract themselves.

Phenomena of nature

The magician can, with the help of the elements and the electromagnetic fluid, produce such types of phenomena in the nature, on a large or small scale. He will, however, need more space in order to be able to project and condense the necessary powers. So by the projection of the air-element, he can influence the movement of the air, i. e., the wind or bring about pelting rain or even steady downpour by projecting the water-element. On the other hand, he can conjure thunderstorms with the help of the electromagnetic fluid, by projecting electric and magnetic "volts" in the air which, when clashing, will cause the lightning. By concentration of the magnetic fluid, he can draw the water-element even from the greatest distance, automatically, making rain in this way. Obviously he is also able to achieve the contrary effect by stopping unwelcome rainfall or by scattering the clouds. Hailstorms may as well be brought about or directed elsewhere, for, through the elements or the electro-magnetic fluid, any influence whatever can be exerted on the nature. This sort of weather-making is successfully practised by the Tibetan lamas. Thus, in this as in so many other ways, the magician knows various methods to cause these phenomena and is able to do this with his own powers after a special training, just as the Tibetan lama brings about with the help of rites, evocational magic, of beings and Tantras.

Power over life and death

A magician who is perfectly mastering the elements and the electro-magnetic fluid is also master over life and death of every human being. But he will never dare to menace the lives of his fellowmen, though he does exactly know how to induce a magical death. There would be a lot of possibilities of doing so, but I desist from quoting such methods, in order not to lead the magician into temptation. According to the universal laws, a magician of illumined spirit and perfect in mastering occult faculties and powers will also be capable to raise the deceased from the dead. Backed by his high mystical experiences and with the help of his well-trained senses, the magician can see not only the working of the elements in the body, the spirit and the soul, but also the effect of the electro-magnetic fluid, moreover he can notice the connecting bond between the material, the astral and the mental body, and he knows how all this can be influenced according to the universal laws. It will be easy for him to restore the two connecting links by means of the elements and the electro-magnetic fluid. In a case where no vital organ has been destroyed, the magician can restore to life, provided he has been destined by the Divine Providence to do so. He can cancel the death of persons or animals killed by an electric shock (lightning or similar events). All he has to do in such cases is to establish the contact with the spirit in akasha, deliberately inducing the electro-magnetic fluid between the spirit and the soul in order to fix the connecting link between the soul and the spirit. Then he has to do the same with the spirit and the soul with respect to the body, thus producing the correct harmony, by means of the elements and the electro-magnetic fluid. The deceased one is restored to life by instantaneously filling the body with the principle of light. This is the synthesis of the resuscitation in the magical way as induced with the powers of the elements and the electro-magnetic fluid, no matter whether willpower or other methods play a role in it. It is wellknown that higher adepts did accomplish such resuscitations.

Before finishing the tenth step, I am going, once more, to point out that not all of the magic faculties described here have to be likewise mastered. In recognition of, and obedience to, the spiritual law which governs the Universe, I have given the magician directions of how to bring about such phenomena bordering on the miracle. It is entirely left to the magician himself how far he is going to specialise in one or the other of the disciplines. A perfectly skilled person, an adept can execute everything and perform even greater magic phenomena than the ones I mentioned here in the light of the universal laws.

Consequently, the complete course of instruction concerning the first tarot-card, the one of the magician, has come to an end. People who have made up their minds to follow this course practically, have been given the opportunity of completing their development. There is no other way to render the practice more understandable than I did. The description I have given, here, responds to the knowledge handed down, up to now, only in the temples of mysteries, and imparted to the most selected and trustworthy scholars. Those who want quick results will be disappointed, for, sometimes, these studies will spread over years. But this fact will not deter the sincere scholar from penetrating the knowledge of this first initiation. For this reason, the first card, the magician, represents the gate to true initiation. A great deal of people who have been smiling ironically about the problem of magic, will probably have to change their minds after reading this book. There are so many misconceptions about magic, and so you should never forget that things are often misinterpreted. Magic is the most difficult knowledge on earth which has to be mastered not only theoretically but first of all practically. It is much easier to attain intellectual knowledge than to become a true Magician.

Summary of all exercises of Step X

I. *Magic Mental Training:*

Elevation of the spirit to higher levels.

II. *Magic Psychic Training:*

1. Conscious communication with the personal God.
2. Communication with deities and so on.

III. *Magic Physical Training:*

Several methods for acquiring magic faculties.

End of the tenth Step

Epilogue

As I have already mentioned in the introduction to this volume, this handbook is not destined to be the stepping-stone in the search after wealth, power and honour, but it has to serve the purpose of studying Man that is, the microcosm in relation to the Universe or the macrocosm together with their laws. So the reader's opinion about magic will undergo a noticeable change and I hope he will nevermore degrade this ancient wisdom to sorcery and similar pieces of devilry. It is understandable that each reader will judge this book from his individual point of view. He who stands upon the purely materialistic position, an unbeliever in religious matter, ignoring supernatural phenomena and only concerned in material interests will, without any doubt, regard this book as sheer nonsense, and I am not purposed to convert such people to any faith or to change their ideas. This work has exclusively been written for those who seek the pure truth and the supreme Wisdom which they will find in it, indeed.

Many times our fellow-men are argued, even persuaded into a special turn of mind, and here we often learn, by experience, that the various representatives of the different ideas cherish revengeful feelings towards each other for professional jealousy or for better knowing. The genuine magician will feel nothing but pity for people and creeds like that, but never will he hate or despise anyone. Whosoever seeks God, and whichever may be the way he chose to lead him toward this goal, him shall be paid the due respect. It is a pity, but also a truth that the clergy, theosophists, spiritualists or whatever they are called are antagonistically inclined just as if not any path were leading to God. All men seeking this path to, and the union with, God should always remember the words of Jesus Christ, great Master of the mystics who said: "Love thy neighbour as thou lovest thyself." This sentence ought to be a sacred command to any seeker of illumination on this spiritual path.

Many of the beings who had to leave our material world and who had no opportunity at all on this planet to attain the true cognition in the Spirit complained in the higher spheres about the fact that the true knowledge reserved so long to the chosen ones in the past, is not obtainable here below. Consequently the mysteries which have been kept as secrets for thousands of years are now revealed by the Divine Providence, step by step, to those inhabitants of this earth who honestly do long for the truth and perception. Evidently the benefits of perception will never come over night, they have got to be acquired in very hard labour and with many difficulties and obstructions. A great number of people —if not most of them—will prefer to become convinced first of the truth of the rules to have faith, and, only then, they will make up their minds to enter the path to initiation. The honest magician will realise that this attitude of Man is the wrong one. He is convinced that one has to be trained and educated for the faith by the initiation. By the mere reading of this work one can, of course, achieve an intellectual knowledge, but not wisdom. Knowledge can be gained by transference, but wisdom must be acquired by experience and recognition, the latter depending on the spiritual maturity of the individual. And this maturity again is determined by the spiritual development which is formed on the path to initiation.

Anybody who has been reading about the *tarot* will know as a fact that there are twentyone more cards, called the great Arcana, beside the first tarot-yard which is symbolized by the magician in the Egyptian mysteries, being the cradle of all wisdom. And each of these tarot-cards again includes an initiation sytem. Apart from the twenty-two great arcana, there are still fifty-six small arcana corresponding to the tarot-cards likewise symbolizing small mysteries, and each of these cards requires a description.

The Divine Providence will decide, what and how much I shall be permitted to write and to publish about the single tarot-cards. Having penetrated to the real inner significance of this book, the reader will have arrived at the conclusion that there is neither a white nor a black magic. In fact, there is no difference at all between magic and mysticism or sciences like that. As I have mentioned at the outset, any science is neither good nor bad, it can, however, become a hindrance or a help according to the use man makes of it. The opinion of the existence of black magic is to be attributed to the fact, that up to now, men had not the least idea of what magic is. In the various chapters and in connexion with the methods I repeatedly pointed out that this type of science is only destined to the most sublime purposes. Furthermore, I have always fully shown that the magician is bound to ennoble his character in the course of his development to the highest degree to avoid an interruption—or even worse—a falling-off in his rise. The ennoblement of the soul is going hand in hand with the rise of the development. Who is only keen on gaining occult faculties and powers to brag of them, will do his work in vain, for inscrutable are the ways of the Divine Providence for ever. He who aspires after occult powers for futile motives will be led away from his path sooner or later, occult faculties being only by-products, sort of a compass of the development and meant for noble purposes and for helping our fellow-men. Consequently, they are reserved exclusively to the true magician.

Who has entered the path to initiation does not have to change his ideology as far as religion is concerned. True religion is in fact nothing else but the practice of the instructions given here, and any religion whatever can be brought into harmony with the present initiation system.

But before entering this path, everyone should ask himself, whether he will regard true initiation practically as his religion, i. e., his life-task which he is intent on fulfilling, inspite of whatever hindrances and difficulties may be put into his way, and whether he will try hard to pursue, and never to run away from, this path as soon as he has entered it. It has to be taken for granted that an enormous, almost superhuman amount of endurance and patience, a tenacious willpower and secrecy regarding his progress are the fundamental conditions.

For all the readers desirous of perfection and who have chosen this book as their leader, I sincerely wish a good success and Divine blessing.

The author.

INDEX

Part II: *Initiation II* — *Practice:*

Further Books by Franz Bardon:

THE PRACTICE OF MAGICAL EVOCATION

The secret of the 2nd Tarot-card. Instructions for invoking and contacting Spirit Beings from the Spheres of the Hierarchy of our cosmic system. From the index:

Magic - Magical aids: The magical circle, the magical cencer, the magical mirror, the magical lamp, the magical sword. The Pentacle, Lamen or Seal. The book of magical spells. In the domain of the Spirit Beings. Advantages and disadvantages of evocational magic. The practice of magical evocation (description of a complete conjuration).

Hierarchy:

The spirits of the four elements. The 360 Heads of the "Zone of the earth". Intelligences of the Moon Sphere. The 72 Genii of the Mercury Zone. Intelligences of the Venus Sphere. Genii of the Sun Sphere. Intelligences of the Mars Sphere. Genii of the Jupiter Sphere. The Saturn Sphere. The Spheres of Uranus and Pluto. Communications with Spirit Beings, Genii and Intelligences of all Spheres by mental travelling. Picture of the 2nd Tarot-card.

ISBN 3-921338-02-6 / 4th Printing. 495 pages, hardb.

****

FRABATO THE MAGICIAN

This occult novel is based on the biography of Franz Bardon. It relates important parts of his life concerning his special mission for human development.

The course of the story shows the inexorable fight between the Magicians of the white and black path and reveals the most intimate practices of black lodges. Six illustrations.

ISBN 3-921338-07-7. 206 pages, pb.

****